Frederick Edward Warren

The Liturgy and Ritual of the Ante-Nicene Church

Frederick Edward Warren

The Liturgy and Ritual of the Ante-Nicene Church

ISBN/EAN: 9783337003920

Printed in Europe, USA, Canada, Australia, Japan

Cover: Foto ©Lupo / pixelio.de

More available books at **www.hansebooks.com**

SIDE-LIGHTS OF CHURCH HISTORY.

THE LITURGY AND RITUAL

OF THE

ANTE-NICENE CHURCH.

BY

F. E. WARREN, B.D., F.S.A.,

RECTOR OF BARDWELL, SUFFOLK; HONORARY CANON OF ELY;
AND FORMERLY FELLOW OF ST. JOHN'S COLLEGE, OXFORD.

PUBLISHED UNDER THE DIRECTION OF THE TRACT COMMITTEE.

LONDON:
SOCIETY FOR PROMOTING CHRISTIAN KNOWLEDGE,
NORTHUMBERLAND AVENUE, W.C.;
43, QUEEN VICTORIA STREET, E.C.
BRIGHTON: 129, NORTH STREET.
NEW YORK: E. & J. B. YOUNG AND CO.
1897.

INTRODUCTION.

IT has been attempted to put together in this volume all that is known about the Liturgy and Ritual of the Ante-Nicene Church, so far as such knowledge can be gathered (1) from Holy Scripture; (2) from ecclesiastical writings prior to A.D. 325; (3) from scanty surviving liturgical remains; and (4) from a few other sources, *e.g.* inscriptions, etc.

A chapter has been added dealing with the interesting but difficult question as to how far the worship and ritual of the Christian Church are of Jewish origin, or are modified by Jewish or other non-Christian influence.

It is hoped that from the material accumulated in the following pages, an answer may be found to the important question, 'How far does the Book of Common Prayer of the Church of England retain or reflect primitive usage, both absolutely as regards itself, and relatively, in comparison with the service-books of other parts of Christendom?'

We can at once lay our finger on many variations from primitive usage, *e.g.* the discontinuance of the Love-feast, and of Infant Confirmation, and of Infant Communion, and of the use of Unction, and of the Kiss of Peace, and of the rite of Exorcism, etc.; in alterations in the mode of singing, including the introduction of instrumental accompaniment, in the general non-separation of the sexes in church, in structural and verbal alterations in the Liturgy and other sacramental offices, etc.

Some changes have been necessitated by altered circumstances; some even by a difference of climate. All changes which involve no violation of any command in Holy Scripture are within the competence of the governing body of Christ's Church on earth.

On many of these points the unchanging Eastern Church adheres more faithfully to primitive practice than either the Church of England or the Church of Rome, and, it is needless to add, than the many Christian bodies which have separated from the Catholic Church within the last three or four centuries.

On the other hand, in the simplicity of her eucharistic, baptismal, confirmation, and ordination ritual, as well as in the use of the vernacular language, the Prayer-book retains and reflects the essential directions of Holy Scripture, and, in some respects, the practice of the primitive church more faithfully, and with less loss or addition, than the corresponding services in any other part of Western Christendom.

No liturgy is perfect, because no liturgy is inspired. It is quite consistent with loyalty to the Anglican Church to wish to see a revival of what has long been discontinued, our Prayer-book itself expressing such a wish in connection with the ancient penitential system of the primitive Church; or to see this or that liturgical detail altered; but while not reaching perfection any more than the Roman Missal and Breviary, or the Greek Euchologion, the Book of Common Prayer enshrines a form of service with which those who are privileged to have been enrolled as the sons and daughters of the English Church may be well content.

F. E. W.

Bardwell Rectory,
    Bury St. Edmunds,
        Lammas Day, 1897.

CONTENTS.

CHAPTER	PAGE
I. TRACES OF LITURGICAL WORSHIP IN THE OLD AND NEW TESTAMENTS ...	1
§ 1. Ritual Allusions in the Old Testament ...	1
§ 2. Reliquiæ Liturgicæ in the Old Testament ...	2
§ 3. Jewish Liturgy and Ritual a Type of the Services of the Chistian Church ...	5
§ 4. The Position and Meaning of Ritual in the Christian Church ...	7
§ 5. Ritual Allusions in the New Testament ...	9
§ 6. Baptism ...	9
§ 7. Benediction ...	16
§ 8. Church furniture ...	17
§ 9. Confirmation ...	19
§ 10. Unction at Baptism and Confirmation ...	20
§ 11. Sign of the Cross at Baptism and Confirmation ...	21
§ 12. Creed ...	23
§ 13. Excommunication ...	23
§ 14. Holy Eucharist ...	25
§ 15. Hymns ...	33
§ 16. Kiss of Peace ...	36
§ 17. Laying on of Hands ...	37
§ 18. Love-feast ...	37
§ 19. Marriage ...	38
§ 20. Offerings ...	39
§ 21. Ordination ...	39
§ 22. Public Prayer ...	42
§ 23. Sunday ...	45
§ 24. Unction of the Sick ...	46
§ 25. Vestments ...	47
§ 26. Washing of Feet ...	48

CHAPTER	PAGE
II. ANTE-NICENE RITUAL	50
Introductory	50
§ 1. Absolution	56
§ 2. Baptism	58
§ 3. Choral Service	74
§ 4. Church Furniture	75
§ 5. Confession	82
§ 6. Confirmation	87
§ 7. Sign of the Cross	98
§ 8. Exorcism	101
§ 9. Fasting	101
§ 10. The Eucharist	105
§ 11. Imposition of Hands	129
§ 12. Incense	129
§ 13. Kiss of Peace	131
§ 14. The Love-feast (*Agapé*)	133
§ 15. Marriage	137
§ 16. Ordination, Holy Orders	139
§ 17. Prayer	141
§ 18. Saints' Days	155
§ 19. Sunday	157
§ 20. Unction	159
§ 21. Vestments	162
§ 22. Vulgar Tongue, Use of the	164
§ 23. Washing of Hands and Feet	164, 165
III. ANTE-NICENE LITURGICAL REMAINS	167
§ 1. A Prayer from the Epistle of St. Clement	167
§ 2. Extract from the Epistle of St. Clement	170
§ 3. Prayers from the *Didaché*	172
§ 4. A Prayer of the Scillitan Martyrs	174
§ 5. Prayers of Origen	175
§ 6. Forms of Creed	177
§ 7. A Hymn to Christ	181
§ 8. The Virgins' Song	182
§ 9. An Evening Hymn	191
§ 10. Prayers and Thanksgivings from the Canons of Hippolytus	192
§ 11. Anthems, etc., of Uncertain Date	195
§ 12. Ancient Liturgies	195

CHAPTER	PAGE
IV. THE CONNECTION BETWEEN THE LITURGY AND RITUAL OF THE JEWISH AND CHRISTIAN CHURCHES	200
§ 1. Introductory	200
§ 2. The Temple Services	202
§ 3. The Synagogue Services	204
§ 4. The Shema	209
§ 5. The Eighteen Benedictions	210
§ 6. The Kadish	214
§ 7. The Kedusha	215
§ 8. The Paschal Supper	216
§ 9. Vitringa's Theory	217
§ 10. Bickell's Theory	218

Detailed resemblances in—

§ 11. Baptism	219
§ 12. Bells	220
§ 13. Benedictions	221
§ 14. Colours	221
§ 15. Confirmation	222
§ 16. Churches, Name of	222
§ 17. Silent Prayer	224
§ 18. Bowing at the Sacred Name	224
§ 19. Removal of Shoes	224
§ 20. Bowing towards the Altar	225
§ 21. Eastward Position	226
§ 22. Ablutions	226
§ 23. Standing at the Gospel	226
§ 24. Procession of the Gospel	227
§ 25. Separation of the Sexes	227
§ 26. Mode of Singing	228
§ 27. Dedication of Churches	228
§ 28. Fasts and Festivals	229
§ 29. Hebrew Language, Use of the	230
§ 30. The Eucharist	231
§ 31. Imposition of Hands	232
§ 32. Holy Orders	233
§ 33. Marriage	235
§ 34. Prayer, Hours of	235
§ 35. Prayer, Attitude at	237
§ 36. Prayer for the Dead	237
§ 37. Vestments	239

CHAPTER		PAGE
IV.	§ 38. Jewish Origin of certain Christian Formulæ of Devotion	242
	§ 39. Gospel for the Tenth Sunday after Trinity	246
	§ 40. Heathen Worship suggested as the Source of some Christian Ritual	247

APPENDIX : From the Apostolic Constitutions 255
§ 1. Gloria in Excelsis 257
§ 2. Triumphal Hymn 260
§ 3. A Widow's Thanksgiving 260
§ 4. A Eucharistic Thanksgiving 261
§ 5. A Post-Communion Thanksgiving 261
§ 6. A Thanksgiving for the Holy Oil 262
§ 7. A General Prayer 262
§ 8. Baptismal Formula of Renunciation 272
§ 9. Baptismal Creed 272
§ 10. Consecration of the Water at Baptism 273
§ 11. Consecration of the Oil at Baptism ... 273
§ 12. A Post-Baptismal Prayer 273
§ 13. A Prayer at the Consecration of a Bishop ... 274
§ 14. The Clementine Liturgy 275
§ 15. Another Description of the Liturgy ... 306
§ 16. A Prayer at the Ordination of a Presbyter ... 311
§ 17. A Prayer at the Ordination of a Deacon ... 312
§ 18. A Prayer at the Ordination of a Deaconess ... 312
§ 19. A Prayer at the Ordination of a Sub-Deacon 313
§ 20. A Prayer at the Ordination of a Reader ... 313
§ 21. A Consecration of Water and Oil ... 314
§ 22. An Evening Prayer 314
§ 23. A Morning Prayer 316
§ 24. A Thanksgiving at the Presentation of the First-fruits 317
§ 25. A Prayer for the Faithful Departed ... 318

INDICES :
1. Index of Biblical Quotations and References ... 321
2. Index of Greek Words 327
3. General Index 331

INDEX OF AUTHORS AND DOCUMENTS.

LIST OF AUTHORITIES.

N.B. This is not a complete index of ante-Nicene literature. With regard to *Acta Sanctorum* and Apocryphal writings, only those works are included of which use has been made in this volume. Heretical writings have been generally omitted, because they are chiefly known to us through extracts in the pages of orthodox writers, and as not containing references bearing on the subject-matter of this volume.

Abercius, St., Bishop of Hierapolis in Phrygia, 2nd cent., Epitaph of. See p. 122.

Acts. *See* Ignatius ; Passion ; Polycarp.

Acts of Apollonius. A senator, martyred at Rome A.D. 180-192. His Acts were published by the Melchitarists of Venice, 1874. They are quoted by Eusebius, *Eccles. Hist.*, Bk. v., cap. 21. Translated from the Armenian by F. C. Conybeare, in *Monuments of Early Christianity* (Lond., 1894), pp. 35-48.

Acts of Eugenia, 3rd cent., in F. C. Conybeare's *Monuments of Early Christianity* (London, 1894).

Acts of Fructuosus, Eulogius, and Augurius, 3rd cent., in Bollandist's *Acta Sanctorum*, Jan. 21, tom. ii. p. 340.

Acts of Paul and Thecla. A religious romance, probably of the second century. Its composition is assigned to A.D. 170-190. Grabe, *Spicilegium*, i. 81, etc. Translated in *A. C. L.*, vol. i., and from the Armenian by F. C. Conybeare in *Monuments of Early Christianity* (London, 1894), pp. 61-88. See Salmon (G.), *Introduction to the New Testament*, 7th ed. (London, 1894), pp. 329-334.

Acts of the Scillitan Martyrs. See p. 175.

Acts of Thomas [the Apostle]. An early unhistorical Gnostic romance. Edition by Max Bonnet (Lipsiæ, 1883).

Acts of Xanthippe, Polyxena, and Rebecca. Recently printed for the first time from Paris, Bibl. Nat. MS. Cod. Græc., 1458, by M. R. James, *Apocrypha Anecdota* (Cambridge), vol. ii. No. 3, pp. 43-85 ; *A. C. L.*, vol. for 1897. It is a romance of Gnostic and Encratite tendency, abounding in the miraculous element, grotesque and otherwise; but not on that account to be assigned to a late date. It resembles in general tone the Acts of Paul and Thecla and the Acts of Thomas.

Africanus, Julius. A writer early in the third century. Fragments only have been preserved by Eusebius.

Apollinaris, Bishop of Hierapolis, in Phrygia, *c.* A.D. 171. A few fragments only of his writings have survived: Routh (J. M.), *Reliquiæ Sacræ*, 2nd ed., i. 160.

Apollonius. *See* Acts of.

Apostolic Canons. These canons, eighty-four in number, are appended at the close of the Eighth Book of the Apostolic Constitutions. They have been sometimes referred to the ante-Nicene period; but in their present form they are certainly later. Bishop Lightfoot thought that they might be as late as the sixth century: *Apostolic Fathers* (London, 1891), vol. i. p. 368. Their first appearance in the Latin language dates from that century: Hefele (C. J.), *A History of the Christian Councils*, 2nd ed. (Edinburgh, 1872), p. 449; but much earlier material is embedded in a large number of them. Mr. F. E. Brightman ascribes them, together with the Apostolic Constitutions, to the pseudo-Ignatius in the latter part of the fourth century: *Liturgies Eastern and Western*, vol. i. p. xxiv. References are to Ueltzen's edition (Suerini et Rostochii, 1853).

Apostolic Constitutions. These Constitutions have been assigned to various dates, from the third to the sixth century A.D.; but it may now be regarded as settled that in their present form they are not earlier than the second half of the fourth century, though they include a great deal of earlier material: Salmon (G.), *Introduction to the New Testament*, 7th ed., p. 553; and Brightman (F. E.), *Liturgies Eastern and Western*, vol. i. pp. xxiv.-xxix. References to pages, unless otherwise specified, are to Ueltzen's edition (Suerini et Rostochii, 1853).

Aristides, Apologist. His Apology was written in the earlier years of the reign of Antoninus Pius (138-161), and may have been presented to that emperor on the occasion of some unrecorded visit by him to Smyrna. Cambridge ed., 1891. *A. C. L.*, vol. for 1897.

Arnobius, Apologist, Presbyter of the Church in Africa. He wrote A.D. 303-313.

Athenagoras, Apologist. He wrote an Apology, and a treatise on the resurrection of the dead, *c.* 176. Otho's ed. (Jena, 1857).

Barnabas, Epistle of. Probably not the work of St. Barnabas the Apostle; written between A.D. 70–150. Ed. Bp. Lightfoot, *The Apostolic Fathers* (London, 1891).

Caius. A Roman ecclesiastic early in the third century, a few fragments of whose writings have been preserved by Eusebius.

Canons of Hippolytus. It is not certain that these canons are the genuine work of Hippolytus (*q.v.*), but they may be assigned to Rome, and to the first half of the third century. Sectional and paginal references are to Gebhardt und Harnack, *Texte und Untersuchungen zur Geschichte der Altchristlichen Literatur* (Leipzig, 1891), Band vi. Heft 4, ss. 38–137, where the difficult questions of their date and genuineness are discussed at length. See also Brightman (F. E.), *Liturgies Eastern and Western*, vol. i. p. xxiii.

Clement, St., of Alexandria, pupil and successor of Pantænus as head of the catechetical school at Alexandria, died *c.* A.D. 220. Ed. Oxford, 1715, unless otherwise specified.

Clement, St., of Rome. The first Epistle which bears his name is in reality an Epistle from the Roman Church to the Corinthian Church written in A.D. 95 or 96. The second Epistle of St. Clement, so-called, is really an ancient homily by an unknown author, written probably at Rome, and certainly between A.D. 110–140. Ed. Bp. Lightfoot, *The Apostolic Fathers* (London, 1891); *A. C. L.*, vol. for 1897.

Clementine Homilies. An Ebionite romance, a somewhat later version of the Clementine Recognitions, *c.* A.D. 218.

Clementine Liturgy. Contained in the Eighth Book of the Apostolic Constitutions. See Appendix, p. 275.

Clementine Recognitions. An Ebionite romance, *c.* A.D. 200.

Commodianus. A Christian poet, middle of third century, and probably an African bishop.

Councils. A large number of Councils were held in various countries, Eastern and Western, before A.D. 325. The names of them will be found in the list of contents of the first volume of Mansi's *Concilia*. It is needless to repeat that list here. These early Councils were local in their character, and some of them very thinly attended, *e.g.* only nineteen bishops were present at the third Roman Council in 313. They were occupied with the more or less local controversies of the day, and throw very little light upon the liturgical language and ritual of the first three centuries. In many cases only the name of the Council is known to us. In few cases have their acts been wholly (though sometimes partly) preserved.

Cyprian, St., Bishop of Carthage, A.D. 200-258. Edition used Parisiis, 1726, unless otherwise specified.

Didaché, The; or, 'Teaching of the Twelve Apostles.' A document of the late first or early second century, most probably between A.D. 80-100. The history of its discovery, and reasons for assigning to it so early a date, are given by Bp. Lightfoot, *The Apostolic Fathers* (London, 1891), pp. 215, 216. Dr. Salmon's remarks on it deserve careful study : *Introduction to the New Testament*, 7th ed. (London, 1894), pp. 551-566.

Diognetus. *See* Epistle to.

Dionysius of Alexandria. Bishop of that see, 248-265. Fragments preserved by Eusebius.

Dionysius, Bishop of Corinth, *c.* A.D. 171-198. Fragments preserved by Eusebius.

Dionysius, Pseudo-Areopagita. His works are printed in Migne's *Patrologia Græca*, tomm. iii., iv., under the first century; but they belong in fact to the latter part of the fifth century, and therefore have no proper place in a list of ante-Nicene authorities.

Egyptian Church Order, The; forming Canons 31-62 of the Sahidic Ecclesiastical Canons, which as a collection date from the middle of the fourth century. This document is later than the Canons of Hippolytus, though largely identical with them, and earlier than the Apostolic Constitutions. Its exact date has not yet been ascertained. A German translation has been printed by Gebhardt und Harnack, *Texte und Untersuchungen zur Geschichte der Altchristlichen!Literatur* (Leipzig, 1891), Band. vi. Heft 4, ss. 38-137. The Sahidic text was previously published by P. de Lagarde, *Ægyptiaca*, Gottingen, 1883; a Greek translation by C. C. J. Bunsen, *Analecta Ante-Nicæna*, vol. ii. pp. 451-477, forming the sixth volume of *Christianity and Mankind* (London, 1854).

Epistle to Diognetus. Authorship unknown; certainly ante-Nicene, and probably written before A.D. 150. Bp. Lightfoot's ed. in *The Apostolic Fathers* (1891). It has been conjecturally assigned to Hippolytus by J. Quarry, *Hermathena*, No. XXII., 1896, pp. 318-357.

Eugenia. *See* Acts of.

Firmilian, St., Bishop of Cæsarea in Cappadocia, A.D. 233-272.

Some of his writing is preserved among the Epistles of St. Cyprian.

Fructuosus, etc. *See* Acts of.

Gregory, Thaumaturgus, St., Bishop of Neo-Cæsarea in Pontus, died *c.* 265.

Hegesippus, Church historian, 2nd cent. Fragments only of his works have survived. They are collected in Routh's *Reliquiæ Sacræ*, 2nd ed., tom. i. pp. 207–219.

Hermas, *The Shepherd* of. Probably not later than A.D. 120; certainly not later than A.D. 150. The work consists of three parts : The Vision, The Commandments, The Similitudes. In Bp. Lightfoot's *The Apostolic Fathers* (London, 1891).

Hippolytus, Bishop of Portus, near Rome, flourished A.D. 190–235. His collected works are in *P. G.*, tom. x. See also Bunsen (C. C. J.), *Analecta Ante-Nicæna*, vol. i. pp. 343-414. *See* Canons of.

Ignatius, St., Bishop of Antioch. Martyred at Rome, *c.* A.D. 110. Writer of seven letters : (1) to the Ephesians, (2) to the Magnesians, (3) to the Trallians, (4) to the Romans, (5) to the Philadelphians, (6) to the Smyrnæans, (7) to Polycarp. Bp. Lightfoot's ed. *The Apostolic Fathers* (London, 1891).

Ignatius, Acts of the Martyrdom of. Not genuine, 4th or 5th cent. Bp. Jacobson's ed. of *Patres Apostolici* (Oxford, 1847), tom. ii. pp. 550–579.

Irenæus, Bishop of Lyons, 177–202. Ed. Benedictine (Paris, 1710).

Justin Martyr, Apologist. He wrote about the middle of the second century, and his martyrdom took place most probably in A.D. 163. *P. G.*, tom. vi. Translated in *A. C. L.*, vol. ii. (Edinburgh, 1879).

Lactantius. The nationality and the date of the birth of this apologist are subjects of dispute ; but he probably died *c.* A.D. 317, and his works are classed as ante-Nicene.

Melito, Bishop of Sardis, *c.* A.D. 317, fragments of whose works have been preserved by Eusebius.

Methodius, Bishop of Tyre. Martyred at Chalcis in Greece, *c.* A.D. 311.

Minucius Felix, Apologist. Flourished in first half of the third century. Ed. C. Halm (Vindobonæ, 1867).

Origen, Presbyter of Alexandria (185–253). Benedictine Edition, ed. C. Delarue, vols. i.–iii. (Paris, 1733–1740), iv. (1759), unless otherwise specified.

Papias (A.D. 60-70—130-140), Fragments of. Bp. Lightfoot's ed. in *The Apostolic Fathers* (1891).
Passion of St. Perpetua. Martyred A.D. 202 or 203. Anonymous, but almost certainly written by Tertullian, and preserving the actual words of St. Perpetua. Cambridge, University Press, 1891. Ed. A. J. Robinson.
Paul and Thecla, SS. *See* Acts of.
Perpetua, St. *See* Passion.
Peter, St., Gospel of. A second century fragment, edit. H. B. Swete, 1893. *A. C. L.*, vol. for 1897.
Peter, St., Archbishop of Alexandria, *c.* 300-311. Fourteen Canons and fragments of his writings have been preserved.
Pliny, Governor of Bithynia, letter of, to the Emperor Trajan, *c.* A.D. 112.
Polycarp, St., Bishop of Smyrna. Martyred in A.D. 155 or 156. Writer of a letter addressed to the Philippians.
Polycarp, St., The Martyrdom of. A very early, perhaps contemporaneous, account in the form of a letter written by the Church of Smyrna to the Church of Philomelium.
Polycrates, Bishop of Ephesus, *c.* A.D. 180-202, a fragment of whose writings has been preserved by Eusebius.
Sahidic Ecclesiastical Canons. *See* Egyptian Church Order.
Sibylline Oracles, The. Partly of pre-Christian and partly of post-Christian date, containing very few liturgical allusions, and none of importance for the purpose of this volume.
Tatian, Apologist, and author of the Diatessaron (*c.* 160), disciple of Justin Martyr, and, after his master's death, a leader of the sect of the Encratites. The date of his death is unknown. He died before 180.
Teaching of the Twelve Apostles. See *Didaché*.
Tertullian, Presbyter at Carthage, 160-220. Ed. Paris, 1842.
Theophilus, Bishop of Antioch, in Syria, 168-182. *P. G.*, tom. vi.
Xanthippe. *See* Acts of.
Zosimus, Narrative of. Third century, but only known to us in late MSS. *A. C. L.*, vol. for 1897, p. 219; *Apocrypha Anecdota* (Cambridge, 1893), vol. ii. No. 3, p. 96.

ABBREVIATIONS.

A. C. L. = *Ante-Nicene Christian Library* (Edin., 1867-1897).
H. = Hammond (C. E.), *Liturgies Eastern and Western* (Oxford, 1878).
P. G. = Migne, *Patrologiæ Græcæ Cursus Completus.*
P. L. = Migne, *Patrologiæ Latinæ Cursus Completus.*

THE LITURGY AND RITUAL

OF THE

ANTE-NICENE CHURCH.

CHAPTER I.

TRACES OF LITURGICAL WORSHIP IN THE OLD AND NEW TESTAMENTS.

§ 1. Ritual allusions in the Old Testament—§ 2. Reliquiæ Liturgicæ in the Old Testament—§ 3. Jewish Liturgy and Ritual a type of the services of the Christian Church—§ 4. The position and meaning of ritual in the Christian Church—§ 5. Ritual allusions in the New Testament—§ 6. Baptism—§ 7. Benediction—§ 8. Church furniture—§ 9. Confirmation—§ 10. Unction at baptism and confirmation—§ 11. Sign of the Cross—§ 12. Creed—§ 13. Excommunication—§ 14. Holy Eucharist—§ 15. Hymns—§ 16. Kiss of peace—§ 17. Laying on of hands—§ 18. Love-feast—§ 19. Marriage—§ 20. Offerings—§ 21. Ordination—§ 22. Public prayer—§ 23. Sunday—§ 24.—Unction of the sick—§ 25. Vestments—§ 26. Washing of feet.

§ 1. THE liturgical element in Jewish worship, and the ritual directions and allusions to the Jewish Scriptures, and more especially in the Pentateuch, are so plain and so generally known, that it is unnecessary here to do more than take their existence for granted. No school of mystical or allegorical or spiritualizing interpretation has, so far as we know, attempted to explain their literal character away.

It may, however, be useful to point out that the liturgical and ritual character of Divine worship was not confined to the Levitical dispensation, but that it was in existence and acceptable to God from the very first age of the world.

By liturgical worship we mean worship which involves material offering or sacrifice, and which expresses itself in audible words as well as in external and visible actions, as distinguished from inaudible, invisible, immaterial worship of the heart only.

In the Book of Genesis we find mention or traces of the following religious observances :—

The institution of the seventh day as the sabbath or holy day of rest.[1]

The offering of the firstfruits of the land and of cattle in sacrifice to God by Cain and Abel.[2]

The clean and unclean animals are distinguished by Noah, who builds an altar, and offers of the former in sacrifice to God.[3]

Abraham, in obedience to Divine direction, offers animals and birds in sacrifice to God.[4]

The rite of circumcision is ordained as the external sign of God's covenant with His people.[5]

Solemn benedictions are bestowed,[6] accompanied by the imposition of hands.[7]

---

[1] Gen. ii. 3.   [2] Gen. iv. 3–5.   [3] Gen. vii. 2 ; viii. 20.
[4] Gen. xv. 8–18.   [5] Gen. xvii. 10–14.
[6] Gen. xxvii. 27–29 ; xxviii. 1–4.   [7] Gen. xlviii. 9–20.

The sacred character of burial is recognized.[1]
The head is bowed as an expression of worship.[2]
An altar is built for the worship of God.[3]
Ceremonial washing and change of dress precede prayer and sacrifice to God.[4]
A pillar is set up, and dedicated by pouring oil upon it.[5]
Vows are solemnly taken in God's presence, and tithes are dedicated by vow to God.[6]

In process of time the patriarchal order gave way to the Mosaic or Levitical dispensation, where, instead of occasional allusions in isolated texts, a complete liturgical system, with most elaborate ritual, is found to be provided for the Jewish nation by God Himself. We do not attempt here to describe that system, or even to recapitulate its leading features. As examples of minuteness of detail with which it was accompanied, readers may be referred to the special directions for the composition of the holy oil[7] and of incense.[8]

§ 2. The only remains of Mosaic liturgical verbal forms are (1) the form of priestly benediction.

'And the Lord spake unto Moses, saying,
Speak unto Aaron and unto his sons, saying, On this wise ye shall bless the children of Israel, saying unto them,
The Lord bless thee, and keep thee :
The Lord make His face shine upon thee, and be gracious unto thee :

---

[1] Gen. xxiii. 17-20; l. 7-13.
[2] Gen. xxiv. 26.
[3] Gen. xxvi. 25.
[4] Gen. xxxv. 2, 3.
[5] Gen. xxviii. 18; xxxv. 14.
[6] Gen. xxviii. 20-22.
[7] Exod. xxx. 22-25.
[8] Exod. xxx. 34-38.

The Lord lift up His countenance upon thee, and give thee peace.'[1]

(2) *The forms of words to be used on offering firstfruits to God.*

On presenting the firstfruits to the priest—

'I profess this day unto the Lord thy God that I am come unto the country which the Lord sware unto our fathers for to give us.'[2]

After the priest has accepted the firstfruits, and is presenting them to the Lord—

'A Syrian ready to perish was my father, and he went down into Egypt, and sojourned there with a few, and became there a nation, great, mighty, and populous:

And the Egyptians evil entreated us, and afflicted us, and laid upon us hard bondage:

And when we cried unto the Lord God of our fathers, the Lord heard our voice, and looked on our affliction, and our labour, and our oppression:

And the Lord brought us forth out of Egypt with a mighty hand, and with an outstretched arm, and with great terribleness, and with signs, and with wonders:

And He brought us into this place, and hath given us this land, even a land that floweth with milk and honey.

And now, behold, I have brought the firstfruits of the land, which Thou, O Lord, hast given me.'[3]

(3) *The form of words to be used on presenting the tithe.*

'I have brought away the hallowed things out of mine house, and also have given them unto the Levite, and unto the stranger, to the fatherless, and to the widow, according

---

[1] Numb. vi. 22–26.   [2] Deut. xxvi. 3.
[3] Deut. xxvi. 5–10.

to all Thy commandments which Thou hast commanded me; I have not transgressed Thy commandments, neither have I forgotten them:

I have not eaten thereof in my mourning, neither have I taken away ought thereof for any unclean use, nor given ought thereof for the dead; but I have hearkened to the voice of the Lord my God, and have done according to all that Thou hast commanded me.

Look down from Thy holy habitation, from heaven, and bless Thy people Israel, and the land which Thou hast given us, as Thou swarest unto our fathers, a land that floweth with milk and honey.'[1]

§ 3. There is an interesting feature which we can only point to the existence of, without attempting to exhibit it in detail, namely, the number of ways in which the ritual, ordinances, and incidents of the Old Testament, and especially of the Levitical Church, were types of various Christian services, and especially of the Holy Eucharist.[2] It is important to note that the Divine care for ritual was not confined to, and did not cease with, the Levitical age. At the time when the Temple was to be built (B.C. 1015), David adds in his parting charge to his son and successor, after an elaborate description of the pattern of the proposed house and of its fittings—

'All this the Lord made me understand in writing by His hand upon me, even all the works of this pattern.'[3]

---

[1] Deut. xxvi. 13-15.
[2] This is the subject of a volume by the Rev. W. E. Heygate, *The Eucharist, its Types*, etc. London, 1874.
[3] 1 Chron. xxviii. 11-19.

And during the actual progress of the work it is said—

'Now these are the things wherein Solomon was instructed for the building of the house of God.'[1]

At its completion God's approbation is conveyed thus:—

'I have heard thy prayer and thy supplication, that thou hast made before Me; I have hallowed this house, which thou hast built, to put My Name there for ever; and Mine eyes and Mine heart shall be there perpetually.'[2]

Within this magnificent temple not only were the ancient Levitical services, sacrifices, and ceremonial carried on, but additional splendour was imparted to Divine service by the introduction, and as time went on the increase and elaboration, of those songs of the sanctuary which are known to us under the title of 'The Psalms of David.' The choral element included both vocal and instrumental music.[3] We get some idea of the enormous size of the temple choir by the fact that the instrumentalists alone numbered four thousand persons.[4] Both male and female singers were included in the choir.[5] The whole of this chapter must be consulted for the number, order, and arrangement of musicians and singers. David's work in this connection has been summarized thus—

'He set singers also before the altar, that by their voices

---

[1] 2 Chron. iii. 3.   [2] 1 Kings ix. 3.
[3] 1 Chron. xiii. 8; xv. 14–16, 28.
[4] 1 Chron. xxiii. 5.   [5] 1 Chron. xxv. 5, 6.

they might make sweet melody, and daily sing praises in their songs.

He beautified their feasts, and set in order the solemn times until the end, that they might praise His holy Name, and that the temple might sound from morning.'[1]

Solomon confirmed and perpetuated the arrangements of his father David.

'He appointed, according to the order of David his father, the courses of the priests to their service, and the Levites to their charges, to praise and minister before the priests, as the duty of every day required.'[2]

Yet the object of all this Divine forethought and kingly care was not a perpetual institution, but a transitory preparation for the world-embracing dispensation of Christianity, which God in the fulness of time intended to unfold.

This fugitive character of the Jewish service and ritual was evident from the typical character of its ceremonial, and especially of its sacrifices and its priesthood. Such was seen to be the case by the Psalmist and prophets, who allude to the impossibility of their being acceptable in themselves,[3] and to the time coming when not among the Jews only, but throughout the whole world, incense and a pure offering should be presented to the Lord.[4] The law was the schoolmaster to educate the Jewish world for Christ,[5] and Christ being its end and object,[6] it was to disappear when He became incarnate.

§ 4. Then the question arises whether at the

---

[1] Ecclus. xlvii. 9, 10.   [2] 2 Chron. viii. 14.   [3] Ps. xl. 8, 9.
[4] Mal. i. 11.   [5] Gal. iii. 24.   [6] Rom. x. 4.

Christian era all external worship, with all ritual and symbolism, were intended to be for ever swept away, and a purely spiritual worship substituted in its place, or whether another and a higher, though simpler, form of worship and ritual was ordained to supersede the Jewish, full of a deeper significance, and possessed of a more real value, because it was no longer the shadow of good things to come,[1] but the pledge and witness of their having arrived.

This question cannot be answered by seizing on one text, such as, 'God is a Spirit: and they that worship Him must worship Him in spirit and in truth,'[2] and then, as some Christian sects do, treating a fixed Liturgy as incompatible with it, and putting a non-literal interpretation on any actions or directions given by our Lord and His Apostles, which seem, if taken literally, to conflict with the purely spiritual religion shadowed forth in the last-quoted text. The more reasonable course is to interpret literally those texts in the New Testament in which some Christian ordinance or usage is referred to or enjoined, and on which a literal interpretation has been placed by the universal, or almost universal, consent of Catholic Christendom; only remembering that such a text as St. John iv. 24 demands of us something much deeper than external compliance with the command to use any rite or ordinance, and that without a spiritual grasp of the purposes for which a rite was ordained, or of the gifts of which it is intended to be the channel, the mere external

---

[1] Heb. x. 1.   [2] St. John iv. 24.

compliance is valueless, and worse than valueless; worse than valueless, because it substitutes the means for the end, and reduces the Christian religion to the mechanical performance of certain actions like the religions of Thibet and Japan.

§ 5. We will therefore put together the passages in the New Testament which bear upon the subject in any way, arranging them under the headings of the particular liturgical forms or ceremonial actions to which they refer. The subjects are referred to in alphabetical order, as a matter of convenience, and in no way referring to their relative importance. It will be found that we not only have general directions forbidding idolatry, irreverence, disorder, neglect, or enjoining decency and order,[1] but that there is a very considerable body of explicit directions with reference to the form and conduct of Christian worship.

ABSOLUTION. *See* Excommunication, p. 23.
AGAPE. *See* Love-feast, p. 37.
ALTAR. *See* Church Furniture, p. 17.
ANOINTING. *See* Unction, p. 46.

§ 6. BAPTISM. Christian Baptism was alluded to by anticipation when our Lord said to Nicodemus—

'Except a man be born of water and of the Spirit, he cannot enter into the kingdom of God.'[2]

But it was not instituted by Him until the immediate eve of His ascension, when He gave this commission to His Apostles—

---

[1] 1 Cor. xi. 34; xiv. 40.   [2] St. John iii. 5.

'Go ye therefore, and teach [make disciples of] all nations, baptizing them in the Name of the Father, and of the Son, and of the Holy Ghost:

Teaching them to observe all things whatsoever I have commanded you: and, lo, I am with you alway, even unto the end of the world.'[1]

Or in the words of another Evangelist—

'Go ye into all the world, and preach the gospel to every creature.

He that believeth and is baptized shall be saved; but he that believeth not shall be damned.'[2]

There is reason to believe that the baptismal powers thus entrusted to the Apostles were not exercised till after the Day of Pentecost.[3] Their previous baptismal acts, recorded in St. John's Gospel,[4] were connected with another baptismal rite, of which we read a good deal in the New Testament, but which must be carefully distinguished from Christian baptism, viz. the baptism of St. John the Baptist. This was called the baptism of repentance,[5] and is believed to have been administered in the name of the Messiah about to come. It was submitted to by our Lord Himself, though sinless, perhaps as the crowning act or seal of the Divine approval of the Baptist's office and ministry, and with surroundings which foreshadowed the mysterious doctrine of the Trinity, which was to be so intimately connected with the baptismal formula to be used hereafter for ever in the Christian Church.

---

[1] St. Matt. xxviii. 19, 20. [2] St. Mark xvi. 15, 16.
[3] Acts i. 5, 8. [4] St. John iii. 22; iv. 1, 2.
[5] St. Mark i. 4; Acts xiii. 24; xviii. 25.

The following are the instances of the administration of baptism recorded in the New Testament:—

Recipients.	Agents.	Authority.
About three thousand persons	St. Peter	Acts ii. 41
Many Samaritans	St. Philip	viii. 12
Simon the sorcerer	St. Philip	viii. 13
The Ethiopian eunuch	St. Philip	viii. 38
Saul	Ananias	ix. 18
Cornelius and others	Not named	x. 47, 48
Lydia and her household	St. Paul	xvi. 15
The jailor of Philippi and his family	St. Paul	xvi. 33
Many Corinthians	Not named	xviii. 8
Certain disciples at Ephesus	St. Paul	xix. 5
Crispus and Gaius	St. Paul	1 Cor. i. 14
The household of Stephanas	St. Paul	i. 16

An examination of the words of institution, of the recorded instances of administration, and of the language in which reference to baptism is made in various Epistles, establishes the following points:—

1. The formula of administration, in accordance with our Lord's explicit direction, was always 'in the Name of the Father, and of the Son, and of the Holy Ghost.'

It has been suggested that side by side with this formula, there are traces of baptism administered 'in the name of Christ' or 'into the death of Christ.' This view is based on such texts as the following:—

'For as yet He was fallen upon none of them; only they were baptized in the name of the Lord Jesus.'[1]

'When they heard this, they were baptized in the name of the Lord Jesus.'[2]

[1] Acts viii. 16.   [2] Acts xix. 5.

'Know ye not, that so many of us as were baptized into Jesus Christ were baptized into His death?'[1]

One possible interpretation of St. Paul's extremely difficult words to the Corinthians may be connected with this subject—

'What shall they do which are baptized for the dead, if the dead rise not at all? why are they then baptized for the dead?'[2]

References to baptism are found in early Christian documents, which are evidently moulded on these passages of Scripture; *e.g.* in the Teaching of the Twelve Apostles we read—

'But let no one eat or drink of your Eucharist except those baptized in the name of the Lord, for regarding this also the Lord hath said, Give not that which is holy to the dogs.'[3]

And in the Apostolic Constitutions—

'Be it known unto you, beloved, that such as are baptized into the death of the Lord Jesus ought to sin no more.'[4]

But these texts of Scripture and passages from early Christian writings are merely general expressions as to baptism and the effects of baptism, and we have no right to press them as indicating an alternative formula, or alternative formulæ, under which baptism was sometimes, or might be, administered. There is no historical evidence for any formula being employed or approved in the Catholic Church

---

[1] Rom. vi. 3.   [2] 1 Cor. xv. 29.   [3] Chap. ix. § 5.
[4] Book ii. chap. 7.

except the Trinitarian formula enjoined by our Lord Himself.[1]

2. The element employed was always and only water. This is not only a natural inference from the word 'baptism,' but is plainly enjoined by Holy Scripture, as in our Lord's words to Nicodemus—

'Except a man be born of water and of the Spirit, he cannot enter into the kingdom of God.'[2]

In the description of the baptism of the Ethiopian eunuch—

'And they went down both into the water, both Philip and the eunuch; and he baptized him.'[3]

In the description of the Church by St. Paul—

'As Christ also loved the Church, and gave Himself for it; that He might sanctify and cleanse it with the washing of water by the word.'[4]

And of Christians by the author of the Epistle to the Hebrews—

'Let us draw near with a true heart in full assurance of faith, having our hearts sprinkled from an evil conscience, and our bodies washed with pure water.'[5]

Therefore such an attempt as that made in Ireland in the twelfth century to substitute milk for water in the case of the baptism of the children of the rich people made their baptism not only irregular but invalid.[6]

3. Immersion, though not expressly ordered, and

---

[1] For variations in bodies external to the Catholic Church, see Bingham, *Antiquities of the Christian Church*, Book xi. chap. 3.
[2] St. John iii. 5. [3] Acts viii. 38. [4] Eph. v. 25, 26.
[5] Heb. x. 22. [6] *Liturgy and Ritual of the Celtic Church*, p. 65.

apparently impossible in the case of the three thousand people baptized on one day by St. Peter,[1] would be the ordinary practice in a hot Eastern climate, and is implied in the symbolism of such passages as these—

'Therefore we are buried with Him by baptism into death: that like as Christ was raised up from the dead by the glory of the Father, even so we also should walk in newness of life.'[2]

And—

'Buried with Him in baptism, wherein also ye are risen with Him through the faith of the operation of God, who hath raised Him from the dead.'[3]

The total immersion of the whole body beneath the baptismal waters symbolizes more completely than any other mode of baptism the burial of our Lord's body in the grave.

Although affusion or aspersion has been accepted by the Church as valid, for climatic or clinical reasons, yet neither of these substitutes for immersion carries out so well as immersion the idea of cleansing so frequently expressed in the New Testament by the word 'washing,' *e.g.*—

'And now why tarriest thou? arise, and be baptized, and wash away thy sins, calling on the name of the Lord.'[4]

'And such were some of you: but ye are washed, but ye are sanctified, but ye are justified in the name of the Lord Jesus, and by the Spirit of our God.'[5]

'Not by works of righteousness which we have done, but

---

[1] Acts ii. 41. [2] Rom. vi. 4. [3] Col. ii. 12.
[4] Acts xxii. 16. [5] 1 Cor. vi. 11.

according to His mercy He saved us, by the washing of regeneration, and renewing of the Holy Ghost.'[1]

4. There are traces of the existence of forms of interrogation in use at baptism, and of a profession of faith, like a short creed, being delivered to and accepted by the candidate.

It is recorded that the Ethiopian eunuch called the attention of Philip to certain water and asked that he might be baptized.

'And Philip said, If thou believest with all thine heart, thou mayest. And he answered and said, I believe that Jesus Christ is the Son of God.'[2]

St. Paul, writing to the Corinthians, said—

'For I delivered unto you first of all that which I also received, how that Christ died for our sins according to the Scriptures;

And that He was buried, and that He rose again the third day according to the Scriptures:

And that He was seen of Cephas, then of the twelve.'[3]

Here the quotation introduced by 'that' (ὅτι) ends. It seems to be a portion of a confession of faith which St. Paul says that he received. From whom did he receive it? If he had received it, as he

---

[1] Tit. iii. 5.
[2] Acts viii. 27. Although this verse is absent from all uncial MSS. except the Codex Laudianus (E.), yet it was known and quoted by many early writers, commencing with Irenæus in the second century. Both Dr. Scrivener and Dr. Jessopp agree in supposing that it contains the words of a very early Church Service-book, first written upon the margin, and thence creeping into the sacred text (*Introduction to the Criticism of the New Testament*, 2nd ed., p. 554; *Expositor*, No. LX. p. 403).
[3] 1 Cor. xv. 3–5.

received the history of the institution of the Eucharist, directly from our Lord, he would surely, in this case as in that,[1] have lent greater dignity and importance to the statement by mentioning that fact. It is more probable that it was part of the faith which he solemnly received at his baptism, and that we have here the germ of what afterwards developed into the solemn ceremonial which preceded baptism called the *Traditio Symboli*, or 'The Delivery of the Creed.'

The faith thus received was professed before many witnesses, to which fact there may be allusion in St. Paul's words to Timothy—

'Fight the good fight of faith, lay hold on eternal life, whereunto thou art also called, and hast professed a good profession before many witnesses.'[2]

The questions and answers in the baptismal service seem to have suggested the form of language in a difficult sentence of St. Peter connected with this same subject—

'The like figure whereunto even baptism doth also now save us (not the putting away of the filth of the flesh, but the answer of a good conscience toward God,) by the resurrection of Jesus Christ.'[3]

§ 7. BENEDICTION.—Two ritual actions are recorded to have been used by our Lord in connection with Benediction on different occasions.

1. The imposition of hands.

'Then were there brought unto Him little children, that

---

[1] 1 Cor. xi. 23. [2] 1 Tim. vi. 12. [3] 1 Pet. iii. 21.

He should put His hands on them, and pray. . . . And He laid His hands on them, and departed thence.'[1]

2. The elevation of hands.

'And He led them out as far as to Bethany, and He lifted up His hands, and blessed them.'[2]

Several formulæ of Benediction occur in the later books of the New Testament, two of which have been incorporated into English Liturgies.

1. 'The grace of the Lord Jesus Christ, and the love of God, and the communion of the Holy Ghost, be with you all. Amen.'[3]

This occurs at the commencement of the anaphora in the Clementine and other Eastern Liturgies,[4] and at the conclusion of Matins and Evensong in the Book of Common Prayer.

2. 'The peace of God, which passeth all understanding, shall keep your hearts and minds through Christ Jesus.'[5]

This forms the first part of the concluding Benediction of the English Liturgy.

CHALICE, or CUP. See p. 18.

§ 8. CHURCH FURNITURE.—As Christian places of worship did not begin to be built within the period covered by the New Testament, we do not find, and we do not expect to find, any reference to the structure, arrangement, furniture,

---

[1] St. Matt. xix. 13, 15.   [2] St. Luke xxiv. 50.   [3] 2 Cor. xiii. 14.
[4] See II., pp. 12, 40, 69, 107, 151, 166, 272. It will be noticed that it is not found in the Alexandrian family of Liturgies, and that in the Armenian Liturgy (p. 272), as in our Prayer-book, the pronoun is changed from the second person to the first person plural.
[5] Phil. iv. 7.

or ornaments of such buildings in its pages. It ought to be unnecessary to add that any attempts to argue against the lawfulness or expediency of Christian Churches, or of the accessories of public worship, from the absence of any mention of them or allusion to them in the New Testament involves an anachronism. Any dispute over the lawfulness of the use of organs, surplices, etc., must be fought out, outside and not inside the four corners of the New Testament. There was, however, one exception. There were two Christian ordinances administered and observed by the disciples from the very first, even while they continued to frequent for ordinary devotional purposes the services of the Jewish Temple. The first of these, Baptism, was administered wherever there was water, and in its original simplicity, and before it came to be administered within a sacred building, it necessitated no external artificial aid for its due performance. The second of these, the Eucharist, celebrated for many years in some private chamber, needed certain accessories for its celebration or administration. Two of these accessories are mentioned in the New Testament.

(*a*) The Eucharistic Chalice, or Cup.

'The cup of blessing which we bless, is it not the communion of the blood of Christ?'[1]

'Ye cannot drink the cup of the Lord, and the cup of devils.'[2]

---

[1] 1 Cor. x. 16.   [2] 1 Cor. x. 21. See also 1 Cor. xi. 25-28.

(*b*) The Eucharistic Table or Altar.

'Ye cannot be partakers of the Lord's table,[1] and of the table of devils.'[2]

'We have an altar, whereof they have no right to eat which serve the tabernacle.'[3]

§ 9. CONFIRMATION, or 'Laying on of hands.'—The practice of confirmation, or the laying on of hands, following upon the reception of baptism, is mentioned in the following passages :—

(*a*) In the case of the Samaritan converts baptized by Philip the Deacon, and afterwards confirmed by St. Peter and St. John—

'But when they believed Philip preaching the things concerning the kingdom of God, and the name of Jesus Christ, they were baptized, both men and women.

Now, when the Apostles which were at Jerusalem heard that Samaria had received the word of God, they sent unto them Peter and John :

Who, when they were come down, prayed for them, that they might receive the Holy Ghost.

Then laid they their hands on them, and they received the Holy Ghost.'[4]

(*b*) In the case of certain disciples at Ephesus, both baptized and confirmed by St. Paul—

'When they heard this, they were baptized in the name of the Lord Jesus.

---

[1] This does not necessarily mean the actual table or altar; some early writers have interpreted it of the Sacramental feast.

[2] 1 Cor. x. 21.

[3] Heb. xiii. 10. This is only one possible interpretation out of many possible interpretations of a difficult passage.

[4] Acts viii. 12, 14, 15, 17.

And when Paul had laid his hands upon them, the Holy Ghost came on them; and they spake with tongues, and prophesied.'[1]

There is also the well-known but difficult passage in the Epistle to the Hebrews, where the doctrine of 'laying on of hands' is enumerated directly after the doctrine of 'baptisms' as among the principles of the doctrine of Christ.

'Therefore leaving the principles of the doctrine of Christ, let us go on unto perfection; not laying again the foundation of repentance from dead works, and of faith toward God,

Of the doctrine of baptisms, and of laying on of hands, and of resurrection of the dead, and of eternal judgment.'[2]

§ 10. UNCTION AT BAPTISM AND CONFIRMATION.—The following passages are sometimes quoted as scriptural evidence for the use of the rite of unction at baptism and confirmation :—

'Now He which stablisheth us with you in Christ, and hath anointed us, is God.'[3]

'But ye have an unction from the Holy One, and ye know all things.'[4]

'But the anointing which ye have received of Him abideth in you, and ye need not that any man teach you: but as the same anointing teacheth you of all things, and is truth, and is no lie, and even as it hath taught you, ye shall abide in Him.'[5]

It is argued that the use of the verb 'to anoint,' and of the substantive 'unction' or 'anointing' in

---

[1] Acts xix. 5, 6.   [2] Heb. vi. 1, 2.   [3] 2 Cor. i. 21.
[4] 1 St. John ii. 20.   [5] 1 St. John ii. 27.

these passages, implies the existence of the practice of unction, and that the existence of such a practice made the choice of such language natural and intelligible. But this argument may be made to cut two ways. It may, with equal probability, be argued that the existence of these metaphorical terms in the New Testament suggested, and rendered easy, the introduction of a literal rite of unction at a very early date in the history of the Church. The word unction (χρίσμα) occurs nowhere else in the New Testament, except in the two above-quoted passages of St. John. The word anoint (χρίειν) occurs in four other passages (St. Luke iv. 18; Acts iv. 27, x. 38; Heb. i. 9), in all of which its use is metaphorical and not literal.

§ 11. SIGN OF THE CROSS AT BAPTISM OR CONFIRMATION.—The following passages are sometimes quoted to prove the scriptural use of the sign of the cross, it being taken for granted that 'to seal' is the same as to sign with the cross, in connection with baptism or confirmation.

'Who hath also sealed us, and given the earnest of the Spirit in our hearts.'[1]

'In whom also after that ye believed, ye were sealed with that Holy Spirit of promise.'[2]

'And grieve not the Holy Spirit of God, whereby ye were (A.V. are) sealed unto the day of redemption.'[3]

But the inference from these texts is equally precarious with the inference as to unction.

---

[1] 2 Cor. i. 22. [2] Eph. i. 13. [3] Eph. iv. 30.

If we examine the three passages in the New Testament (outside the Apocalypse) in which the word seal (σφραγίς) occurs, we shall see that it is used once of circumcision, and in the other two passages distinctly and necessarily in a metaphorical, and not in a literal sense.

Its use as a description of circumcision, strongly suggests that in the above-quoted passages, St. Paul is referring to its Christian counterpart, Holy Baptism.

'And he received the sign of circumcision, a seal of the righteousness of the faith which he had yet being uncircumcised.'[1]

'For the seal of mine apostleship are ye in the Lord.'[2]

'Having this seal, The Lord knoweth them that are His.'[3]

If we examine the passages in the New Testament (outside the Apocalypse) in which the verb 'to seal' (σφραγίζειν) occurs, in addition to the three passages, above quoted, we shall find that they are four in number. In one passage it is used literally, but certainly with no allusion to the sign of the cross; in the other three passages its use is plainly metaphorical.

'Sealing the stone, and setting a watch.'[4]

'He that hath received His testimony hath set to his seal that God is true.'[5]

'For Him hath God the Father sealed.'[6]

'When therefore I have performed this, and have sealed to them this fruit, I will come by you into Spain.'[7]

---

[1] Rom. iv. 11. [2] 1 Cor. ix. 2. [3] 2 Tim. ii. 19.
[4] St. Matt. xxvii. 66. [5] St. John iii. 33. [6] St. John vi. 27.
[7] Rom. xv. 28.

We conclude, therefore, that the use of the sign of the cross as a ritual act, though found, as will be seen afterwards, in the most primitive time of Christianity, is not referred to in Holy Scripture.

§ 12. CREED.—We have already (p. 16) called attention to what are believed to be fragments of an early baptismal creed. In addition to the passages there quoted, the following texts may be adduced as containing allusions to the existence of a settled form of words of sound doctrine in the shape of a received creed.

'Ye have obeyed from the heart that form of doctrine which was delivered you.'[1]

'Hold fast the form of sound words, which thou hast heard of me, in faith and love which is in Christ Jesus.'[2]

'Let us hold fast the profession of our faith without wavering.'[3]

'Whosoever transgresseth and abideth not in the doctrine of Christ, hath not God. He that abideth in the doctrine of Christ [$\dot{\epsilon}\nu$ $\tau\hat{\eta}$ $\delta\iota\delta\alpha\chi\hat{\eta}$ $\tau o\hat{\upsilon}$ $X\rho\iota\sigma\tau o\hat{\upsilon}$], he hath both the Father and the Son.'[4]

'It was needful for me to write unto you, and exhort you that ye should earnestly contend for the faith which was once delivered unto the saints.'[5]

§ 13. EXCOMMUNICATION.—The power of excommunication from, and the correlative power of re-admitting to the visible Church of Christ on earth, was given by our Lord on one occasion to St. Peter singly, and afterwards with equal fulness to all the Apostles.

---

[1] Rom. vi. 17.   [2] 2 Tim. i. 13.   [3] Heb. x. 23.
[4] 2 St. John 9.   [5] St. Jude 3.

He said to St. Peter alone—

'And I will give unto thee the keys of the kingdom of heaven: and whatsoever thou shalt bind on earth shall be bound in heaven: and whatsoever thou shalt loose on earth shall be loosed in heaven.' [1]

And afterwards with equal fulness to all the Apostles—

'Verily I say unto you [ὑμῖν], Whatsoever ye shall bind on earth shall be bound in heaven: and whatsoever ye shall loose on earth shall be loosed in heaven.' [2]

The same power was once again committed to the Apostles, if possible, in yet more solemn action and language.

It was after His resurrection that—

'Then said Jesus to them again, Peace be unto you: as My Father hath sent Me, even so send I you.

And when He had said this, He breathed on them, and saith unto them, Receive ye the Holy Ghost.

Whose soever sins ye remit, they are remitted unto them; and whose soever sins ye retain, they are retained.' [3]

Instances of its exercise are found in the case of the incestuous Corinthian, whose excommunication is recorded in 1 Cor. v. 3-5, and his absolution in 2 Cor. ii. 6-11; also in the case of Hymenæus and Alexander.[4]

The absolution, or reception back into the visible fold of the excommunicate person, was, in primitive times, accompanied by the outward sign of the laying on of hands. There is one passage in the New

---

[1] St. Matt. xvi. 19.
[2] St. Matt. xviii. 18.
[3] St. John xx. 21-23.
[4] 1 Tim. i. 20.

Testament which possibly refers to this imposition of hands,[1] though most commentators interpret it of ordination rather than of absolution.

'Lay hands suddenly on no man, neither be partaker of other men's sins.'[2]

§ 14. HOLY EUCHARIST.—We have preserved for us, in the New Testament, four records of the institution of this, the most distinctive rite of the Christian dispensation. (See table, p. 26.)

It has been doubted whether 1 Cor. xi. 26 contains St. Paul's own words, or words spoken by our Saviour at the institution of the Holy Eucharist. Most commentators take the former view for granted. It seems a natural inference from the change from the first to the third person, and from the reference to Christ as the Lord (ὁ Κύριος). But it is not a necessary inference. Christ uses the third person of Himself when He asks—

'When the Son of Man cometh, shall He find faith on the earth?'[3]

And the title of Lord (ὁ Κύριος) is sometimes used by Christ Himself, as where He says—

'If I then, your Lord [ὁ Κύριος] and Master, have washed your feet; ye also ought to wash one another's feet.'[4]

And again—

'The Lord [ὁ Κύριος] hath need of them.'[5]

The liturgical evidence preponderates overwhelm-

---

[1] So Bp. Jeremy Taylor, Works, ed. 1824, vol. ix. p. 197.
[2] 1 Tim. v. 22.   [3] St. Luke xviii. 8.   [4] St. John xiii. 14.
[5] St. Matt. xxi. 3.

St. Matt. xxvi. 26–28.	St. Mark xiv. 22–24.	St. Luke xxii. 19, 20.	I Cor. xi. 23–26.
And as they were eating,	And as they did eat,	And	The Lord Jesus the same night in which He was betrayed took bread :
Jesus took bread, and blessed it, and brake it, and gave it to the disciples, and said, Take, eat ; this is My body.	Jesus took bread, and blessed, and brake it, and gave to them, and said, Take, eat ; this is My body.	He took bread, and gave thanks, and brake it, and gave unto them, saying,	and when He had given thanks, He brake it, and said, Take, eat : this is My body which is broken for you ;
		This is My body which is given for you : this do in remembrance of Me.	this do in remembrance of Me.
And He took the cup, and gave thanks, and gave it to them,	And He took the cup, and when He had given thanks, He gave it to them : and they all drank of it. And He said unto them,	Likewise also the cup after supper,	After the same manner also He took the cup, when He had supped,
saying, Drink ye all of it ; for this is My blood of the new testament, which is shed for many for the remission of sins.	This is My blood of the new testament, which is shed for many.	saying, This cup is the new testament in My blood, which is shed for you.	saying, This cup is the new testament in My blood ; this do ye, as oft as ye drink it, in remembrance of Me. For as often as ye eat this bread, and drink this cup, ye do shew the Lord's death till He come.

ingly in favour of the view that they are Christ's own words. As such they are interwoven, or were once interwoven, along with the words of institution, into the consecration prayer of the large majority of ancient Liturgies, as the following table will show:—

I. WESTERN LITURGIES.

Inserted in
1. The Mozarabic.[1]
2. The Gallican.[2]
3. The Ambrosian.[3]

Omitted in
1. The Roman.[4]
2. The Anglican.[5]

II. EASTERN LITURGIES.

(a) *West Syrian.*

1. The Clementine.[6]
2. Greek St. James.[7]
3.   „   St. Basil.[8]
4. Syriac St. James.[9]
5.   „   Lesser St. James.[10]
6.   „   St. Xystus.[11]
7.   „   St. Peter.[12]

1. St. Chrysostom.[13]

[1] *P. L.*, tom. lxxxv. col. 117.
[2] *Liturgy and Ritual of the Celtic Church*, p. 237. This is a Gallican insertion into a Roman text, by the Irish scribe Moel Caich. In the older MSS. of the Gallican Liturgy the words of institution are not printed in full, but only indicated by two or more of the opening words, 'Qui pridie quam pateretur,' etc.
[3] Ceriani's print of the oldest extant MS. Ambrosian text, 10th cent., p. 171. This is an Ephesine survival in a Romanized Milanese text. It has dropped out of the Ambrosian Missals of the present day.
[4] Both in its so-called Gelasian and Gregorian forms.
[5] This Liturgy, together with its Scottish and American derivatives, owes this omission, together with certain other features, both for better and for worse, to its Roman descent.
[6] H., p. 17.   [7] *Ibid.*, p. 41.   [8] *Ibid.*, p. 112.   [9] *Ibid.*, p. 70.
[10] Renaudot, *Liturg. Orien. Coll.*, tom. ii. p. 127.
[11] *Ibid.*, p 136.   [12] *Ibid.*, p. 147.
[13] H., p. 109. But St. Chrysostom himself held these words to

Inserted in	Omitted in

8. St. Peter II.[1]
9. St. John Evangelist.[2]
10. The Twelve Apostles.[3]
11. St. Mark.[4]
12. St. Clement.[5]
13. St. Dionysius Areopagita.[6]
14. St. Ignatius.[7]
15. St. Julius.[8]
16. St. Eustathius.[9]
17. St. John Chrysostom I.[10]
18. St. John Chrysostom II.[11]
19. St. Marutas.[12]
20. St. Cyril.[13]
21. St. Dioscorus (Alexandrinus).[14]
22. St. Philoxenus I. (Mabugensis).[15]
23. St. Philoxenus II. (Hieropolitanus).[16]
24. Severus Antiochenus.[17]
25. St. James Baradatus.[18]
26. St. Matthew the Shepherd.[19]
27. St. James of Botnan.[20]
28. St. James of Edessa.[21]
29. St. Thomas of Heraclea.[22]

be our Lord's (Hom. in Eph. sect. 4). Were they in the Liturgy of Constantinople in his time? They are not in the earliest extant MS. text (Barberini MS., early 9th cent.).

[1] Renaudot, p. 156. [2] *Ibid.*, p. 164. [3] *Ibid.*, p. 171.
[4] *Ibid.*, p. 178. [5] *Ibid.*, p. 189. [6] *Ibid.*, p. 205.
[7] *Ibid.*, p. 216. [8] *Ibid.*, p. 228. [9] *Ibid.*, p. 235.
[10] *Ibid.*, p. 244. [11] *Ibid.*, p. 256. [12] *Ibid.*, p. 262.
[13] *Ibid.*, p. 277. [14] *Ibid.*, p. 288. [15] *Ibid.*, p. 301.
[16] *Ibid.*, p. 311. [17] *Ibid.*, p. 323. [18] *Ibid.*, p. 335.
[19] *Ibid.*, p. 348. [20] *Ibid.*, p. 359. [21] *Ibid.*, p. 373. [22] *Ibid.*, p. 384.

All (8–41) these are Syriac Liturgies. See Brightman (F. E.), *Eastern Liturgies*, pp. lviii, lix.

I.] LITURGICAL WORSHIP IN H. SCRIPTURE. 29

Inserted in	Omitted in
30. St. Moses Bar-Cephas.[1]	2. The Armenian Liturgy.[13]
31. St. Philoxenus III. (Bag-dadensis).[2]	
32. The Holy Doctors.[3]	
33. St. John Basorensis.[4]	
34. St. Michael of Antioch.[5]	
35. St. Dionysius Barsalibi.[6]	
36. St. Gregory (Catholicus.)[7]	
37. St. John the Patriarch.[8]	
38. St. Dioscorus of Cardou.[9]	
39. Ignatius the Patriarch.[10]	
40. Ignatius of Antioch.[11]	
41. St. Basil (ex Versione Andreæ Masii).[12]	

(b) *East Syrian.*

Nestorius.[14]   Theodore the Interpreter.[15]

(The Liturgy of SS. Adæus and Maris is omitted as uncertain, the words of institution being absent from the text as known to us, though they are used in practice.)[16]

(c) *Alexandrian.*

1. St. Mark.[17]   1. The Ethiopic Liturgy.[20]
2. Coptic St. Basil.[18]
3.   „   St. Cyril.[19]

[1] Renaudot, p. 392. [2] *Ibid.*, p. 401. [3] *Ibid.*, p. 411.
[4] *Ibid.*, p. 424. [5] *Ibid.*, p. 440. [6] *Ibid.*, p. 449.
[7] *Ibid.*, p. 459. [8] *Ibid.*, p. 475. [9] *Ibid.*, p. 493.
[10] *Ibid.*, p. 511. [11] *Ibid.*, p. 527. [12] *Ibid.*, p. 548.
[13] H., p. 153.
[14] Renaudot, *Liturg. Orien. Coll.*, tom. ii. p. 623.
[15] *Ibid.*, p. 613.
[16] H., p. 274; Brightman (F. E.), *Eastern Liturgies*, pp. 246, 285.
[17] H., p. 187. [18] *Ibid.*, p. 211. [19] *Ibid.*, p. 220.
[20] Both in the Canon Universalis (H., *ut supra*, p. 258), and in the shorter Liturgy, forming part of the Ethiopic Apostolic Constitutions (*Ibid.*, p. 235).

| Inserted in | Omitted in |

4. Coptic St. Gregory.¹
5. Greek St. Basil.²
6.   ,,   St. Gregory.³
7. Ancient Fragment.⁴

The following titles are given to this service :—

(*a*) 'The breaking of bread.'

'And they continued stedfastly in the Apostles' doctrine and fellowship, and in [the] breaking of bread, and in [the] prayers.'⁵

(*b*) 'The Lord's Supper.'

'When ye come together therefore into one place, this is not to eat the Lord's supper.'⁶

The title 'Communion,' or 'Holy Communion,' does not occur in the New Testament, but, no doubt, was suggested by St. Paul's words—

'The cup of blessing which we bless, is it not the communion of the blood of Christ? The bread which we break, is it not the communion of the body of Christ?'⁷

The word 'Liturgy' (λειτουργία) occurs several times in the New Testament, but never in a technical sense with exclusive reference to this Christian service.⁸

The word 'Eucharist' (εὐχαριστία) occurs frequently

---

¹ Renaudot, *Liturg. Orien. Coll.*, tom. i. p. 30.
² *Ibid.*, p. 67.   ³ *Ibid.*, p. 97.
⁴ Georgius (F. A. A.), *Fragmentum Evangelii*, etc. (Rome, 1789), p. 315.
⁵ Acts ii. 42. See, also, ii. 46, and xx. 7.   ⁶ 1 Cor. xi. 20.
⁷ 1 Cor. x. 16.
⁸ The verb λειτουργεῖν occurs once in Acts xiii. 2. 'As they ministered (λειτουργούντων) to the Lord, and fasted.' The word here may include, but cannot be confined to, the celebration of the Christian Eucharist.

I.] *LITURGICAL WORSHIP IN H. SCRIPTURE.* 31

in the New Testament; but though there are one or two cases (*e.g.* 1 Cor. xiv. 16; 1 Tim. ii. 1) in which it may include the offering of the Eucharistic Sacrifice, it is evident that the word had not yet assumed exclusively a technical sense, as a title for that particular service.[1]

It would be a natural inference from the language used in 1 Cor. xii. 26—whether we regard the words as spoken by Christ or composed by St. Paul—that this service was intended to be celebrated frequently, not infrequently. We are, therefore, not surprised to find that the two practices for which there is directly scriptural authority, are daily and weekly reception of the Holy Communion. The former was the practice of the first Christians immediately after the Day of Pentecost.

'And they, continuing daily with one accord in the temple, and breaking bread from house to house [or 'at home'], did eat their meat with gladness and singleness of heart.'[2]

The latter was the practice at Troas, where the Eucharist apparently formed part of the Sunday as distinguished from the week-day worship.

'And upon the first day of the week, when the disciples came together to break bread, Paul preached unto them.'[3]

---

[1] St. Augustine interprets the whole of 1 Tim. ii. 1 of the Holy Eucharist (*Epist. ad Paulinum*, 149, sect. 16). His words are so important that they would be quoted here, were they not outside the limit, as to date, which has been imposed upon this volume. They are quoted in note 1 of J. H. Blunt's *Dict. of Theology*, p. 255. See *P. L.*, tom. xxxiii. col. 636.

[2] Acts ii. 46; but Dr. P. Gardner interprets this verse of the Agapé (*The Origin of the Lord's Supper*, p. 15: London, 1893).

[3] Acts xx. 7.

Communion in both kinds was ordered by our Lord at the original institution, and the following texts prove (what, without them, could hardly have been doubted) that it was the practice of the Church in apostolic times :—

'Ye cannot drink the cup of the Lord, and the cup of devils.'[1]

'Wherefore whosoever shall eat this bread, and[2] drink this cup of the Lord, unworthily, shall be guilty of the body and blood of the Lord.

But let a man examine himself, and so let him eat of that bread, and drink of that cup.

For he that eateth and drinketh unworthily, eateth and drinketh damnation to himself, not discerning the Lord's body.'[3]

There remain two points on which there has been much controversy and some diversity of practice in later Christendom, and about which no direction is explicitly laid down in Holy Scripture, viz. the use of leavened or unleavened bread, and the use of a mixed or unmixed cup. But though explicit directions with reference to Christian Eucharistic usage are wanting, we know, with certainty, that the bread in use at the Paschal Supper was unleavened ;[4] and

---

[1] 1 Cor. x. 21.

[2] The truer reading is 'or,' but our translators only followed the reading of the older Vulgates, and of the older Roman Missals, in printing 'and' [*et*]. They were not actuated by any doctrinal motive, as has been sometimes supposed.

[3] 1 Cor. xi. 27-29.

[4] Exod. xii. 15, 18-20. Even if the feast, at which our Lord was present, was not the Paschal Supper, but an anticipation of it, unleavened bread and the mixed cup would probably have been used.

we know, with something approaching to certainty, that the cup contained wine mingled with water.[1]

§ 15. HYMNS.—The word 'hymn' (ὕμνος), and the verb to sing 'hymns' (ὑμνίζειν), occur several times in the New Testament. In the case of the hymn recorded to have been sung by our Saviour and His disciples after the institution and reception of the first Christian Eucharist[2] it is generally supposed to have been Pss. cxv.-cxviii., which formed the second part of the Hallel, and were sung by every Jewish family or company at the conclusion of the Paschal Supper. But this does not seem to be necessary or certain though most probable.

When Paul and Silas were imprisoned at Philippi, it is recorded that 'about midnight they were praying and singing hymns unto God, and the prisoners were listening to them.'[3] It is not known, and there are no means of knowing, what psalms or hymns were sung then. In a well-known Latin hymn attributed to St. Gregory the Great, but probably composed in the seventh or eighth century, and assigned, in most Breviaries, both secular and monastic, to be sung at Matins on Wednesday, these midnight devotions of Paul [and Silas] are somewhat fancifully referred to as authority or the institution of the midnight service of nocturns.[4]

---

[1] Lightfoot (J.), *Horæ Hebraicæ*, on St. Matt. xxvi. 26, 27, and on 1 Cor. xi. 25. Oxford, 1859, vol. ii. p. 351; vol. iv. p. 247.
[2] St. Matt. xxvi. 30; St. Mark xiv. 26.   [3] Acts xvi. 25 (R.V.).
[4] 'Mentes manusque tollimus
  Propheta sicut noctibus
  Nobis gerendum præcipit,
  Paulusque gestis censuit.'
  Fourth stanza of 'Rerum Creator Optime.'

There are two passages in the Epistles in which hymns are enumerated as something distinct from psalms—

'Speaking to yourselves in psalms and hymns and spiritual songs.' [1]
'Teaching and admonishing one another in psalms and hymns and spiritual songs.' [2]

It has been suggested that the three Persons in the blessed Trinity are referred to as addressed in the three different kinds of sacred song,[3] and from the words 'to yourselves' that they were antistrophically arranged and rendered;[4] but these are merely conjectures.

There are good grounds for believing that there exist embedded in the text of the New Testament actual fragments of some of the earliest Christian hymns as distinguished from the recognized and inspired Psalms and Canticles of Holy Scripture. The metrical ring is so much more obvious in the Greek than in the English language, that we offer no apology for printing the Greek original and an English line for line version side by side.

(1) Fragment of an Advent Hymn—

Ὥρα ἡμᾶς ἤδη	'This the hour already
ἐξ ὕπνον ἐγερθῆναι,	to waken out of sleep,
νῦν γὰρ ἐγγύτερον	for nearer now
ἡμῶν ἡ σωτηρία	is our salvation
ἢ ὅτε ἐπιστεύσαμεν·	than when we believed;

[1] Eph. v. 19.   [2] Col. iii. 16.
[3] Blunt (J. H.), *Annotated Prayer-book*, revised edition, p. 53.
[4] Bp. Ch. Wordsworth's *Commentary*, 3rd ed., on Eph. v. 19, p. 303.

ἡ νὺξ προέκοψεν, the night is far spent,
ἡ δὲ ἡμέρα ἤγγικεν. the day is nigh at hand.'[1]

(2) Fragment of a Hymn on Penitence—

Ἔγειρε ὁ καθεύδων, 'Awake thou that sleepest,
καὶ ἀνάστα ἐκ τῶν νεκρῶν, and arise from the dead,
καὶ ἐπιφαύσει σοι ὁ Χριστός. and Christ shall give thee light.'[2]

(3) Fragment of a Hymn or Antiphonal Composition on Christ—

[Θεὸς or] Ὃς   'Who
ἐφανερώθη ἐν σαρκί,   was manifest in the flesh,
ἐδικαιώθη ἐν πνεύματι,   justified in the Spirit,
ὤφθη ἀγγέλοις,   seen of angels,
ἐκηρύχθη ἐν ἔθνεσιν,   preached unto the Gentiles,
ἐπιστεύθη ἐν κόσμῳ,   believed on in the world,
ἀνελήφθη ἐν δόξῃ.   received up into glory.'[3]

(4) Another fragment on Christ—

Πιστὸς ὁ λόγος·   'It is a faithful saying:
Εἰ συναπεθάνομεν, καὶ συζή-   If we be dead with Him, we
  σομεν·   shall also live with Him;
εἰ ὑπομένομεν, καὶ συμ-   if we suffer, we shall also
  βασιλεύσομεν·   reign with Him;
εἰ ἀρνούμεθα, κἀκεῖνος ἀρνή-   if we deny Him, He also
  σεται ἡμᾶς·   will deny us;
εἰ ἀπιστοῦμεν, ἐκεῖνος πισ-   if we believe not, yet He
  τὸς μένει·   abideth faithful;
ἀρνήσασθαι ἑαυτὸν οὐ δύναται.   He cannot deny Himself.'[4]

We append two more quotations apparently from early Christian formularies, yet of a didactic, rather than a liturgical character; they are both introduced

[1] Rom. xiii. 11, 12.   [2] Eph. v. 14.   [3] 1 Tim. iii. 16.
[4] 2 Tim. ii. 11-13.

by St. Paul as faithful sayings, the first as worthy of all acceptation (πιστὸς ὁ λόγος καὶ πάσης ἀποδοχῆς ἄξιος), and the second as incumbent upon Titus to affirm constantly (πιστὸς ὁ λόγος καὶ περὶ τούτων βούλομαί σε διαβεβαιοῦσθαι).

(5) Εἰς τοῦτο γὰρ καὶ κοπιῶμεν καὶ ὀνειδιζόμεθα, ὅτι ἠλπίκαμεν ἐπὶ Θεῷ ζῶντι, ὅς ἐστι σωτὴρ πάντων ἀνθρώπων, μάλιστα πιστῶν.

'For, therefore we both labour and suffer reproach, because we trust in the living God, who is the Saviour of all men, specially of those that believe.'[1]

(6) Ἵνα φροντίζωσι καλῶν ἔργων προΐστασθαι οἱ πεπιστευκότες τῷ Θεῷ· ταῦτά ἐστι τὰ καλὰ καὶ ὠφέλιμα τοῖς ἀνθρώποις.

'That they which have believed in God might be careful to maintain good works: these things are good and profitable unto men.'[2]

There remain some other passages in the New Testament which may be quotations from early liturgical or other authorized formularies, but the case with regard to them is too uncertain for their insertion here.[3]

§ 16. THE KISS OF PEACE.—The use of the kiss as an emblem of Christian love and peace is frequently referred to in the apostolic writings, e.g.—

'Salute one another with an holy kiss.'[4]
'Greet ye one another with an holy kiss.'[5]
'Greet one another with an holy kiss.'[6]

---

[1] 1 Tim. iv. 10.   [2] Titus iii. 8.
[3] On the whole subject see a paper by Dr. Jessopp, in the *Expositor*, No. LX., pp. 401–422.
[4] Rom. xvi. 16.   [5] 1 Cor. xvi. 20.   [6] 2 Cor. xiii. 12.

'Greet all the brethren with an holy kiss.'[1]
'Greet ye one another with a kiss of charity.'[2]

It is true that there is no liturgical position assigned to this kiss, but the epithet 'holy' always applied to it by St. Paul indicates that it was not merely the ordinary Eastern mode of salutation, but that it partook of a religious character, and we find it from the very earliest post-scriptural times associated with the approach to the Holy Eucharist. Its Eucharistic connection can hardly fail to have been suggested by these words of our Lord—

'Therefore if thou bring thy gift to the altar, and there rememberest that thy brother hath ought against thee;

Leave there thy gift before the altar, and go thy way; first be reconciled to thy brother, and then come and offer thy gift.'[3]

§ 17. LAYING ON OF HANDS.—See Benediction (p. 16); Confirmation (p. 19); Excommunication (p. 23); Ordination (p. 39).

§ 18. LOVE-FEAST.—The love-feast, or agapé, was a common meal, at which the first Christians met together in token of love and brotherly kindness. It was partly of a religious, partly of a social, but not of sacramental character.

It is evident from St. Paul's language in 1 Cor. xi., that it was closely associated with, and it is almost certain that in scriptural times it preceded, the Holy Eucharist. But the gross scandals which this close connection was liable to cause, and did cause in the Corinthian church, led to their very early severance.

[1] 1 Thess. v. 26.   [2] 1 Pet. v. 14.   [3] St. Matt. v. 23, 24.

Some commentators have thought that the expression 'the Lord's supper,' in 1 Cor. xi. 20, refers to the love-feast and not to Holy Communion.

Further allusions to this love-feast are found in the Epistle of St. Jude—

'These are spots in your feasts of charity (ἀγάπαις), when they feast with you, feeding themselves without fear.'[1]

Possibly also in St. Peter's exhortation—

'Greet ye one another with a kiss of charity' (ἀγάπης)[2]— the kiss of charity being part of the ceremonial observed at the feast called the agapé.

And in another passage, where ἀπάταις may be a false reading for ἀγάπαις—

'Spots they are and blemishes, sporting themselves with their own deceivings, [ἀπάταις, but *read* 'ἀγαπάις,' in their love-feasts] while they feast with you.'[3]

§ 19. MARRIAGE.—Our Lord's language with reference to marriage, and the language employed by St. Paul in reference to the same subject, imply that marriage is a religious union; but there is no reference to any special ceremony to be used in connection with the marriage service.

Our Saviour says—

'What therefore God hath joined together, let not man put asunder.'[4]

St. Paul says—

'The wife is bound by the law as long as her husband liveth; but if her husband be dead, she is at liberty to be married to whom she will; only in the Lord.'[5]

[1] St. Jude 12.   [2] 1 Pet. v. 14.   [3] 2 Pet. ii. 13.
[4] St. Mark x. 9.   [5] 1 Cor. vii. 39.

And the comparison of the union between husband and wife to the union between Christ and His Church might be also quoted.[1]

§ 20. OFFERINGS.—The principle of a weekly Sunday collection, or offering, for charitable purposes is found in the direction given by St. Paul to the Churches of Corinth and Galatia—

'Now concerning the collection for the saints, as I have given order to the Churches of Galatia, even so do ye,

Upon the first day of the week let every one of you lay by him in store, as God hath prospered him, that there be no gatherings when I come.'[2]

§ 21. ORDINATION.—Our Lord selected a human ministry for the purpose of preaching the gospel, founding the Christian Church, and carrying on through it, after His own departure, the work which He came on earth to do.

He specially chose and empowered twelve of His followers in the first instance—

'And when He had called unto Him His twelve disciples, He gave them power against unclean spirits, to cast them out, and to heal all manner of sickness and all manner of disease. . . .

And as ye go, preach, saying, The kingdom of heaven is at hand.

Heal the sick, cleanse the lepers, raise the dead, cast out devils: freely ye have received, freely give. . . .

He that receiveth you receiveth Me, and he that receiveth Me receiveth Him that sent Me.'[3]

[1] Eph. v. 22-32.   [2] 1 Cor. xvi. 1, 2.
[3] St. Matt. x. 1, 7, 8, 40.

On another occasion He chose and sent forth seventy disciples—

'After these things the Lord appointed other seventy also, and sent them two and two before His face into every city and place, whither He Himself would come.'[1]

Then follow commissions and instructions similar to those given to the twelve.

A further commission and mission were given to the Apostles after our Lord's resurrection. It was on the evening of the same day on which He had risen from the grave, that our Saviour suddenly appeared in the midst of His ten Apostles gathered together in an upper chamber in Jerusalem, for fear of the Jews, and said to them—

'Peace be unto you: as My Father hath sent Me, even so send I you.

And when He had said this, He breathed on them, and saith unto them, Receive ye the Holy Ghost:

Whose soever sins ye remit, they are remitted unto them; and whose soever sins ye retain, they are retained.'[2]

The act of breathing was sacramental. It was the outward visible sign accompanying the gift of the Holy Spirit to the Apostles, to give them strength for the work of the Apostleship, to which they were then sent forth. The act seems to betoken that He who so breathed was the source, and not only the channel of sacramental grace. Possibly for this reason it was not repeated or retained, for at

---

[1] St. Luke x. 1. [2] St. John xx. 21-23.

all the ordinations of which we have any record, or to which there is any allusion in the New Testament, we find that the imposition or laying on of hands takes its place—

As at the ordination of the seven deacons—

'Whom they set before the Apostles: and when they had prayed, they laid their hands on them.'[1]

At the ordination of Barnabas and Saul—

'And when they had fasted and prayed, and laid their hands on them, they sent them away.'[2]

At the ordination of Timothy—

'Neglect not the gift that is in thee, which was given thee by prophecy, with the laying on of the hands of the presbytery.'[3]

'Wherefore I put thee in remembrance that thou stir up the gift of God, which is in thee by the putting on of my hands.'[4]

At the ordination of those whom Timothy was to ordain—

'Lay hands suddenly on no man, neither be partaker of other men's sins.'[5]

Fasting was a practice closely connected with ordination, as may be seen in the passage quoted above from Acts xiii. 3, and from the following account of ordinations held by SS. Barnabas and Paul—

'And when they had ordained them elders in every

---

[1] Acts vi. 6.   [2] Acts xiii. 3.   [3] 1 Tim. iv. 14.
[4] 2 Tim. i. 6.
[5] 1 Tim. v. 22. For another interpretation of this passage, see p. 25.

church, and had prayed with fasting, they commended them to the Lord, on whom they believed.'[1]

The following is a list of the various ministerial titles or descriptions used in the New Testament:—

Greek word.	Meaning.	Where used.	English word.
Ἀπόστολος	One sent	*Frequently*	Apostle
Ἐπίσκοπος	An overseer	Acts xx. 28	Bishop
Ἄγγελος	A messenger	Rev. ii. 1	Angel
Πρεσβύτερος	An elder	Acts xv. 23	Presbyter, or Priest
Διάκονος	A servant	1 Tim. iii. 12	Deacon
Λειτουργός	One who performs a public duty	Rom. xv. 16	Minister
Εὐαγγελιστής	A bearer of good news	2 Tim. iv. 5	Evangelist
Ἡγούμενος	A ruler	Heb. xiii. 17	Ruler
Κῆρυξ	A herald	1 Tim. ii. 7	Preacher
Οἰκονόμος	Manager of house	1 Cor. iv. 1, 2	Steward
Προφήτης	One who declares God's will	1 Cor. xiv. 29	Prophet
Διδάσκαλος	A teacher	1 Cor. xii. 29	Teacher
Ποιμήν	A shepherd	Eph. iv. 11	Pastor
Προϊστάμενος	Presiding	1 Thess. v. 12	President

The titles of Ἱερεύς (= Priest) and Ἀρχιερεύς (= High Priest or Arch-Priest) are given to our Lord only (Heb. iv. 14; x. 21).[2] But all Christians are called Priests (1 Pet. ii. 5, 9; Rev. i. 6; v. 10), and all Jews (Exod. xix. 6).

§ 22. PUBLIC PRAYER.—During our Lord's lifetime on earth, He and His Apostles frequented the services of the Jewish temple at Jerusalem and of the synagogues in country places,[3] and this continued to be the practice of the Apostles and first Christian converts after the Ascension and after the Day of Pentecost.

[1] Acts xiv. 23.

[2] The verb ἱερουργεῖν, 'to minister as a priest,' or 'about sacred things,' is once used by St. Paul of his own work in connection with the gospel (Rom. xv. 16).

[3] St. Matt. xxi. 12, 13; St. Mark xi. 15; xiv. 49; St. Luke iv. 16, 33; vi. 6; xix. 45; St. John ii. 13-16, etc.

After the Ascension, the Apostles—

'Returned to Jerusalem with great joy:
And were continually in the temple, praising and blessing God.'[1]

After the Day of Pentecost, we find it still recorded that—

'Peter and John went up together into the temple at the hour of prayer, being the ninth hour.'[2]

St. Paul says of himself—

'It came to pass, that, when I was come again to Jerusalem, even while I prayed in the temple, I was in a trance.'[3]

This custom of frequenting the temple services prevailed throughout the period covered by the New Testament; but, from the very first, there was one addition or exception necessarily made. The distinctively Christian ordinance of the Eucharist could not be celebrated in any Jewish place of worship. Christian places of worship did not begin to be built till long afterwards. The difficulty was met by celebrating the Eucharist in private houses or at home—

'And they, continuing daily with one accord in the temple, and breaking bread from house to house,[4] did eat their meat with gladness and singleness of heart.'[5]

Round these home Eucharists there would naturally gather the elements of teaching, exhortation, praise, and prayer.

---

[1] St. Luke xxiv. 52, 53.   [2] Acts iii. 1.   [3] Acts xxii. 17.
[4] Κατ' οἶκον, better translated, as in the R.V., 'at home.'
[5] Acts ii. 46.

These elements are implied when we are told that the first converts—

'Continued steadfastly in the Apostles' doctrine and fellowship, and in breaking of bread, and in prayers.'[1]

And that—

'Upon the first day of the week, when the disciples came together to break bread, Paul preached unto them.'[2]

In Palestine, after the destruction of Jerusalem, and in Gentile countries where there were neither synagogue nor temple before that time, these elements of Christian worship grew, were regulated, were ultimately systematized into settled forms of worship.

Very few directions as to the arrangement and external forms of such worship are to be found in the New Testament.

St. Paul delivered certain ordinances or traditions to the Corinthians, and praised them for keeping them;[3] but we do not know what these ordinances were.

They included—

The uncovering of men's heads in prayer.[4]
The covering or veiling of women in prayer.[5]
The use of a language understood by the people.[6]
The prohibition of women from speaking in church.[7]
Weekly collection of alms for charitable purposes.[8]

---

[1] Acts ii. 42.   [2] Acts xx. 7.   [3] 1 Cor. xi. 2.
[4] 1 Cor. xi. 4.   [5] 1 Cor. xi. 5.   [6] 1 Cor. xiv. 19.
[7] 1 Cor. xiv. 34, 35. Compare 1 Tim. ii. 11, 12.
[8] 1 Cor. xvi. 2.

And, generally speaking, decency and order.[1]

The Jewish name of 'synagogue' was used at first to denote the place of Christian assembly.

St. James said—

'If there come unto your assembly (συναγωγήν) a man with a gold ring,' etc.[2]

He had made use of the same word previously in a strictly Jewish sense and connection in his speech at the Council of Jerusalem.[3]

The author of the Epistle to the Hebrews, speaking of the duty of public Christian worship, says—

'Not forsaking the assembling (ἐπισυναγωγήν) of ourselves together, as the manner of some is.'[4]

The expression 'synagogue of Satan' is twice used in the Book of Revelation to denote the gathering together of wicked worshippers.[5]

§ 23. SUNDAY.—There are distinct traces, from the very earliest times, of the first day of the week taking the place of the seventh day of the week as the Christian day of rest and worship, although there is no Divine or apostolic command authorizing the change of day. It may have been among the unrecorded directions given by our Saviour to His disciples during the forty days before His ascension.[6]

Thus we find how at Troas—

[1] 1 Cor. xiv. 40.   [2] St. Jas. ii. 2.   [3] Acts xv. 21.
[4] Heb. x. 25.   [5] Rev. ii. 9; iii. 9.   [6] Acts i. 3.

'Upon the first day of the week, when the disciples came together to break bread, Paul preached unto them.'[1]

St. Paul recommends systematic almsgiving upon the same day—

'Upon the first day of the week let every one of you lay by him in store, as God hath prospered him.'[2]

As the day on which our Lord had risen from the dead, it was pre-eminently the Lord's day, and as such it became known, and is believed to be referred to in the passage in which St. John says—

'I was in the Spirit on the Lord's day.'[3]

TABLE OF THE LORD. See p. 19.

§ 24. UNCTION OF THE SICK. Unction of the sick is plainly mentioned in two passages. Firstly, as the practice of the Apostles in our Lord's lifetime—

'And they cast out many devils, and anointed with oil many that were sick, and healed them.'[4]

Secondly, as recommended by St. James, to be used in the case of sick people—

'Is any sick among you? let him call for the elders of the Church; and let them pray over him, anointing him with oil in the name of the Lord.
And the prayer of faith shall save the sick, and the Lord shall raise him up; and if he have committed sins, they shall be forgiven him.'[5]

For Unction at Baptism or Confirmation, see p. 20.

[1] Acts xx. 7. [2] 1 Cor. xvi. 2.
[3] Rev. i. 10. It is doubtful whether 'the Lord's day' (ἡ Κυριακὴ ἡμέρα) in this passage means 'Sunday' or 'the Day of Judgment.'
[4] St. Mark vi. 13. [5] St. Jas. v. 14, 15.

§ 25. VESTMENTS.—There is no allusion in the New Testament to any distinctive dress as worn either by the Apostles or by persons of any grade in the Christian ministry, either while engaged in Divine service or in everyday life.

There is, indeed, one passage which has sometimes been referred to, especially in recent times,[1] as possibly referring to an article of ecclesiastical dress; but there is no ground whatever for such an interpretation—

'The cloke ($\phi\alpha\iota\lambda\acute{o}\nu\eta s$) that I left at Troas with Carpus, when thou comest, bring with thee, and the books, but especially the parchments.'[2]

St. Chrysostom knew nothing of a chasuble theory. He interpreted the cloke to mean the ordinary article of attire which now goes by that name. It is in his first homily on the Philippians, where he is replying to the objections of some mean persons who excused themselves from providing a suitable maintenance for their clergy on the ground of such texts as St. Matt. x. 9, 10: 'Provide neither gold, nor silver, nor brass in your purses, nor scrip for your journey, neither two coats, neither shoes,' etc.

'What?' he says, 'had not Peter a girdle, and a cloke, and shoes? (Acts xii. 8). And Paul too, when he writes

---

[1] Rock (D), *Hierurgia*, 2nd ed. (London, 1851), p. 438; Neale (J. M.), *Essays on Liturgiology*, p. 414. Cardinal Bona was doubtful whether this cloke was a sacerdotal vestment or not (*Rer. Liturg.*, lib. i. cap. 24, tom. ii. p. 235: Turin, 1749). Sala appends a long note ([1]) in favour of the chasuble theory (*Ibid.*, p. 237).

[2] 2 Tim. iv. 13.

to Timothy: "Do thy diligence to come before winter," and then gives him instructions: "The cloke which I left at Troas," etc. There now! he says, *the cloke;* and no one would pretend to say that he had not a second, namely, the one he was wearing. For if he was not in the habit of wearing one, it would be superfluous for him to bid Timothy bring this one; but if he did wear one, and could not help wearing one, it is clear that he had another besides.'[1]

Tertullian's reference to the same passage (2 Tim. iv. 13),[2] makes it evident that he understood 'the cloke' in the same sense as St. Chrysostom.

§ 26. THE WASHING OF FEET.—After our Lord had washed the feet of His Apostles in the upper chamber on the evening of Maundy Thursday, He used these words—

'Ye call Me Master and Lord: and ye say well; for so I am.

If I then, your Lord and Master, have washed your feet; ye also ought to wash one another's feet.

For I have given you an example, that ye should do as I have done to you.'[3]

It has generally been believed that our Lord's words and actions are metaphorical and symbolical, and that it was not His design to institute a ceremony to be observed hereafter in the Church. But a literal interpretation has caused the washing of the feet of

[1] Quoted in Field (F.), *Otium Norvicense*, pars tertia, 1881, p. 133.
[2] *De Oratione*, cap. xvi.; *P. L.*, tom. i. col. 1171.
[3] St. John xiii. 13-15.

catechumens, or of poor men, to form part of the ceremonial of Maundy Thursday; and the washing of the feet of the newly baptized has also formed an integral part of certain ancient baptismal offices.[1]

[1] *E.g.* The ancient Gallican (Neale and Forbes'-edition, pp. 97, 189, 267); the ancient Irish (F. E. Warren, *Lit. and Rit. of the Celtic Church*, p. 217); the ancient Spanish (Mansi, *Concil*, tom. ii. p. 14).

CHAPTER II.

ANTE-NICENE RITUAL.

Introductory—§ 1. Absolution—§ 2. Baptism—§ 3. Choral Service —§ 4. Church furniture.—§ 5. Confession—§ 6. Confirmation —§ 7. Sign of the Cross—§ 8. Exorcism—§ 9. Fasting—§ 10. The Eucharist—§ 11. Imposition of hands—§ 12. Incense— § 13. Kiss of peace—§ 14. The Love-feast (Agapé)—§ 15. Marriage—§ 16. Ordination, Holy Orders—§ 17. Prayer—§ 18. Saints' Days—§ 19. Sunday—§ 20. Unction—§ 21. Vestments —§ 22. Use of the vulgar tongue—§ 23. Washing of hands and feet.

WE pass from the evidence which is yielded by Holy Scripture as to the character of the worship and ritual of the Apostolic Church, to describe the liturgy and ritual of the ante-Nicene Church, so far as they can be gathered from the writings of the ante-Nicene Fathers or from other genuine documents which may bear upon the subject of a date prior to A.D. 325.

But before going into details, we will quote at length some passages of a general character, either describing the worship of the early Christian Church or explaining or defending certain broad features which it possessed.

The following description of Christian worship was given by Pliny, Governor of Bithynia, writing to the Emperor Trajan, A.D. 112. Pliny said that he had obtained his information from certain apostates from the Christian faith whom he had examined.

'They asserted that this was the sum and substance of their fault or their error; namely, that they were in the habit of meeting before dawn on a stated day, and singing alternately a hymn to Christ as to a god, and that they bound themselves by an oath [1] not to the commission of any wicked deed, but that they would abstain from theft, and robbery, and adultery; that they would not break their word; and that they would not withhold a deposit when reclaimed. This done, it was their practice, so they said, to separate, and then to meet together again for a meal, which, however, was of the ordinary kind, and quite harmless. But even from this they had desisted after my edict; in which, in pursuance of your commands, I had forbidden the existence of clubs.' [2]

The following description of the Eucharistic Service is given by Justin Martyr, in his First *Apology*, most probably written and addressed to the Emperor Antoninus Pius in A.D. 148:—

'CAP. LXV.

'But we [Christians], after we have thus washed him who has been convinced and has assented [to our teaching] lead him to the place where those who are called brethren

---

[1] 'Sacramento.' The word 'Sacramentum,' in early Christian writings, has two senses—(1) 'a sacred ordinance, or doctrine, or fact,' (2) 'a solemn oath.' It is impossible to decide in which sense it is used here. If it is used in the former sense the reference is obviously to the Eucharist. See Bp. Lightfoot's exhaustive note, *The Apostolic Fathers* (London, 1891), pt. ii. vol. i. p. 51.

[2] *Epp.*, lib. x, No. 97 (ed. Frankfort, 1611), p. 364.

are assembled, in order that we may offer hearty prayers in common for ourselves and for the illuminated [*i.e.* baptized] person, and for all others in every place, that we may be counted worthy, now that we have learned the truth, by our works also to be found good citizens and keepers of the commandments, so that we may be saved with an everlasting salvation. Having ended the prayers, we salute one another with a kiss. Bread and a cup of wine mingled with water are then brought to the president of the brethren; and he, taking them, gives praise and glory to the Father of the Universe, through the Name of the Son and of the Holy Ghost, and offers thanks at considerable length for our being counted worthy to receive these things at his hands. And when he has concluded the prayers and thanksgivings, all the people present express their consent by saying, "Amen." This word "Amen" answers in the Hebrew language to [the Greek] γένοιτο [*i.e.* So be it]. And when the president has given thanks, and all the people have expressed their assent, those who are called by us deacons give each of those present the bread and wine mixed with water, over which the thanksgiving was pronounced, and they carry away a portion to those who are not present.

Cap. LXVI.

And this food is called among us "the Eucharist," of which no one is allowed to partake but he who believes that the things which we teach are true, and who has been washed with the washing that is for the remission of sins and unto regeneration, and who is so living as Christ hath enjoined. For we do not receive these [elements] as common bread and common drink, but in like manner as Jesus Christ our Saviour, having been made flesh by the word of God, had both flesh and blood for our salvation, so likewise have we been taught that the food which is blessed by the prayer of the word which comes from Him, and from which our blood and flesh are nourished by transmutation, is the flesh and blood of that Jesus who was made flesh. For the Apostles in the memoirs composed by them, which are called Gospels, have thus delivered unto us what was enjoined upon them that Jesus took bread, and gave thanks, and said, "Do this in remembrance of Me: this is My body;" and that after the same manner He took the cup, and gave thanks, and said, "This is My blood," and gave it to them alone. The wicked devils have also imitated this in the mysteries of Mithras, commanding the same thing to be done. For you know, or can learn, that bread and a cup of water are employed with certain incantations in the mystic rites which accompany the initiation of a member.

Cap. LXVII.

And we afterwards continually remind each other of these things. And the wealthy among us help the needy, and we always keep together. And we bless the Creator of all things, through His Son Jesus Christ, and through the Holy Spirit, for all things wherewith we are supplied. And on the day called Sunday all who live in cities or in the country gather together to one place, and the memoirs of the Apostles [*i.e.* the Gospels], or the writings of the Prophets, are read, as long as time permits. Then, when the reader has ceased, the president verbally instructs and exhorts [the people] to the imitation of these good things. Then we all rise together and offer prayers. And, as we have said before, when we have finished the prayer, bread and wine and water are brought, and the president in like manner offers prayers and thanksgivings with all his might,[1] and the people assent, saying, "Amen," and there is a distribution to each, and a participation in the Eucharistic elements, and portions are sent to those who are not present

---

[1] Ὅση δύναμις αὐτῷ. The bearing of this expression is referred to hereafter, p. 106.

by the deacons. And the well-to-do and the willing give what each person thinks fit, and the collection is deposited with the president, who succours orphans and widows, and those who are in want through sickness or any other cause, and those who are in prison, and the strangers sojourning among us, and, in a word, he takes care of all who are in any need. We all hold our common assembly on Sunday, because it is the first day on which God having wrought a change in darkness and chaos made it cosmos, and because Jesus Christ our Saviour rose from the dead on the same day. For they crucified Him on the day before the day of Saturn [Saturday], and on the day after Saturday, which is Sunday, He appeared to His Apostles and disciples, and taught them these things, which we have submitted to you for your consideration.'[1]

Such is the description of simple Christian worship just before the middle of the second century. Its very simplicity was sometimes in early days urged as an argument against, or made a ground for, disputing the efficacy of the sacraments of the Christian Church. This is the way in which Tertullian meets the objection in the case of baptism; but the argument would apply equally well in the case of any or all of the sacraments or sacramental ordinances of Christ's Church. He says—

'But how great is the power of perversity in weakening or totally undermining faith, that it should find a ground of attack in those very elements on which that faith rests! There is nothing which so hardens men's minds against accepting the truth as the simplicity of the Divine operations, as seen in action, contrasted with the magnificence of the promised results. Take the case of Baptism. With the

[1] *P. G.*, tom. vi. coll. 427-431.

greatest simplicity, without parade, without any new or magnificent equipment, without any expense, a man is immersed in the water; a few words are said over him while he is dipped; he emerges very little, if at all, cleaner outwardly than he was before; therefore it is considered incredible that he should have acquired the heirship of eternal life. It would be untrue not to state, on the other hand, in connection with the worship of idols, that it is the solemnity and the secrecy and the expense of the preparations and of the performances which command confidence and submission.

Alas for a miserable incredulity which denies to God His own proper attributes—simplicity and power! What then? Is it not a wonderful thing that death should be washed away in the laver [of baptism]? Yes; but so far from not being believed because it is wonderful, it is on that account the more to be believed. For of what sort ought Divine works to be, except works of surpassing wonder? We also ourselves wonder; but we wonder because we believe. Unbelief wonders but does not believe. It wonders at simple rites as if they were empty of power or meaning; it wonders at magnificent rites as impossibilities. Be it as you think, the Divine pronouncement has anticipated both results. God has chosen the foolish things of this world to confound its wisdom, and what is impossible among men is possible with God. For if God is both wise and powerful, which those who neglect Him do not deny, it is not incongruous that He should lay the foundations of His operation in the opposites of wisdom and power, that is to say, in folly and impossibility, for all virtue originates in those elements from which it is evoked.'[1]

Throughout this chapter Tertullian is contrasting the simplicity of Christian worship as it existed in his

---

[1] *De Baptismo,* cap. ii.; *P. L.,* tom. i. col. 1201.

time with the gorgeousness of idolatrous ceremonial. One must allow that after the elaboration of Christian ritual in later ages, this argument lost some of its force; but one must insist, likewise, on the fact that Christian worship in Tertullian's time, with its unctions, its frequent use of the sign of the cross, its prolonged vigils, its midnight Easter celebration of the Eucharist, etc., was elaborateness itself compared with some modern forms of Christian worship.

Variety in ritual and in ecclesiastical usage began to be in evidence at a very early date. It was defended by St. Firmilian writing to St. Cyprian, c. 255. He pointed out that those who lived at Rome did not observe in all points their original traditions; that it was useless for the Church of Rome to claim apostolic authority for all its practices, as, for instance, on the question of the proper day for the celebration of Easter; also with regard to many unspecified points of liturgical arrangements, one way prevailed at Jerusalem, another at Rome. In most provinces there were diversities caused by the varieties of locality and of human nature; but the peace and unity of the Catholic Church were never imperilled by this fact.[1]

We now pass on from general descriptions to review in detail the particular usages of the primitive Church.

§ 1. ABSOLUTION.—Imposition of hands was the outward sign which accompanied the formal bestowal of absolution, or the public reconciliation to the

[1] *Inter Cypriani Epistolas*, No. 75, p. 145.

Church of one who had lapsed into schism or heresy, or who for some other cause was excommunicate.

St. Cyprian says—

'In the case of baptized members of the Church lapsing into heresy, and afterwards recognizing their sin, renouncing their error, and returning to the truth and to their mother, it will be sufficient to use imposition of hands,[1] as a token of the reception of the penitent, that so the shepherd may receive back into the fold, to which it once belonged, the alienated and wandering sheep.'[2]

Stephen I., Bishop of Rome, held that in the case of a convert coming over from heresy, re-baptism was unnecessary, and that he need only be received with imposition of hands as a token of penitence.[3]

The following passage describes the penitential system of the African Church:—

'In the case of lesser faults, sinners [ordinarily] do penance for a proper period, and then, according to the order of discipline, come to [public] confession,[4] and by the imposition of the hands of bishop and clergy receive the right of communion; but now, in this rough time, with persecution still prevalent, and peace not yet restored to the Church, people are admitted to communion, and the Eucharist is given to them, with no penance yet performed, no confession yet made, and the hands of bishop and clergy not yet laid upon them.'[5]

[1] 'Imponere manum.' It is almost always 'manum,' not 'manus,' in Latin writers.

[2] *Ep.* 71; *P. L.*, tom. iv. col. 423.

[3] The words of St. Stephen are quoted by St. Cyprian, and combated by him in Ep. 74; but the Roman view and practice on this point finally prevailed throughout the whole Church.

[4] Exomologesis.

[5] *Ep.* ix. p. 18. See also p. 19, *et passim*, for allusions to this use of the laying on of hands.

The imposition of hands is mentioned in the Apostolic Constitutions (but not in the Canons of Hippolytus, xi. 65 ; xiv. 74; xv. 79), as used in the restoration of an excommunicate person to Church membership.[1] See § 5, p. 82.

§ 2. BAPTISM.—We will first quote some general descriptions of the administration of baptism before producing evidence in detail on particular points of interest connected with it.

The baptism of Xanthippe, in answer to her request to St. Paul, 'Even now hasten to seal me,' is thus described—

'He led her by the hand into the house, and baptized her in the Name of the Father, and of the Son, and of the Holy Ghost. Then taking the bread of the Eucharist, he gave it to her, saying, " Let this be to thee for the remission of sins, and for the renewing of thy soul." Then the blessed Xanthippe, having received the Divine gift of holy baptism, returned to her own home, rejoicing and praising God.'[2]

Afterwards the baptism of her husband, Probus, is thus told—

'Rising early in the morning, he went to Paul, and found him baptizing many in the Name of the life-originating Trinity,[3] and said, If I am worthy, my master, to receive baptism, lo ! the hour is come. Paul replied to

---

[1] Lib. ii. cap. 18. Bp. Jeremy Taylor's interpretation of 1 Tim. v. 22 has been already referred to (p. 25). Compare the following words of Bp. Andrewes: ' By the Holy Ghost we are regenerate first in baptism ; by Him after confirmed in the imposition of hands; by Him after renewed to repentance when we fall away by a second imposition of hands' (*Sermons*, 1865, vol. iii. p. 194).

[2] Page 78.   [3] Εἰς τὸ τῆς ζωαρχικῆς τριάδος ὄνομα.

him, My son, behold, the water is ready for the cleansing of those who approach to Christ. Forthwith, then, eagerly stripping off his clothes, Paul holding his hand, he leaped into the water, saying, Jesus Christ, Son of God, and God eternal, may all my sins be done away by this water. And Paul said, We baptize thee in the Name of Father, Son, and Holy Ghost; and then he made him partake of the Eucharist of Christ.'[1]

Later on, Polyxena and Rebecca are described as baptized by the same Trinitarian formula, the former having thus made her request, 'Seal me, as Paul sealeth people, through the laver of regeneration.'[2]

In these passages the scriptural titles given to baptism, its administration where water could be found, the administration at once of the Eucharist to the newly baptized, without the mention of any intervening rite corresponding in any way to confirmation,[3] are to be remarked as noteworthy in themselves, and as pointing to an early date for the composition of the story.

Baptism by any other formula than in the Name of the Trinity, and especially baptism into the death of the Lord, was forbidden by the Apostolic Canons XLIX., L. These canons are post-Nicene, but they point to some irregular forms of the administration of baptism having sprung up at a very early date.[4]

The following account of baptism is given by Justin Martyr in his first *Apology* :—

[1] Page 73.   [2] Page 78.   [3] See p. 87, § 6.
[4] See chap. i. p. 11.

'As many as are persuaded and believe that these things which are taught and said by us are true, and promise that they are able to live thus, are taught to pray and ask God, with fasting, for the forgiveness of their former sins, while we pray and fast with them. Then they are led by us where there is water, and are regenerated after the same manner of regeneration with which we ourselves were regenerated. For they then make their bath in the water, in the Name of God the Father, and Lord of all, and of our Saviour Jesus Christ, and of the Holy Ghost. For Christ said, Except ye be born again, ye shall not enter into the kingdom of heaven.[1] Now, it is manifest to all that it is impossible for those who have once been born to enter again into their mothers' wombs. But Esaias the prophet has declared how those who have sinned and repent shall escape from their sins, saying thus: "Wash you, make you clean," etc. . . .[2]

We have learned from the Apostles the following reasons for this [rite of baptism]. Since we have received our first birth without our knowledge or consent . . . and have fallen into vicious customs and evil modes of education; therefore, in order that we may not remain children of necessity or of ignorance, but of free-will and understanding, and may obtain forgiveness of sins formerly committed, the Name of God the Father and Lord of all is named in the water over him who chooses to be regenerated and repents for his sins, no other description [of God] being given by him who leads the man to be washed to the laver. This laver is called "illumination,"[3] because those who learn these things have their minds illuminated. I should add that the person illuminated washes also in the Name of Jesus Christ, who was crucified under Pontius Pilate; and in

---

[1] St. John iii. 3.   [2] Isa. i. 16.
[3] Φωτισμός, *illuminatio*, 'enlightenment.'

the Name of the Holy Ghost, who, through the prophet, proclaimed beforehand all things concerning Jesus.'[1]

Then, after three chapters which are devoted to show how Christian baptism was counterfeited by demoniacal agency, Justin Martyr proceeds in the sixty-fifth chapter, which has been printed on page 51—

'But we, after we have thus washed the man who has been convinced and has given his consent [to our teaching], lead him to the place where those who are called brethren are assembled, etc. . . . Having ended the prayers, we salute one another with a kiss. . . .'[2]

Here Justin Martyr passes on to a description of the Eucharist in words already quoted.[3] It is difficult to decide whether the kiss of peace just referred to is the last baptismal or the first Eucharistic action. The kiss of peace occurs at the commencement of the Clementine Liturgy, before the expulsion of the catechumens and others, as well as just before the offertory.[4]

Baptism bore many titles. Justin Martyr calls it the 'water of life,'[5] and 'the illumination.'[6] In the *Acts of Paul and Thecla* it is called 'the seal of Christ;'[7] and in *The Shepherd* of Hermas, 'the seal of the Son of God.'[8] Tertullian calls it 'the seal of

---

[1] Cap. 61 ; *P. G.*, tom. vi. col. 421.
[2] Cap. 65; *P. G.*, vi. col. 427.   [3] Page 52.   [4] H., pp. 3, 10.
[5] Ὕδωρ ζωῆς, *Dial.*, cap. 14 ; *P. G.*, tom. vi. col. 504.
[6] Φωτισμός, *Apol.*, i. cap. 61 ; *P. G.*, tom. vi. col. 421.
[7] Ἡ ἐν Χριστῷ σφραγίς, Grabe, *Spicilegium* (Oxford, 1698), tom. i. p. 106.
[8] Ἡ σφραγὶς τοῦ υἱοῦ τοῦ Θεοῦ, *Simil.* 9, cap. xvi.

faith,'[1] 'the sacrament of water,'[2] 'the enrolment of God.'[3] It is also called 'the seal of the bath,'[4] and 'the seal of baptism.'[5] St. Clement of Alexandria calls it 'the seal of the Lord,'[6] a title which is also used in the Apostolic Constitutions,'[7] and he also calls it 'grace,' 'illumination,' 'the perfect work,' and 'the bath.'[8]

Passing from general descriptions, we find proofs or traces of the following practices existing in ante-Nicene times:—

(a) *Infant baptism.*—This practice is implied in the language of Polycarp to the heathen proconsul. When urged at his trial by the latter to renounce Christ, Polycarp replied—

'Fourscore and six years have I been His servant, and He hath done me no wrong. How then can I blaspheme my King who saved me?'[9]

Justin Martyr, in his first *Apology*, speaks of there being many men and women in existence then (that is, in the middle of the second century) who were

---

[1] 'Signaculum fidei,' *De Spectac*, cap. 24; *P. L.*, tom. i. col. 656.
[2] 'Sacramentum aquæ,' *De Baptismo*, cap. i.; *P. L.*, tom. i. col. 1197.
[3] 'Dei census,' *Ibid.*, cap. xvi.; *P. L.*, tom. i. col. 1218.
[4] Ἡ σφραγὶς τοῦ λουτροῦ, *Acts of Thomas*, ed. M. Bonnet, Leipzig, 1883, cap. 26, p. 19.
[5] Canons of Hippolytus, xxix. § 251, p. 135.
[6] 'Quis dives salvetur,' cap. xlii.; *P. G.*, tom. ix. col. 647.
[7] Lib. ii. cap. 14, p. 22.
[8] Χάρισμα, καὶ φώτισμα, καὶ τέλειον, καὶ λουτρόν, *Pædagog.*, lib. i. cap. 6; *P. G.*, tom. viii. col. 281. The whole chapter, which is both beautiful and curious, should be read.
[9] Letter of the Smyrnæans on the martyrdom of St. Polycarp, cap. ix., Lightfoot (J. B.), *The Apostolic Fathers*, 1891, pp. 193, 206.

made disciples to Christ from their childhood.[1] The childhood of people who were old people, c. A.D. 150, must have extended back to within the lifetime of some of the Apostles.

Irenæus used these words—

'Therefore as He [Jesus Christ] was a master, He had also the age of a master; not disdaining or going in a way above human nature; not breaking in His own Person the law which He had set for mankind, but sanctifying every age by the likeness which it has to Him. For He came to save all persons through Himself—all, I say, who through Him are regenerated unto God—infants, and little ones, and boys and youths, and old people. Therefore He went through every age; for infants being made an infant, sanctifying infants; for little ones being made a little one, sanctifying those of that age, and at the same time being made an example to them of godliness, justice, and dutifulness,' etc.[2]

Elsewhere he speaks more plainly of 'infants newly-born and spiritually born again.'[3]

St. Cyprian pleaded for the baptism of infants at a very early age indeed, while yet only two or three days old, not even advising delay till the eighth day, in accordance with the analogy of circumcision. He argued—

'If adults are admitted to the font, how much more should those be baptized at once who have not sinned,

---

[1] Οἱ ἐκ παίδων ἐμαθητεύθησαντῷ Χριστῷ. The verb is the same which was employed in the commission to baptize, as recorded by St. Matthew, πορευθέντες μαθητεύσατε πάντα τὰ ἔθνη, xxviii. 19 (W. Wall, *The History of Infant Baptism* (Oxford, 1862), vol. i. p. 43).

[2] *Contra Hæreses*, lib. ii. cap. xxii. § 4; *P. G.*, vii. 783.

[3] Ὡς παιδία νεόγονα πνευματικῶς ἀναγεννώμενοι, Gk. Fragm. 33, *Opera* (ed. W. W. Harvey, Cambridge, 1857), tom. ii. p. 497.

except so far as by natural descent from Adam they have contracted, in the moment of birth, the infection of ancient death, who for this very reason may come more easily to the remission of sins, because it is the sins of another and not their own which are remitted to them.'[1]

St. Clement of Alexandria speaks of 'children that are drawn up out of the water.'[2]

In the Apostolic Constitutions we find this injunction—

'Baptize your children, and bring them up in the nurture and admonition of the Lord, for He saith, "Suffer little children to come unto Me, and forbid them not."'[3]

The testimony of Origen to the practice of infant baptism is repeated and explicit. He says that—

'Baptism is administered even to infants, according to the custom of the Church.'[4]

And again that—

'Infants are baptized for the remission of sins. Of whose sins? or at what time have they sinned? or how can any reason exist for the use of the baptismal laver in the case of infants, except in that sense about which we have spoken a short time before? It is because the birth pollution is washed away in baptism that infants are baptized, For except a man be born of water and the Spirit, he cannot enter into the kingdom of heaven.'[5]

---

[1] *Ep.* lix., *Ad Fidum de infantibus baptizandis*, pp. 97–99. The whole Epistle should be read. It is written by St. Cyprian in his own name and in the names of sixty-five bishops assembled in council.
[2] *Pædagog.*, lib. iii. cap. ii.; *P. G.*, tom. viii. col. 633.
[3] Lib. vi. cap. 15.
[4] Hom. viii., *In Levit.*, tom. ii. p. 230.
[5] St. John iii. 5 ; Hom. xiv. *In Luc.*; *P. G.*, tom. xiii. col. 1831.

Elsewhere he calls baptism 'a second circumcision.'[1]

Again, after pointing out that according to the Jewish law an offering had to be made for the new-born infant,[2] and after referring to David's assertion, 'Behold, I was shapen in wickedness; and in sin hath my mother conceived me,'[3] Origen proceeds to state that—

'For this reason too the Church has received it as a tradition from the Apostles to administer baptism even to infants.'[4]

(b) *Profession of faith and renunciations.*—A profession of faith, which at a very early time assumed the form of a definite creed, was made by candidates for baptism.

Justin Martyr says that before men are regenerated they must both profess to believe the truth of those things which they had been taught, and also promise to live answerably to their knowledge.[5]

Tertullian uses language which implies that articles relating to the Father, Son, and Holy Ghost, and the Church, were part of the interrogations at baptism.[6]

For the interrogative form of creed provided in the Canons of Hippolytus, see chap. iii. § 6, p. 181.

[1] Hom. v., *In Lib. Jesu Nave*, § 6, tom. ii. pp. 408, 409.
[2] Lev. xii. 6-8.   [3] Ps. li. 5.
[4] Comment. in *Ep. ad. Rom.*, lib. v. § 9; *P. G.*, tom. xiv. col. 1047.
[5] *Apol.* ii. p. 93, as quoted at length by Bingham, *Antiqq. of the Christian Church* (London, 1865), vol. i. p. 520.
[6] *De Baptismo*, cap. 6; *P. L.*, tom. i. col. 1206.

F

Irenæus speaks of the 'canon of truth which every one received at his baptism.'[1]

One of the questions in the African Baptismal Service of the third century was—

'Dost thou believe in eternal life, and remission of sins through the holy Church?'

This was naturally pressed by St. Cyprian with great force against the validity of heretical baptism.[2]

Tertullian also mentions the solemn and triple renunciation of the devil, his pomp, and his angels, as made twice—firstly, on a person's admission to be a catechumen, and, secondly, at his actual baptism.[3]

(c) *Sponsors*, who are necessarily introduced if questions are used at the baptism of infants, are mentioned by Tertullian, who refers to the danger that there was of sponsors failing to fulfil their promises, either by their own death, or through the evil dispositions which might be developed in the person for whom they have acted as sponsors.[4] Throughout this chapter, Tertullian is arguing against the baptism of infants, which was evidently the established church practice at this time. In the *Academy* of February 15, 1896, Mr. Whitley Stokes turns the argument the

---

[1] Quoted without a reference in Smith's *Dictionary of Christian Antiqq.*, i. 489.

[2] *Ep.* lxx. (ed. Antwerp, 1568), p. 172; Routh (J. M.), *Reliquiæ Sacræ*, 2nd ed. vol. iii. p. 108.

[3] *De Spectaculis*, cap. iv.; *De Corona*, cap. iii.; *De cultu feminarum*, cap. ii.

[4] *De Baptismo*, cap. 18; *P. L.*, tom. i. col. 1221.

other way, and takes the fact that Tertullian argued against it to be a proof that the practice of infant baptism was then a novel introduction, and suggests that it was derived from imitation of the lustral ceremony performed over infants in heathen rites, with which Christianity was now fast coming into contact. This is a most unlikely suggestion, for heathenism was the deadly enemy of Christianity, and its abominations and puerilities had been and were the constant theme of Christian apologists; and in the attitude and temper then existing it is morally impossible that the Christian Church should have adopted a rite from the religion of their persecutors.[1]

Sponsors are mentioned in the Canons of Hippolytus.[2]

(*d*) *Milk and honey.*—Tertullian mentions that on leaving the font the newly baptized tasted a mixture of milk and honey,[3] a piece of symbolism probably suggested by the Old Testament description of the promised land as a land flowing with milk and honey, into which the Israelites entered through the waters of the river Jordan; but the explanation given in the Canons of Hippolytus, where the rite is also enjoined, is that the newly baptized may remember that they have become as little children, whose natural food is milk and honey.[4]

---

[1] See chap. iii. § 40, p. 247.

[2] 'Qui pro infantibus parvis respondent,' Canon xix. § 113, p. 94.

[3] *De Corona*, cap. iii.; *Adv. Marcionem*, lib. I, cap. xiv.; *P. L.*, tom. ii. col. 79; tom. ii. col. 262.

[4] Canon xix. § 144, but § 148 explains it of the future life, and the sweetness of its blessings.

St. Clement of Alexandria refers to the same custom in these words—

'As soon as we are born we are nourished with milk, which is the nutriment of the Lord. And when we are born again we are honoured with the hope of rest by the promise of Jerusalem which is above, where it is said to rain milk and honey. For by these material things we are assured of that sacred food.'[1]

(e) *Sign of the cross and Unction.*—The sign of the cross, which was in such general use in the earliest days of Christianity, would naturally be included in the ceremonial of baptism. Tertullian says—

"The flesh is washed that the soul may be rid of its stains; the flesh is anointed that the soul may be consecrated; the flesh is sealed (*i.e.* signed with the cross) that the soul also may be protected; the flesh is overshadowed by the imposition of hands, that the soul may be illuminated by the Spirit; the flesh is fed with the Body and Blood of Christ, that the soul may be made fat from God.'[2]

Elsewhere he says—

'Then when we come out of the bath [of baptism] we are anointed with the holy unction, according to the ancient practice by which men were wont to be anointed for the priesthood with oil poured out of a horn.'[3]

How far the anointing and sealing in these passages belong to the Baptismal Service, and how far they belong to the Confirmation Service it is not

---

[1] *Pædagog.*, lib. i. cap. 6; *P. G.*, tom. viii. col. 504.
[2] *De Resurrectione carnis*, cap. viii.; *P. L.*, tom. ii. col. 806.
[3] *De Baptismo*, cap. vii.; *P. L.*, tom. i. col. 1206.

easy to say. The two rites of baptism and confirmation were administered in close succession, and formed almost one complex rite throughout the ante-Nicene period; in fact, for the first thousand years and more of the Church's existence. It is perhaps with special reference to this use of the sign of the cross that baptism is called 'the seal' or 'the seal of Christ,' as where Thecla is represented as saying to St. Paul—

'Grant me only the seal of Christ, and no temptation shall affect me.'[1]

And in the words of Polyxena previously quoted from the Acts of Xanthippe.[2]

(*f*) *Immersion.*—Baptism by immersion was both the custom and the rule, but the validity of baptism by affusion or aspersion, in the case of sick people, is defended at length by St. Cyprian, who quotes in support of it Num. viii. 7; xix. 18; Ezek. xxxvi. 25, and concludes that a person so baptized is to be reckoned as a legitimate Christian.[3]

Cornelius, Bishop of Rome (251-2), records that Novatian had been baptized on a sick-bed by affusion. He does not dispute the validity of such baptism, but he objects to Novatian as not having afterwards complied with Church regulation as to the reception of confirmation from the hands of a bishop. This he calls being signed by the bishop,

[1] Cap. vi. 14; Hone (W.), *Apocryphal New Test.*, 1820, p. 105. For further information about unction, see sub-sect. (*g*).
[2] Page 59. See § 7, *ad finem*, p. 101.
[3] *Ep.* 76, § 12; *P. L.*, tom. iii. coll. 1194-1196.

apparently alluding to the sign of the cross which was made by the bishop on the forehead of each person confirmed.[1]

Baptism by affusion had been recognized in the *Didaché*, in which it was laid down—

'But if thou hast not either, pour water thrice upon the head in the Name of the Father, and of the Son, and of the Holy Ghost.'[2]

When St. Fructuosus baptized Rogatianus in prison, immersion must have been an impossibility.[3]

Baptismal immersion is specially stated by Tertullian to have been triple. He says—

'We dip not once but three times, at the mention of each of the three Persons of the Trinity.'[4]

(*g*) *Unction.*—The rite of unction in immediate connection with baptism is mentioned both by Tertullian and St. Cyprian. The former, after describing the actual baptism with water, proceeds thus—

'Then on stepping forth from the font we are anointed with consecrated oil, a custom derived from the old dispensation, in which men used to be anointed priests with oil out of a horn, since the time when Aaron was anointed by Moses;[5] from which he is called "a christ" from the chrism, that is, the unction employed. And this unction

---

[1] Σφραγισθῆναι ὑπὸ τοῦ ἐπισκόπου, Routh (J. M.), *Reliquiæ Sacræ*, iii. 25. Dr. Routh argues that to sign (*consignare*, σφραγίζειν) and to lay on hands (*manum imponere*) are the same thing (*ibid.*, p. 69), but the argument is not convincing.

[2] Cap. vii. § 3.   [3] Fructuosi, etc., *Acta*, p. 340.

[4] 'Ter mergitamur,' *De Corona*, cap. iii. ; *P. L.*, tom. ii. col. 79.

[5] Exod. xl. 15.

gave his name to our Lord, being spiritually performed; because He was anointed with the Spirit by God the Father, as it is said in the Acts: "For of a truth they were gathered together in that state against thy Holy Child whom thou hast anointed."[1] Thus too in our case, though the unction takes place in the flesh, yet it benefits us spiritually; just as in the act of baptism itself the immersion in water is a carnal transaction, but the effect is a spiritual one, namely, the deliverance from our sins.'[2]

A reference to this unction is to be found in another passage of Tertullian, quoted previously.[3]

Elsewhere he mentions after the baptismal washing, 'the oil with which God anoints His people.'[4]

St. Cyprian speaks thus of the same unction—

'The man who has been baptized needs also to be anointed, in order that in receiving the chrism, that is, the unction, he may be one of God's anointed ones, and have within himself the grace of Christ. And the oil, moreover, wherewith the baptized are anointed is consecrated upon the altars by the Eucharist; but those who have neither altar nor church could not consecrate the creature of oil. Wherefore, there can be no spiritual unction among heretics, as it is evidently impossible for there to be any consecration of oil or any celebration of the Eucharist among them.'[5]

This is not the only unction mentioned in connection with the baptism in the ante-Nicene period. A twofold unction, one before and one after baptism, is

---
[1] Acts iv. 27.
[2] *De Baptismo*, cap. vii. ; *P. L.*, tom. i. col. 1206. [3] Page 68.
[4] *Adv. Marcionem*, lib. i. cap. 14; *P. L.*, tom. ii. col. 262.
[5] *Ep.* lxx. p. 125.

prescribed in the Canons of Hippolytus,[1] as well as in the Apostolic Constitutions.[2]

(*h*) *Fasting.*—Fasting is mentioned in connection with preparation for baptism from the earliest times. In the *Didaché* there is this direction given—

'Before baptism let him that baptizeth fast, and any others who are able, and thou shalt order him that is baptized to fast a day or two before.'[3]

The Canons of Hippolytus order the candidate to fast on the Friday preceding his baptism.[4]

This pre-baptismal fast is enforced at great length in the Apostolic Constitutions, where it is somewhat awkwardly connected with, while it is distinguished from, the post-baptismal fast of our Lord.[5]

There are frequent allusions to the fast before baptism both in the Clementine Recognitions[6] and in the Clementine Homilies.[7]

A reference of Justin Martyr to the same subject has been already quoted.[8]

Tertullian states that candidates for baptism should prepare themselves by prayer, fasting, and confession of sin.[9]

(*i*) *Time for Baptism.*—Tertullian, while allowing that every Lord's day—in fact, every day and every hour—is suitable for the administration of baptism, points out that the festivals, firstly, of Easter, and

---

[1] Canon xix., §§ 116–135.
[2] Lib. vii. capp. 42–44. See p. 68, sub-sect. (*e*). [3] Cap. vii.
[4] Canon xix., § 106, p. 92. [5] Lib. vii. cap. 22.
[6] Lib. vii. capp. 34, 37. [7] Lib. iv. cap. 73; xii. 35; xiii. 11.
[8] Page 60. [9] *De Baptismo*, cap. xx.; *P. L.*, tom. i. col. 1222.

secondly, of Pentecost, are the most appropriate occasions.[1] To these two seasons the Epiphany was added at a very early date in the East, and it has also been found connected with baptism in certain parts of the West. Its first introduction into Egypt as a baptismal festival was due to the followers of Basilides in the second century.[2]

(*k*) *Washing of Feet.*—See § 23, p. 165, and chap. i. § 26, p. 48.

(*l*) *Consecration of the Water.*—The element of water was consecrated for use at baptism, as the elements of bread and wine were consecrated for use in the Eucharist, by words of invocation of the Holy Spirit.

Tertullian said—

' The waters are made the sacrament of sanctification by the invocation of God. The Spirit immediately descends from heaven, and resting upon them, sanctifies them by Himself, and they being so sanctified, imbibe the power of sanctification.' [3]

St. Cyprian said—

'The water must first be cleansed and sanctified by the priest, that it may have power by baptism to wash away the sins of the person who is baptized.' [4]

(*m*) *Minister of Baptism.*—The proper minister of baptism, according to Tertullian, is the bishop, but presbyters and deacons, and in case of necessity,

---

[1] *De Baptismo*, cap. xx. ; *P. L.*, tom. i. col. 1222.
[2] Clemens Alex., *Stromata*, cap. xxi. ; *P. G.*, tom. viii. col. 888.
[3] *De Baptismo*, cap. iv. ; *P. L.*, tom. i. col. 1204.
[4] *Ep.* 70, ad Januarium, *Opera* (ed. Baluz. Paris, 1726), p. 125.

laymen, but not women, are permitted to baptize.[1] This was an instance of the exercise of those priestly powers which belong to all the faithful, and about which Irenæus said—

'All just men possess the order of the priesthood;'[2]

and about which Tertullian asked, referring to Rev. i. 6—

'And are not we laity priests?'[3]

The rest of this passage should be studied. Tertullian pushes the doctrine of the priesthood of the laity to its extremest limits in order to press home his Montanistic theory, that as the clergy might not marry twice, no more might the laity.

Justin Martyr described all Christians as a true race of priests of God.[4] Origen has a fine passage on the same subject.[5]

It is not within the object of these pages to describe the baptismal doctrine of the early Church; but for a clear passage connecting the gift of the Holy Spirit with baptism we would refer our readers to a passage in the writings of Origen.[6]

§ 3. CHORAL SERVICE.—It would follow naturally

[1] *De Baptismo*, cap. xvii.; *P. L.*, tom. i. col. 1218.
[2] *Contra Hæres*, lib. iv. cap. 8; *P. G.*, tom. vii. col. 995.
[3] *Lib. de Exhortatione Castitatis*, cap. vii.; *P. L.*, tom. ii. col. 922.
[4] *Dial. cum Tryphone*, § 116; *P. G.*, tom. vi. col. 746.
[5] Hom. ix. in Levit., § 1, tom. ii. p. 236. See also § 9 of the same Homily, where he refers to the unction which all Christians have received as conferring on them their priesthood.
[6] Hom. vi. in Levit., § 2, tom. ii. p. 216, left col., lines 8–14. For a later but similar passage, see Ambrose, *De Mysteriis*, cap. ix. § 59, *ad finem*.

from the musical instincts of human nature, as well as from the precedent of the Jewish temple services in the Old Testament, and from the allusions to singing in the New Testament, that the choral element would enter into primitive Christian worship. The analogy of chorus singing in the Greek theatre, as well as of the psalmody in the Jewish temple, would likewise suggest that the singing would be antiphonal in its character. According to a tradition first found in the pages of the historian Socrates, the antiphonal mode of singing originated with St. Ignatius the Martyr, who 'saw a vision of angels, praising the Holy Trinity in antiphonal hymns, and left the fashion of his vision as a custom to the Church in Antioch, whence this custom spread likewise through all the churches.'[1] Yet, as Pliny in his letter to the emperor Trajan describes the Christians of Bithynia as in the habit of singing hymns to Christ as God 'alternately,'[2] it may be inferred that antiphonal singing was already a custom in the Christian Church in the earlier part of the second century, though there is later evidence for the early prevalence of a responsorial mode of chanting or singing as well. Instrumental music was not employed in Divine service,[3] and, as is well known, the conservative Eastern Church has never departed from primitive practice in this respect up to the present day.

§ 4. CHURCH FURNITURE.—During a great part

---

[1] *Hist. Eccles.*, vi. 8. Socrates wrote in the fifth century.
[2] *Epp.*, lib. x. No. 97. See p. 51.
[3] Clemens Alex., *Pædagog.*, lib. ii. cap. 4 ; *P. G.*, tom. vii. col. 443.

of the period with which we are concerned, Christians possessed no churches, but met for worship in the privacy of their chambers, or in dens and caves of the earth. Throughout the Roman empire Christianity was for a long time a proscribed religion, and though the penal laws against it were left at times to slumber, they were liable at any time to be evoked and put in force.[1] Hence it was the Christians' object to worship God as unobtrusively as possible, and we are not surprised to find that as, for the most part, there were no Christian churches, so there are but scanty references to Church furniture, or to the ordinary accessories of Divine worship in writers of the first three centuries.

Minucius Felix mentions it as a charge made against Christians that they had no churches or altars. It was a cruel charge to be brought against Christianity by its heathen opponents, because, though it was true, yet, so far as it was true, it was due to the persecutions of heathenism, and the necessity of avoiding publicity. However, Minucius Felix defends the non-existence among Christians of churches and altars on other grounds, and in a passage of such spiritual beauty, that we quote it at length—

'But do you think that we conceal what we worship if we have not temples and altars? And yet what image of

[1] Christianity was first made a *religio licita* under Gallienus in 261, but it did not obtain complete recognition and toleration till after the conversion of Constantine the Great in 313.

God shall I make, since, if you think rightly, man himself is the image of God? What temple shall I build to Him, when the whole world, fashioned by His work, cannot receive Him? And when I, a man, dwell far and wide shall I shut up the might of so great majesty within one little building? Were it not better that He should be dedicated in our minds, consecrated in our inmost heart? Shall I offer victims and sacrifices to the Lord, such as He has produced for my use, that I should throw back to Him His own gifts? Is it ungrateful when the victim fit for sacrifice is a good disposition, and a pure mind, and a good conscience? Therefore, he who cultivates innocence supplicates God; he who cultivates justice makes offerings to God; he who abstains from fraudulent practices propitiates God; he who snatches men from danger slaughters the most acceptable victim. These are our sacrifices; these are our rites of God's worship; thus, among us, he who is the more just is the more religious.'[1]

The same charge against Christians is referred to, and is met in a similar manner, in the writings of Arnobius.[2] Yet some buildings set apart for Divine worship must have existed in the third century, when we find St. Cyprian reproaching a rich woman for coming into the Lord's house without a sacrifice.[3] Churches are also mentioned by Tertullian[4] and Origen[5] under the names of 'ecclesia' and 'domus Dei.' Both Eusebius[6] and Optatus[7] refer to the

[1] *Octavius*, capp. xxvi., xxxii. ; *P. L.*, tom. iii. col. 339.
[2] *Disputationes adv. Gentes*, bks. vi., viii.
[3] ' Quæ in dominicum sine sacrificio venis,' *Lib. de opere et eleemosynis*, cap. xv. ; *P. L.*, tom. iv. col. 613.
[4] *De Idololatria*, cap. vii. ; *P. L.*, tom. i. col. 699.
[5] Hom. x. in *Librum Jesu Nave*, § 3 ; *P. G.*, tom. xii. col. 881.
[6] *Hist. Eccles.*, lib. x. capp. ii., iii., etc.
[7] Optatus mentions the existence of forty churches at Rome at this

existence of many churches at Rome and elsewhere at the beginning of the fourth century; and Constantine, in his letter to Eusebius on the subject of building Christian churches, refers to the small size and the ruin of previously existing sacred buildings.[1]

We now pass to the consideration of certain passages in the writings of the Apostolic Fathers, in which the word 'altar' (θυσιαστήριον) occurs, and which are sometimes quoted in connection with this subject to prove that Christians had altars in the second century.

St. Ignatius, writing to the Ephesians, says—

(*a*) 'Let no man be deceived. If any one be not within [the precincts of] the altar, he lacketh the bread of God.'[2]

Writing to the Magnesians, he says—

(*b*) 'Hasten to come together all of you as to one temple, even God; as to one altar, even to one Jesus Christ, who came forth from one Father, and is with One, and departeth unto One.'[3]

Writing to the Trallians, he says—

(*c*) 'He that is within [the precincts of] the altar is clean; he that doeth aught without the bishop, the presbytery, and the deacon, this man is not clean in his conscience.'[4]

(*d*) Writing to the Romans, he says—

'Grant me nothing more than that I may be poured out a libation to God, while there is still an altar ready.'[5]

time (*De Schismate Donatistarum*, lib. ii. cap. 4; *P. L.*, tom. xi. col. 951).

[1] Theodoret, *Hist. Eccles.*, lib. i. cap. 14; *P. G.*, tom. lxxii., col. 951.
[2] Ἐντὸς τοῦ θυσιαστηρίου, cap. v.
[3] Ὡς ἐπὶ ἓν θυσιαστήριον, cap. vii.
[4] Ἐντὸς θυσιαστηρίου, cap. vii.
[5] Ὡς ἔτι θυσιαστήριον ἕτοιμόν ἐστιν, cap. ii.

(*e*) Writing to the Philadelphians, he says—

'Be ye careful, therefore, to observe one Eucharist (for there is one flesh of our Lord Jesus Christ, and one cup unto union in His blood; there is one altar, as there is one bishop, together with the presbytery and the deacons, my fellow-servants), that whatsoever ye do, ye may do it after God.'[1]

(*f*) Polycarp, writing to the Philippians, says—

'Our widows must be sober-minded as touching the faith of the Lord, . . . knowing that they are God's altar, and that all sacrifices are carefully inspected, and that nothing escapeth Him either of their thoughts or intents, or any of the secret things of the heart.'[2]

Of these six passages four of them, (*b*), (*c*), (*d*), and (*f*), are obviously metaphorical. (*a*) may be literal; but if so the word altar must mean the church, or that portion of the church within which the altar stands.[3] (*e*) must be classed as metaphorical,[4] but the employment of this metaphor may be taken to prove that the word 'altar' was not unfamiliar to the Christian ear in connection with the Eucharistic service.

The word altar (*altare*)[5] occurs in the following

[1] *Ἐν θυσιαστήριον*, cap. iv.   [2] *Θυσιαστήριον Θεοῦ*, cap. iv.

[3] 'Altar' is used in this sense in the 19th and 44th canons of the Council of Laodicea, A.D. 320 (Mansi, *Concil*, tom. ii. coll. 587, 589).

[4] So Bp. Lightfoot, *Apostolic Fathers*, vol. ii. p. 258, 2nd ed. (London, 1889).

[5] Βωμὸς (like *altare* = raised place) is generally used in the LXX. and earlier Greek Fathers for heathen altars (*e.g.* 1 Macc. i. 54, and Clem. Alex., *Strom.*, vii. 717), and *ara* (? = place of victim), its equivalent in the Vulgate, is also sometimes rejected as heathen (*e.g.* Min. Felix, *Octavius*, cap. 32). But *θυσιαστήριον* (= place of offering, whether bloody or unbloody) seems from the beginning to have had a wider application than to heathen or even Hebrew rites (cf. Matt. v. 24; Heb. xiii. 10; Ign. Phil. iv., and Mag. vii. Dict. of C.A., i. 61).

passage of Irenæus, where still the reference may be to the heavenly rather than to the earthly altar :—

'We offer to Him, not as standing in need of an offering, but giving thanks for His rule, and sanctifying His creature. . . . Thus He wills that we accordingly should offer the gift at His altar frequently, without intermission. There is, therefore, an altar in heaven, for thither our prayers and oblations are addressed,' etc.[1]

The word 'altar' is used by St. Clement of Alexandria, in a metaphorical sense to denote 'the assembly of worshippers.'[2]

In Africa, in the time of Tertullian and St. Cyprian, the word 'altar' in its literal signification had come into established use. Tertullian speaks of 'the altar of God.'[3] St. Cyprian says—

'Another altar cannot be reared, a new priesthood cannot be constituted, beside the one altar, and the one priesthood. He who gathers [people] elsewhere scatters.'[4]

And again—

'As if after ministering at the altars (*aras*) of the devil it were lawful to approach the altar of God.'[5]

So he speaks of the altar being placed in the church,[6] of assisting at God's altar,[7] of the sacerdotal

---

[1] *Contra Hæres*, lib. iv. cap. xviii. § 6.
[2] *Stromata*, lib. vii. cap. 6 ; *P. G.*, ix. 443.
[3] 'Ara Dei,' *De Oratione*, cap. xix.; *P. L.*, i. 1182. Bede uses *altare* for the Christian 'altar,' and *ara* for a heathen altar (C. Plummer's ed., vol. ii. p. 60); but this distinction of words was not always observed by the African writers.
[4] *Ep.* xl. p. 53. The preceding sentence on the unity of the Church should be read.
[5] *Ep.* lxiv. See also *Epp.* xlii., lv.
[6] *Ep.* xlii. p. 56.   [7] *Ep.* lviii. p. 96.

order being wholly occupied in serving at the altar and at the sacrifice;[1] of one who is an enemy to the altar, and a rebel against the sacrifice of Christ.[2] Origen also speaks of the altar and its adornment,[3] and of altars.[4]

Instances of the use of the word 'table,' or 'holy table,' are rare in ante-Nicene literature, but the two following instances can be adduced from the writings of Dionysius of Alexandria. In a letter addressed to Basilides, he says—

'In former days, as seems most probable, women used to enter the sanctuary and partake of the holy table.'[5]

In another letter addressed to Xystus II., Bishop of Rome, he refers to 'one who has heard the words of the Eucharist, and has joined in uttering the "Amen," and has stood by the table, and has extended his hands to receive the holy food,' etc.[6]

In the Canons of Hippolytus the bishop communicating the newly baptized is described as 'standing at the table.'[7]

There is no direct contemporary evidence as to the material of which the altar or 'holy table' was

---

[1] *Ep.* lxvi. p. 114.   [2] *De Unitate Ecclesiæ,* § xvii. p. 200.
[3] Hom. x. in *Librum Jesu Nave,* § 3; *P. G.,* xii. 881.
[4] *Ibid.,* § i. There is a very fine passage about the spiritual altar (*Ibid.,* Hom. ix.).
[5] Τὸ παλαιὸν εἰσήρχοντο γυναῖκες εἰς τὸ θυσιαστήριον καὶ ἀπὸ τῆς ἁγίας τραπέζης μετελάμβανον. Gallandius, *Bibliotheca, Vet. Pat.* iii. 505. Θυσιαστήριον here is evidently not the altar, but the part of the church where the holy table stood.
[6] Quoted by Eusebius, *Hist. Eccles.* lib. vii. cap. 9 (ed. Oxford, 1856), p. 227.
[7] 'Stans ad mensam,' Canon xix. § 143.

made; but from later references to the introduction of stone altars, and to the existence of wooden altars in the fourth century, and later, it is evident that the earliest material was wood.[1]

The only other article of Church furniture of which we have certain mention is the 'pulpit,' or 'ambo,' from which the gospel was read.[2]

Indirectly it may be inferred that a font was employed, when among the works of St. Cyprian we find an African bishop speaking of water consecrated in the church by the prayer (*prex*) of the priest.[3]

§ 5. CONFESSION.—There is no trace of private confession to a priest, as a sacramental ordinance of obligation in the ante-Nicene Church, but public confession in the presence of the clergy and of the congregation was part of the disciplinary or penitential system of the early Church, and was in constant practice. The name by which it was known was not 'confessio,' but 'exomologesis,' a word found in the writings of Tertullian,[4] St. Cyprian,[5] and Origen.[6]

---

[1] Heales (A), *The Archæology of the Christian Altar* (London, 1881), p. 4, where see references in footnotes.

[2] Cyprian, *Ep.* xxxiii. ; *P.L.*, iv. 388. The Latin word is ' pulpitum.'

[3] The bishop was Sedatus of Thuburbum (*Sententiæ episcoporum de hæreticis baptizandis*), No. 18, p. 332.

[4] Exomologesis est qua delictum Domino nostrum;confitemur, etc. (*De Pænitentia*, cap. ix. ; *L. P.*, i. 1243. The whole chapter should be read).

[5] *De Lapsis*, p. 190 ; *Epp.* x. *ad Martyres*, p. 20; xiii. *ad Clerum*, p. 23 ; xi. *ad Plebem*, p. 21 ; lii. *ad Antonianum*, p. 71, etc.

[6] *Select. in Psalm* cxxxv. tom. ii. p. 833. 'Sed si malorum tibi conscius aliquorum fueris, noli occultare, sed per exomologesim, id est, confessionem revela ea Domino, et spera in eum, et ipse faciet' (*Select. in Psalm* xxxvi., Hom. i. § 5, tom. ii. p. 659. The rest of the passage should be read). The word ἐξομολόγησις does not occur in the N.T., but ἐξομολογεῖσθαι occurs frequently.

St. Ignatius speaks of the Lord forgiving all penitent persons if they have recourse to the unity of God and the council of the bishop.[1] Submission to the presbyters is counselled by St. Clement.[2]

Tertullian describes the penitent as 'throwing himself on the ground before the presbyters.' The whole passage must be quoted; it will be seen that it is the description of a public and not of a private act.

'This confession is a disciplinary act of great humiliation and prostration of the man; it regulates the dress, the food; it enjoins sackcloth and ashes; it defiles the body with dust, and subdues the spirit with anguish; it bids a man alter his life, and sorrow for past sin; it restricts meat and drink to the greatest simplicity possible; it nourishes prayer by fasting; it inculcates groans and tears and invocations of the Lord God day and night, and teaches the penitent to cast himself at the feet of the presbyters, and to fall on his knees before the beloved of God, and to beg of all the brethren to intercede on his behalf.'[3]

Sackcloth and ashes as part of the symbols of penitence are also mentioned by Commodianus.[4]

St. Cyprian speaks of confession made before the priests of God,[5] and of remission thus obtained being pleasing in God's sight.[6]

Origen's allusions to confession are either expressly

[1] *Ad Philad.* cap. viii.   [2] *Ep.* i. cap. 57.
[3] *De Pœnitentia*, cap. ix.
[4] His hexameters, which are difficult to scan, are these—
  'Idcirco commoneo vulneratos cautius ire
  Barbam comamque fœdare in pulvere terræ
  Volutarique saccis et petere summo de rege.'
      Instructiones, xlix.; *P. L.*, v. 239.
[5] 'Apud sacerdotes Dei confitentes,' etc. (*De Lapsis*, pp. 190, 191).
[6] *Ibid.*, cap. 29.

or inferentially connected with public discipline. He exhorts sinners—

'Look around diligently for one to whom you should confess your sins;'[1] to find a physician 'learned and merciful, who will judge if the sickness is of such a nature that it ought to be exposed in the meeting of the whole Church.'[2] And again—

'If we reveal our sins not only to God, but also to those who can heal our sins and wounds, our sins will be blotted out by Him who says, "Behold, I will blot out like a cloud."[3]

'Consider,' he says, 'what the Holy Scripture teaches us; that we ought not to conceal our sin within our own breast. For, perhaps, as they who are inwardly oppressed with the humour of phlegm or undigested meat, which lies heavy upon the stomach, if they vomit it up, are relieved; so they who have sinned, if they hide and conceal their sin within themselves, are inwardly oppressed, and almost suffocated with the phlegm and humour of sin; but if any one become his own accuser and confess his sin, in so doing he, as it were, vomits up his sin, and digests and removes the cause of his distemper. Only be circumspect in the choice of him to whom it will be fit to confess thy sin. Try first the physician to whom thou art to reveal the cause of thy distemper, and see that he be one who knows how to be weak with him that is weak, and weep with him that weeps; one who understands the discipline of consoling and compassionating; that so, at length, if he shall say anything, who hath first shewed himself to be both a skilful and a merciful physician, and give thee counsel, thou mayest observe and follow it. If he discerns and foresees

---

[1] Hom. in *Psalm* xxxvii. § 6, tom. ii. p. 688.

[2] *Ibid.*, xxvi. § 6, tom. ii. p. 688; *P. G.*, xii. 1386.

[3] Hom. in *Luc.* xvii. tom. iii. p. 953. See also Hom. ii. in *Levit.*, tom. ii. p. 191, and Hom viii. in *Levit.*, tom. ii. p. 228. The whole of this latter homily should be read through. See also a curious interpretation of St. John xx. 23 in *De Oratione*, § 28, tom. i. p. 255.

thy distemper to be such as will need to be declared and cured in the full assembly of the Church, whereby, perhaps, others may be edified, and thou thyself healed, this is to be done with great deliberation, and the prudent advice of such a physician.'[1]

This private confession to a presbyter was, then, not with the view to obtaining immediate and private absolution, but with the view of obtaining advice or direction as to whether a person should seek absolution after public confession in the open penitential system of the Church. Quotations both from Tertullian and Origen—especially from the latter, from whose writings more passages bearing on the subject might be culled—must be read with their context, and read as a whole, in order to be understood. If isolated, or read in the light of the practice of later centuries, they might sometimes be supposed to refer to private confession and absolution, whereas they are connected with the ancient public penitential system of the primitive Church.

Forgiveness following on 'exomologesis' or confession to God only is described by Origen in Hom. i. in *Psalm* xxxvi. § 5, tom. ii. p. 659.

In the following curious passage[2] Origen enumerates seven different ways as provided in the Gospels for obtaining absolution from sin :—

'1. The first is that by which we are baptized for the remission of sins.

2. The second remission is in suffering martyrdom.

3. The third remission is that which is given for alms-

[1] Hom. ii. in *Psalm* xxxvii. § 6, tom. ii. p. 688.
[2] Hom. ii. in *Levit.* § 4, tom. ii. p. 190.

giving; for the Saviour says, "But [rather] give alms [of such things as ye have]; and, behold, all things are clean to you."[1]

4. The fourth remission of sins accrues to us in return for our forgiving the sins of our brethren. For thus speaks our Lord and Saviour: "For if ye forgive men their trespasses, your heavenly Father will also forgive you: but if ye forgive not men their trespasses, neither will your Father forgive your trespasses.[2] And as he has taught us to say in prayer, "Forgive us our debts, as we forgive our debtors."[3]

5. The fifth remission of sins takes place when any one converts a sinner from the error of his ways, for thus saith Holy Scripture: "He which converteth the sinner from the error of his way shall save his soul from death, and shall hide a multitude of sins."[4]

6. The sixth remission takes place through abounding love, as the Lord Himself saith, "Verily I say unto thee, Her sins, which are many, are forgiven; for she loved much."[5]

7. There is also still a seventh remission of sins, though hard and laborious, through penitence, when the sinner waters his couch with his tears, and his tears become his meat day and night, and when he is not ashamed to lay bare his sin to the priest of the Lord, and to seek medicine, according to him who saith, "I will confess my sins unto the Lord, and so thou forgivest the wickedness of my sin."[6] Wherein is fulfilled too that which James the Apostle saith, "Is any sick among you? let him call for the elders of the Church; and let them lay their hands upon him, anointing him with oil in the Name of the Lord: and the prayer of faith shall save the sick; and if he have committed sins, they shall be forgiven him."'[7]

[1] St. Luke xi. 41.   [2] St. Matt. vi. 14, 15.   [3] St. Matt. vi. 12.
[4] St. James v. 20, but reading 'salvat' and 'cooperit.'
[5] St. Luke vii. 47.
[6] Ps. xxxii. 6, but reading 'et tu remisisti impietatem cordis mei.'
[7] St. James v. 14, 15.

It is strange that while enumerating the different modes of obtaining remission of sins under the gospel dispensation, Origen should not have added as an eighth mode, the partaking of the Eucharistic cup, of which our Lord said, 'Drink ye all of it, for this is my blood of the new testament, which is shed for many for the remission of sins.'[1] It is also strange that in support of number seven he should not have quoted St. John xx. 23 and St. James v. 16, instead of or in addition to Ps. xxxii. 6 and St. James v. 14, 15.

§ 6. CONFIRMATION.—During the whole of the period of which we are treating Baptism and Confirmation were closely connected, the latter being always administered immediately after the former, whatever might be the age of the person baptized and confirmed. Origen unites, almost identifies, the two ordinances in the following sentence:—

'In the Acts of the Apostles the Holy Spirit was given in baptism through the imposition of the hands of the Apostles.'[2]

Hence, it is not always easy to separate baptism from confirmation, or to distinguish the baptismal unction from the unction of confirmation. Indeed, the one unction with chrism of earlier days developed into two unctions in later days; and in still later days an interval of years came to separate the two rites; and the imposition of hands, of which we have clear proof in primitive times, dropped out of

---
[1] St. Matt. xxvi. 27, 28.
[2] *De Principiis*, lib. i. cap. 3, § 2; *P. G.*, xi. 147.

use altogether, so far as confirmation is concerned, in both the Western and Eastern Churches.[1]

In the Acts of Thomas 'the seal of the bath' is immediately followed by the reception of 'the seal of oil.'[2]

The following description of Baptism, Confirmation, and First Communion is taken from the Canons of Hippolytus (Canon xix.) :—

§§ 112. The time is to be about cock-crow.

113–115. Unvesting of the candidates for baptism.

116–118. Consecration of two oils by the bishop, and the delivery of them to the presbyter, viz. 'the oil of exorcism' and 'the oil of unction or thanksgiving.'

119. The candidate is directed to face westward and to renounce Satan.

120. Unction by the presbyter with the oil of exorcism.

121, 122. The candidate faces eastward, and declares his belief in Father, Son, and Holy Spirit.

123–133. Then he enters the water, and the presbyter, laying his hand on the candidate's head, immerses him thrice, asking him at each immersion whether he believes in the Three Persons of the Blessed Trinity, successively, the presbyter repeating the formula of baptism at each immersion.

134. Then the presbyter anoints him with the oil of thanksgiving, in the name of the Trinity, and in the form of the cross, on the forehead, mouth, breast, whole body, head, and face.

---

[1] An imposition of hands is retained to this day in the Roman Church, as part of the baptismal office, as testified by the rubric, 'Mox imponit manum super caput infantis;' but it has disappeared for centuries from the Order of Confirmation. This baptismal imposition of hands is, however, totally unconnected both in origin and meaning with the laying on of hands in confirmation.

[2] Caps. 26, 27, p. 20.

135. The candidate is wiped, clothed, and introduced into the church.

136–139. The bishop lays his hands on the heads of all the recently baptized, with prayer.[1]

139, 140. The bishop signs each of them on the forehead with the sign of the cross, and gives to each the kiss of peace, this mutual salvation passing—

    V. The Lord be with you.
    ℟. And with thy spirit.

141. The kiss of peace is then exchanged between the newly-baptized and all the congregation.

142–147. The bishop then communicates them with the reserved eucharistic elements, separately, using these formulæ of administration.

    Bishop. This is the body of Christ.
    ℟. Amen.
    Bishop. This is the blood of Christ.
    ℟. Amen.

148. The candidates then partake of milk and honey, which have been brought in chalices by the presbyters, or, in their absence, by the deacons. The milk and honey are represented as having a double symbolism; firstly, as teaching the newly baptized that they are babes in Christ; secondly, as typifying the world to come, and the sweetness of all good things.

149. They are now designated 'Christiani perfecti'— 'perfect Christians.'

Tertullian, in his treatise *De Baptismo*, describes baptism as consisting of three parts: (1) Immersion in water; (2) anointing with oil; (3) imposition of hands. After describing the first part, he proceeds—

'Then on stepping forth from the font we are anointed

[1] The words of this prayer will be found in chap. iii. § 10 (*a*).

with consecrated oil. This is a custom derived from the Old Testament dispensation, in which men used to be anointed to the priesthood with oil out of a horn, since the time when Aaron was anointed by Moses, from which he is called "a christ," from the chrism, that is, the unction employed; and this unction gave his name to our Lord, being spiritually performed, because he was anointed with the Spirit by God the Father, as it is written in the Acts, "For of a truth against Thy holy Child Jesus, whom Thou hast anointed, were they gathered together."[1] Thus, in our case also, though the unction takes place in the flesh, the benefit is spiritual, just as in baptism itself the immersion in water is a carnal transaction, but the effect is spiritual, namely, the deliverance from our sins. After that, the hand is laid upon us, invoking and inviting the Holy Ghost. If human skill can bring wind into water, and then by application of hands from above can make the conjunction of those elements breathe out another wind which produces a loud music, shall we say that God is unable in his own organ [*i.e.* man] by means of holy hands to awaken strains of spiritual sublimity? This rite also comes from the Old Testament dispensation, in which it is recorded how Jacob blessed his grandsons by Joseph, Ephraim and Manasseh, by placing his hands upon their heads, and at the same time crossing them so as to represent Christ, and to foreshadow the blessing which was to come through Him. Then that most Holy Spirit comes down willingly from the Father upon the bodies which have been cleansed and blessed.'[2]

Elsewhere Tertullian refers to the same rite in a passage which has been already quoted.[3]

St. Clement of Alexandria advances a curious

---

[1] Acts iv. 27.
[2] *De Baptismo*, capp. vii., viii.; *P. L.*, i. 1206–1209.
[3] *De Resurrec. Carnis*, cap. viii.; *P. L.*, ii. 806. See p. 68.

argument against the use of false hair. He condemns it, because when the presbyter lays on his hands [in confirmation] and blesses, he will not be laying his hands upon the woman who is so adorned, but on some one else's hair, and so upon somebody else.[1]

St. Cyprian of Carthage frequently and plainly alludes to the imposition of hands. He writes—

'And, therefore, because they (*i.e.* the Samaritans) received legitimate and ecclesiastical baptism, there was no need for them to be further baptized, but that only was wanting which was done for them by Peter and John, viz. the invoking and the outpouring on them of the Holy Spirit, with prayer on their behalf, and the laying on of hands. This custom is also now observed among ourselves. Those who are baptized in the church are brought to the chief officers of the church, and through our prayers and the imposition of hands receive the Holy Spirit, and are consummated with the sign [or seal] of the Lord' [*i.e.* the sign of the cross.] [2]

Again, arguing that, if the validity of heretical baptism is admitted, the validity of heretical confirmation must be admitted as well, he employs these words—

'If they attribute the effect of baptism to the majesty of the name, so that those who are baptized in the Name of Jesus Christ, anywhere and anyhow, are to be considered renewed, and consecrated, why does not the baptized person, in the Name of the same Christ, receive the imposition of hands also there, to the receiving of the Holy Ghost? Why does not the same majesty of the

---

[1] *Pædagog.*, lib. iii. p. 291. [2] *Ep.* 73, p. 132.

same Name avail in the imposition of hands, which, as they contend, availed in the baptismal consecration?'

And so on, pursuing the argument at great length.[1] He also wrote thus to Jubaianus—

'This is our custom now. Those who are baptized in church are brought to the presidents of the church that they may receive the Holy Spirit by our prayer, and by the imposition of our hands, and that they may receive the sign of the Lord.'[2]

At the Carthaginian council of eighty-seven bishops, who supported St. Cyprian in his attitude on the question of the re-baptism of heretics, Nemesianus of Thubunæ said—

'Our Lord Christ spoke with His own Divine voice, saying, "Except a man be born again of water and the Spirit, he cannot enter into the kingdom of God." This is the Spirit which moved in the beginning over the water. For neither can the Spirit work separately without the water, nor the water without the Spirit. It is, therefore, a wrong interpretation which some give, who say that they ought to receive the Holy Ghost by the imposition of hands, and so be admitted into the Church, when it is manifest that they ought to be born again, by both sacraments of the Catholic Church.'[3]

On the same occasion Secundinus of Carpos (or Carpis) said that—

'It is impossible for the Holy Ghost to descend through the imposition of hands alone upon strange children, and the progeny of Antichrist, it being clear that heretics have no baptism.'[4]

[1] *Ep.* 74, p. 139.
[2] *Ibid.*, 72, p. 132.
[3] Cypriani *Opera*, p. 330.
[4] *Ibid.*, p. 333.

Firmilian, Bishop of Cæsarea in Cappadocia, writing to St. Cyprian in support of the Cyprianic attitude on the subject of the validity of heretical baptism, thus bears witness to the rite of laying on of hands in confirmation in Asia Minor, in the middle of the third century—

'Heretics, if they cut themselves off from the Church of God, can have no power or grace at all, since all power and grace is placed in the Church in which elders preside (ubi præsident majores natu), who have the power both of baptizing, and of laying on of hands, and of ordaining. For as a heretic may not ordain, nor lay on hands, so neither may he baptize, nor perform anything in a holy and spiritual manner, since he is an alien from spiritual and Divine holiness. . . . Forasmuch as Stephen [Bishop of Rome, 253-257] and those who think with him contend that remission of sins and the second birth can take place in the baptism of heretics, among whom they themselves confess that there is no Holy Ghost, let them consider and understand that there cannot be any spiritual birth without the Spirit. Accordingly the blessed Apostle Paul baptized again with spiritual baptism those who had been baptized by John before the Holy Ghost was sent by the Lord, and so laid his hand upon them that they might receive the Holy Ghost. . . . Was Paul less great than these bishops of to-day, that they should be able to give the Holy Ghost to heretics who come over by the imposition of hands alone, while Paul was not qualified to give the Holy Ghost to those baptized by John by imposition of hands, without first having also baptized them with the Church's baptism?'[1]

'What does Stephen mean by saying that those baptized

---
[1] Inter Cypriani *Epistolas*, No. lxxv., *Opera*, p. 145.

among heretics have with them the presence and sanctity of Christ? If the Apostle does not lie when he says, "As many of you as are baptized into Christ have put on Christ," then surely he who is baptized into Christ then has put on Christ. But, if he has put on Christ, he could also have received the Holy Ghost, who has been sent by Christ, and it is vain to lay hands upon him on coming over, that he may receive the Spirit, unless Christ and the Spirit can be so divided, as to let heretics have Christ among them, but not the Holy Ghost.'[1]

'If baptism outside the church availed in the name of Christ for purifying the man, the laying on of hands might also have availed there in the Name of the same Christ for receiving the Holy Ghost.'[2]

The whole letter, which is a long one, should be read. It dates from a time before it was anywhere thought or said 'Roma locuta est, causa est finita,' although in this particular controversy the Roman view, as maintained by Stephen, has justly and universally prevailed over the African view upheld by Cyprian, and over the Asiatic view, agreeing with the African, and upheld by Firmilian. But our purpose in quoting these passages has been to prove that the laying on of hands was the outward sign of confirmation in the African and in the Eastern Church in the middle of the third century.

The third Council of Carthage, A.D. 256, distinctly mentions the imposition of hands (in confirmation) as following after baptism, and as connected with the gift of the Holy Spirit.[3]

---

[1] Inter Cypriani *Epistolas*, No. lxxv., *Opera*, p. 147.
[2] *Ibid.*, p. 148.
[3] Canons, 5, 24 ; Mansi, *Concil*, tom. i. cols. 953, 956.

In the synodical letter sent by St. Cyprian and his colleagues from Carthage in the same year, addressed to St. Stephen, Bishop of Rome, they inform him that they have decided that, in the case of converts from heresy, it was not sufficient to receive them by the imposition of hands for the reception of the Holy Ghost, but that it was necessary that they should receive the baptism of the Church as well.[1]

But, as has been already stated, the Roman view and practice prevailed against the practice of the Church of Africa; *e.g.* we find the Synod of Arles in Gaul, A.D. 314, laying down in its eighth canon that in the case of converts from heresy, if it be proved that they have been baptized in the Name of the Father, and of the Son, and of the Holy Ghost, they should be received into the Church with the imposition of hands only, that they may receive the Holy Ghost.[2]

Origen refers twice to this subject, but both times historically to the practice as recorded in the New Testament. These passages prove that the laying on of hands was sometimes spoken of as part of baptism, sometimes as following after baptism. They do not prove, but they go some way to imply, that the laying on of hands was practised in Egypt in Origen's day; at least, if it had dropped into desuetude, we might have expected some reference to the

---

[1] *Ep.* lxxii. inter Cypriani *Opera*, p. 128.
[2] Hefele (C. J.), *A History of the Christian Councils*, 2nd ed. (Edinburgh, 1872), p. 188.

fact, if not some explanation of the reason. He says—

'In the Acts of the Apostles, through the laying on of the apostolic hands, the Holy Ghost was given in baptism.'[1]

And again—

'Lastly, it is for this reason that the grace and revelation of the Holy Ghost were delivered through the laying on of the hands of the Apostles after baptism.'[2]

We obtain information, incidentally, through Clement of Alexandria, that imposition of hands was practised by the Gnostics, in connection with baptism, in the middle of the second century. Theodotus, the Valentinian, giving a fanciful interpretation of 1 Cor. xv. 29, mentions that the formula which accompanied the imposition of hands in his sect included the phrase 'into angelic redemption.'[3]

In the Apostolic Constitutions confirmation is still spoken of under the title of 'the laying on of hands.'[4]

We will for once travel beyond our proper time limit to say that the latest Eastern Father who is quoted as testifying to this practice of laying on of hands is St. Athanasius (ob. 373), who says—

'Likewise also all the saints having received the Holy Spirit in the Name of the Father, and of the Son, and of

---

[1] *De Principiis*, lib. i. cap. iii., § 2 ; *P. G.*, xi. 147.
[2] *Ibid.*, § 7 ; *ibid.*, 153.
[3] Διὸ καὶ ἐν τῇ χειροθεσίᾳ λέγουσιν ἐπὶ τέλους· Εἰς λύτρωσιν ἀγγελικὴν, τοῦτ' ἐστιν, ἣν καὶ ἄγγελοι ἔχουσιν, Inter *Opera*, Clem. Alex., p. 974.
[4] Χειροθεσία, lib. ii. cap. 32. The word occurs twice in this chapter. It occurs again in lib. vii. cap. 44, where the imposition of hands is stated to be a necessary sequel of baptism. The word for 'confirmation' in a modern Greek service book is χρίσμα.

the Holy Ghost, through the laying on of the hands of the priest of God, are restored to that primitive state in which they were before Adam fell.'[1]

Western evidence for the practice continues to a much later date—as late as the twelfth century—but with gradually dwindling frequency and force. A passage from St. Jerome is so exactly descriptive of modern Anglican practice that we venture to quote it. It is put into the mouth of an orthodox person disputing with a Luciferian.

'I do not deny that this is the usage of the churches, that the bishop should make excursions to those who have been baptized a long way off in the smaller towns by presbyters and deacons, to lay his hands upon them for the invoking of the Holy Ghost. But if the bishop lays on his hands, he lays them upon those who have been baptized in the right faith.'[2]

St. Isidore of Seville entitled a chapter (cap. 26) in his second book on Ecclesiastical Offices 'Of the Imposition of Hands or Confirmation,' and opens it thus—

'But since after baptism the Holy Spirit is given through the bishops along with the imposition of hands,' etc.[3]

Evidence for the use of unction in confirmation

---

[1] *De Trinitate et Spiritu Sancto*, § 21; *P. G.*, xxvi. 1217.

[2] *Dialogus contra Luciferianos*, §9; *P. L.*, xxiii. 164. We are indebted for this, as well as for other quotations on this subject, to Dr. A. J. Mason's work on *The Relation of Confirmation to Baptism* (London, 1890).

[3] The plural word 'manum' is, contrary to the general rule, used here. Hittorpius, *De Cathol. Eccles. Divin. Offic.* (Romæ, 1591), p. 31.

has been already given in a passage from Tertullian.[1] Elsewhere he says—

'As soon as we are come out of the water we are anointed with the blessed unction, and then we receive imposition of hands, invocating the Holy Spirit by a benediction.'[2]

Origen mentions unction when he speaks of 'all those baptized with visible water and visible chrism,'[3] drawing no clear line of demarcation between the unction of baptism and the unction of confirmation.

In both the Greek and Roman Churches, while the unction remains, the use of the imposition of hands has disappeared for many centuries.

For the use of the sign of the cross in confirmation, see next paragraph.

§ 7. SIGN OF THE CROSS.—The sign of the cross was in constant use among the early Christians, not only in baptism and confirmation or while praying, but also as an accompaniment of the commonest actions of everyday life. They thought that they saw or could see the sign of the cross almost anywhere and everywhere. Justin Martyr bade people see it in the cross masts of a ship, in the cross handle of a plough, in the shape of tools used by diggers and mechanics, in the shape of the human form as it stands erect with arms extended,[4] and especially

---
[1] *De Resurrectione Carnis*, cap. 8; *P. L.*, ii. 806. See p. 68.
[2] *De Baptismo*, caps. 7, 8; *P. L.*, i. 1206, 1207.
[3] In Rom. v. §8; *P. G.*, xiv. 1038.
[4] *Apol.* i. cap. lv.; *P. G.*, vi. 411.

in the case of the extended arms of Moses while the Israelites defected the Amalekites.¹

Tertullian describes how

'In all our travels and movements, in all our coming in and going out, in putting on our shoes, at the bath, at the table, in lighting our candles, in lying down, whatever employment occupies us, we mark our foreheads with the sign of the cross.'²

In deprecating mixed marriages, he asks how the Christian wife will be able to escape detection by the heathen husband, when she makes the sign of the cross over her body, or over her bed, or to banish evil thoughts, or when she rises at night to pray.³

St. Cyprian, speaking of the necessity for the Christian to be armed at all points, says—

'Let thy forehead be protected that the sign of the cross may be preserved intact.'⁴

This may be either a general reference to the use of the sign of the cross, or a special reference to its use in confirmation, about which he elsewhere says that—

'Those who are baptized are brought to the bishops (*præpositis*) of the Church, and obtain the Holy Spirit through our prayer and the imposition of hands, and are consummated by the sign of the Lord.'⁵

Minucius Felix says—

'We see the sign of the cross naturally in a ship, borne

---

¹ *Dial. cum Tryphone*, capp. xc., xcvii. ; *P. G.*, vi. 690, 703.
² *De Corona Militis*, cap. iii. ; *P. L.*, ii. 80.
³ *Ad Uxorem*, lib. ii. cap. v. ; *P. L.*, i. 1296.
⁴ *Ep.* lvi. p. 93.   ⁵ *Ep.* lxxiii. p. 132.

along with bellying sails; we see it when the ship glides forward with outstretched oars, and when the yard is hoisted; we see it when a pure-hearted man worships God with extended arms.'[1]

Origen thought that the shape of the letter *tau*

'bore a resemblance to the figure of the cross, and that therein was contained a prophecy of the sign which is made by Christians upon the foreheads, for all the faithful make this sign in commencing any undertaking, and especially at the commencement of prayer or of reading Holy Scripture.'[2]

In early Acts of the Saints reference is made to the use of this sign in offering prayer;[3] it was made by Thecla on leaving her mother's home.[4]

A two-fold symbolism is ascribed to it in the Canons of Hippolytus—firstly, as a sign of conquest over Satan; secondly, as a sign of glorying in our faith.[5]

The sign of the cross was, as we have seen,[6] connected with baptism. St. Cyprian speaks of 'those persons who have been regenerated, and signed with the sign of Christ,'[7] and says, 'Let thy brow be fortified [with the cross] that the sign of God [*i.e.* once imprinted at baptism] may be preserved intact.'[8]

---

[1] Octavius, cap. 29, ed. 1672, p. 287.
[2] *Select. in Ezek.*, cap. ix. tom. iii. p. 424.
[3] *Acts of Xanthippe*, p. 62.
[4] *Acts of Paul and Thecla*, x. 10; Grabe, *Spicilegium* (Oxford, 1714), p. 116.
[5] Canon xxix. § 247, p. 134. See also § 245.   [6] Page 68.
[7] *Lib. ad Demetrianum*, cap. xxii. ; *P. L.*, iv. 580.
[8] *Ep.* lviii. [al. lvi.] ; *P. L.*, iv. 367.

It is referred to in the Apostolic Constitutions.[1] Origen represents the devil at the Day of Judgment claiming a man as his own in these words—

'Lo! this man was called a Christian, and was signed on the forehead with the sign of Christ; but he bore my will and my mark in his heart. Behold a man who renounced me and my works at his baptism, but again occupied himself in my works, and obeyed my laws!'[2]

§ 8. EXORCISM.—No external action is mentioned in the New Testament in connection with the act of exorcising or casting out evil spirits (St. Matt. xii. 27; Acts xix. 13); but the practice of the imposition of hands in connection with it evidently obtained at a very early date.

Origen speaks of the imposition of the hands of the exorcists which unclean spirits found heavy upon them.[3]

Vincentius of Thibaris mentions the imposition of hands in exorcism as the first rite to be received by a man on his way to become a full Christian.[4] From this we gather that the imposition of hands in exorcism was practised in Africa in the third century.

All extant offices of exorcism mention and provide for it; but none of these offices, as we know them, are ante-Nicene.

§ 9. FASTING. — Fasting on Wednesday and

[1] Ἡ σφραγίς ἀντὶ τοῦ σταυροῦ, lib. iii. cap. xvii. p. 88.
[2] *Select. in Psalmos*, Ps. xxxviii.; Hom. ii. § 5, tom. ii. p. 698.
[3] *Hom. in Jesu Fil. Nave*, xxiv. cap. 1; *P. G.*, xii. 940.
[4] 'Inter Sententias Episcoporum lxxxvii.,' 'De Hæreticis Baptizandis,' Cypriani *Opera*, p. 334.

Friday is recognized and ordered in the Teaching of the Twelve Apostles—

'But let not your fasts be together with the hypocrites, for they fast on the second and fifth days of the week; but fast ye on the fourth day [Wednesday], and on the preparation day [Friday].'[1]

The same injunction occurs in the Apostolic Constitutions, with a very practical definition of the object of fasting appended to it—

'We enjoin you to fast every fourth day of the week [Wednesday], and every day of the preparation [Friday], and bestow the surplusage of your fast upon the needy.'[2]

The custom is mentioned by Tertullian,[3] by St. Clement of Alexandria,[4] and by Origen.[5] In *The Shepherd* of Hermas the reason for fasting is set forth at greater length—

'This fasting,' saith he, 'if the commandments of the Lord are kept, is very good. This, then, is the way that thou shalt keep the fast. First of all, keep thyself from every evil word and every evil device, and purify thy heart from all the vanities of this world. If thou keep these things, thy fast shall be perfect for thee. And thus shalt thou do. Having fulfilled what is written, on that day on which thou fastest, thou shalt taste nothing but

---

[1] *Didaché*, cap. viii. § 1.
[2] Bk. v. cap. 20. In the same place fasting upon the Lord's day and at certain other times is forbidden.
[3] *Lib. de Oratione*, cap. 19, where he argues that the reception of the Eucharist on these days (*stationum diebus*) does not break the fast; *P. L.*, i. 1181.
[4] *Stromata*, lib. vii. cap. 12; *P. G.*, ix. 504. The whole chapter as to the true meaning of the observance of Feast-days and Fast-days is a beautiful one.
[5] Hom. x. *in Levit.*, tom. ii. p. 246.

bread and water; and from thy meals which thou wouldest have eaten, thou shalt reckon up the amount of that day's expenditure, which thou wouldest have incurred, and shalt give it to a widow, or an orphan, or to one in want, and so shalt thou humble thy soul, that he that received from thy humiliation may satisfy his own soul, and may pray for thee to the Lord. If then thou shalt so accomplish this fast, as I have commanded thee, thy sacrifice shall be acceptable in the sight of God, and this fasting shall be recorded; and the service so performed is beautiful and joyous, and acceptable to the Lord.'[1]

The *Apology* of Aristides contains this passage, among others, which describe the life of the early Christians—

'If there is among them a man that is poor and needy, and they have not an abundance of necessaries, they fast two or more days, that they may supply the needy with their necessary food.'[2]

An early reference to the strict view of the binding character of the Wednesday and Friday fast, irrespective of eleemosynary considerations or other such purposes, occurs in the Acts of St. Fructuosus. When that saint was on the way to martyrdom, he refused to touch a cup of wine offered him by his friends, because it was only 10 a.m. on a Wednesday, and he would not break the fast which on Wednesday and Friday was protracted till 3 p.m.[3]

St. Peter of Alexandria explains the origin of

[1] *Similitude*, No. 5, § 3.
[2] Cap. xv. p. 49. This chapter contains a beautiful description of the simple, pure, self-denying life of the early Christians.
[3] *Fructuosi Acta*, p. 340.

these two fast-days, saying that it was usual to fast on Wednesday 'because of the Jews taking counsel for the betrayal of our Lord,' and on Friday, 'because He then suffered for our sake.'[1]

Origen says—

'We have the forty days of Lent (*Quadragesimæ dies*) consecrated to fasting; we have the fourth and sixth days of the week (Wednesday and Friday) on which to keep our solemn fasts.'[2]

Lent and Wednesdays and Fridays are mentioned as times of fasting by Tertullian,[3] in the Canons of Hippolytus,[4] and, it may be added, in the later Apostolic Canons, where they are ordered to be observed, both by clergy and laity, under severe penalties.[5]

In the second century there was variety of custom with regard to the duration of Lent, some observing it for one day (*i.e.* Good Friday), some for two days (*i.e.* Good Friday and Easter Even), some for more days than these two, some for forty days.[6]

There are traces of a strict and continuous fast being observed on Good Friday and Easter Even. This was supposed to be literally carrying out our Lord's words, 'But the days will come, when the bridegroom shall be taken from them, and then

[1] Routh (M. J.), *Reliquæ Sacræ*, 2nd ed. p. 45.
[2] Hom. x. in *Levit.*, tom. i. p. 246.
[3] Lib. *de Jejuniis*, cap. xiv. ; *P. L.*, ii. 973.
[4] Canon xx. § 154.   [5] Canon 69.
[6] Irenæus, Gr. Fragm. iii., ed. W. W. Harvey (Cambridge, 1857), tom. ii. p. 475. Irenæus goes on to remark that diversity of practice in this matter caused no break of friendship between the Eastern Polycarp, the disciple of St. John, and the Western Anicetus, Bishop of Rome, though neither could win the other over to his practice.

shall they fast.'[1] It was a prolonged preparation for the midnight celebration of the Eucharist on Easter Morning. Lactantius speaks of the night of Holy Saturday being passed in watchfulness on account of the Saviour's body coming to life again, and on account of the second coming of our Lord and King.[2] Tertullian refers to the difficulty which would be experienced by a Christian wife in absenting herself all night from her heathen husband on account of the paschal solemnities.[3] The all-night watch on Easter Even is specially mentioned in the Canons of Hippolytus.[4] Zosimus narrates that the feast of the resurrection of the Lord is performed with much watching, for we continue watching for three days and three nights.[5]

For fasting as a preparation for the reception of baptism, see p. 72; of the Holy Eucharist, see p. 127.

§ 10. THE EUCHARIST.—We do not propose to discuss fully the much-debated and difficult question as to the time when the Liturgy of the Christian Church was first committed to writing. But it should be stated that there is not sufficient evidence to prove the existence of any written liturgical books before A.D. 325, and that there are certain facts and statements which tend to disprove, without amounting to positive disproof of their existence.

The facts referred to are these—

[1] St. Matt. ix. 15.
[2] *Div. Institt.*, lib. vii.; *De Vita Beata*, cap. xix.; *P. L.*, vi. 797.
[3] *Ad Uxorem*, lib. ii. cap. iv.; *P. L.*, i. 1294.
[4] Canon xxxviii. § 255, p. 136.
[5] *Narrative of Zosimus*, cap. xii.; *A. C. L.*, vol. for 1897, p. 222.

There is no allusion to the surrender, or to any demand for the surrender, of liturgical books during the early persecutions, though the surrender, or the demand for the surrender, of copies of Holy Scripture is frequently mentioned.

No appeal is made to the authority of a settled liturgical text during the controversies of the first three centuries.

Some phrases used in early descriptions of Christian worship point to the extempore character of the prayers used, *e.g.* in the Teaching of the Twelve Apostles it is said—

'Suffer the prophets to give thanks *as much as they will.*'[1]

Justin Martyr, describing the Eucharistic Service, tells us that—

'Bread and a cup of wine mingled with water are then brought to the president of the brethren; and he, taking them, gives praise and glory to the Father of the universe through the Name of the Son and of the Holy Ghost, and *offers thanks at considerable length* for our being counted worthy to receive these things at his hands.'[2]

And in another description he says—

'When we have finished the prayer, bread and wine and water are brought, and the president in like manner *offers prayers and thanksgivings with all his might.*'[3]

We have put in italics the phrases which seem to

---

[1] Ὅσα θέλουσιν. This seems to mean 'in what words they will.' Εὐχαριστία and εὐχαριστεῖν, having a general sense connected with thanksgiving, as well as a technical sense connected with the Eucharist, are the cause of much ambiguity and difficulty of interpretation.

[2] *First Apology*, cap. lxv. See p. 52.

[3] *Ibid.*, cap. lxvii. Ὅση δύναμις αὐτῷ has also been translated 'according to his ability.' See p. 53.

imply, if they do not prove, the use of extempore devotional language.

In the Acts of Thomas there is an extremely interesting account of the communion of the newly baptized, the Eucharist being celebrated for that purpose by the Apostle, who is represented as employing words of consecration which are evidently extempore.[1]

We append one more passage from a later writer, which has been taken to mean, and which, as far as language goes, may mean, but which does not necessarily mean, that the Liturgy had not yet been written down in the fourth century.

St. Basil of Cæsarea (*ob.* 379) says—

'Which of the saints has left us in writing the words of invocation at the consecration of the bread of the Eucharist, and of the cup of blessing? For we are not content with those mentioned by the Apostle or the Gospel, but we also say some words before them and after them, as being of great force for the purpose of the sacrament, which we have received from unwritten tradition.'[2]

Language may, however, have become fixed before it was written. We can trace the 'Sursum corda,' as an integral portion of the Eucharistic Service, as far back as the time of St. Cyprian, who says—

---

[1] Capp. 46, 47, pp. 35, 36.
[2] *De Spiritu Sancto*, cap. xxvii. § 66; *P. G.*, xxxii. 188. The passage is quoted in full by W. Maskell, *Ancient Liturgy of the Church of England*, 3rd ed. p. xxvii. He seems to agree with Renaudot in thinking that it may only mean that the words of Eucharistic consecration are not found in Holy Scripture. Probst (F.) argues that Liturgies were written at a very early date, at least as early as the *Didaché*. *Die aeltesten roemischen Sacramentarien*, Münster, i. W. 1892, pp. 1-12.

'The priest, in the preface which is said before the Prayer [of Consecration], prepares the minds of the brethren by saying,

    Lift up your hearts,

that when the people answer,

    We lift them up unto the Lord,

they may be warned that they ought to think of nothing but the Lord.'[1]

And more fully still in the Canons of Hippolytus—

'And let the bishop say:
    The Lord be with you all.*
Let the people reply:
    And with thy spirit.
Let him say:
    Lift up your hearts.*
Let the people reply:
    We lift them up unto the Lord.*
The bishop:
    Let us give thanks unto the Lord.*
Let the people reply:
    It is meet and right so to do.'*[2]

The formulæ of administration mentioned in the same canons are these—

---

[1] *De Oratione Dominica*, p. 213.

[2] Canon iii. §§ 21–26, pp. 48–50. The sentences marked with an asterisk are given in the Greek language, a proof of the early nature of this document. Other Greek words, written in Greek characters, which occur in these Canons, are—ἐξομολόγησις (ii. 9), ἀναγνώστης (vii. 48, etc.), ὑποδιάκονος (vii. 49, etc.), θεατρικός, κυνηγός (xii. 67), γραμματικός (xii. 69), οἰωνιστής (xv. 76), πάλλιον (xvii. 98), παράκλητος (xix. 131), εὐχαριστία (xix. 134, etc.), ἀρραβών (xix. 138), κυριακή (xxxii. 164, etc.), ἀνάμνησις (xxxiii. 169), ἐξορκισμός (xxxiii. 170, etc.), πάσχα (xxii. 197, etc.), κλῆρος (xxi. 218), κοιμητήριον (xxiv. 220), λυχνικός (xxv. 237).

'This is the body of Christ. ℟. Amen.
This is the blood of Christ. ℟. Amen.'[1]

In the Egyptian Church Order the formula has become slightly enlarged—

'This is the bread of heaven, the body of Jesus Christ. ℟. Amen.
This is the blood of Jesus Christ our Lord. ℟. Amen.'[2]

Titles of the Service.—(a) The Breaking of Bread. The earliest and scriptural title of this service, 'the breaking of bread,' occurs in a passage of the Epistle of St. Ignatius to the Ephesians, in which he bids them—

'Assemble yourselves together in common, every one of you severally, ... breaking one bread, which is the medicine of immortality, and the antidote that we should not die, but live for ever in Jesus Christ.'[3]

And in the following passage in the Teaching of the Twelve Apostles—

'And on the Lord's day come together, and break bread, and give thanks, after confessing your transgressions, that your sacrifice may be pure.'[4]

In the Acts of Paul and Thecla St. Paul is described, on his arrival at the house of Onesiphorus, as offering prayer, breaking bread, and preaching the word of God.[5]

In the Acts of Thomas we find the expression 'breaking the eucharistic bread.'[6]

---

[1] Canon xix. §§ 146, 147, pp. 100, 101. There are similar, not identical, short formulæ in the Clementine Liturgy (H., p. 21). See p. 304.
[2] Canons of Hippolytus, pp. 101, 102. [3] Cap. 20. [4] Cap. 14.
[5] Cap. 2; Gallandius, *Bib. Vet. Pat.*, tom. i. p. 178.
[6] Κλάσας ἄετον τῆς εὐχαριστίας, cap. 27, p. 20; cap. 29, p. 22.

(*b*) *The Eucharist.* The word 'Eucharist' is first found as a distinct title of 'Holy Communion' in the writings of St. Ignatius. He says to the Philadelphians—

'Be ye careful, therefore, to observe one Eucharist (for there is one flesh of our Lord Jesus Christ, and one cup unto union in His blood; there is one altar, as there is one bishop, together with the presbytery, and the deacons, my fellow-servants), that whatsoever ye do, ye may do it after God.'[1]

He thus describes, among other ways, certain heretics in his Epistle to the Smyrnæans—

'They abstain from Eucharist and prayer, because they allow not that the Eucharist is the flesh of our Saviour Jesus Christ, which flesh suffered for our sins, and which the Father, of His goodness, raised up.'[2]

In the same Epistle he adds—

'Let that be held a valid Eucharist which is under the bishop, or one to whom he shall have given a commission. ... It is not lawful, apart from the bishop, either to baptize or to hold a love-feast.'[3]

A few years afterwards the use of the word 'Eucharist' as a title is definitely fixed by Justin Martyr. After describing the partaking of the consecrated bread and wine and water, he goes on to say—

'And this food we call the Eucharist, which nobody may partake of, except,' etc.[4]

[1] Cap. 4.   [2] Cap. 6.
[3] Cap. 8. The expression love-feast (ἀγάπη) probably includes the Eucharist. See Bp. Lightfoot's note, *in loco*.
[4] *Apol.* i. 65 ; also in *Dialogus cum Tryphone*, cap. xli., etc. ; *P. G.*, vi. 563.

St. Irenæus, reproving Victor, Bishop of Rome, who had broken off communion with the bishops of Asia Minor because they kept Easter always on the fourteenth day of the month, whether it was a Sunday or not, claiming to follow the practice of the Apostle St. John, tells him that his predecessors 'sent the Eucharist to the Asiatic bishops,' in accordance with a custom of that time, as a mark of intercommunion between the two Churches.[1] In the same letter he perhaps uses the word 'Eucharist' to denote the whole service, telling Victor that his predecessor, Anicetus, conceded the Eucharist to Polycarp, *i.e.* permitted Polycarp to celebrate the Eucharist at Rome.[2] Elsewhere Irenæus says—

'For as the bread from the earth, when it receives the invocation of God, is no longer common bread, but the Eucharist,' etc.[3]

In the Clementine Homilies the curious expression 'to break the Eucharist' is found.[4]

St. Clement of Alexandria says that Melchisedech gave consecrated bread and wine for a type of the Eucharist.[5]

Origen says that the symbol of gratitude towards God is that bread which is called the Eucharist.[6]

---

[1] *Epist. ad Victorem* apud Eusebii, *Hist. Eccles.*, lib. v. cap. 24.
[2] *Ibid.*
[3] *Contra Hæres*, iv. 18. 5.
[4] Lib. xi. cap. 36 : Εὐχαριστίαν κλάσας, 'Eucharistiam fregit.'
[5] *Stromata*, lib. iv. cap. 25 ; *P. G.*, viii. 1371 ; also *Pædagog*, lib. ii. cap. 2 ; *Ibid.*, 411.
[6] *Contra Celsum*, lib. viii. cap. 57 ; also Hom. ii. in Ps. xxxvii. § 6.

Tertullian[1] and Cyprian[2] both use the word
'Eucharistia.' Tertullian also uses 'gratiarum actio,'
or 'giving of thanks,' as its Latin equivalent.[3] In
the Acts of Thomas it is called 'the Eucharist of
Christ.'[4]

It is this widespread and preponderating use of
the term 'Eucharistia' in ante-Nicene literature,
which has caused us to select the title of 'the
Eucharist' as the heading for this section of the
second chapter.

Among other titles which were given to this
sacrament there should be mentioned the following:—

(c) *Sacrifice*, either absolutely by itself,[5] or with
some epithet attached to it, *e.g.* 'the pure sacrifice,'[6]
'the pure and spiritual oblation,'[7] 'the Lord's
sacrifice.'[8]

At the trial of Apollonius—

'the prefect said to the Christian martyr, "Come and
sacrifice to Apollo, and to the other gods, and to the
emperor's image." Apollonius replied, "As to my change
of mind, and as to the oath, I have given thee answer;
but as to sacrifices, I and all Christians offer a bloodless
sacrifice to God, Lord of heaven and earth,"' etc.[9]

Not that the title of 'sacrifice' was confined to

[1] *De Præscript adv. Hæret.*, cap. 36; *P. L.*, ii. 50.
[2] *Ep.* liv. p. 77.
[3] *Adv. Marcion*, lib. i. cap. 23; *P. L.*, ii. 274.
[4] Cap. 27, p. 20.   [5] Θυσία, *Didaché*, cap. xiv.
[6] Irenæus, *Contra Hæres*, lib. iv. cap. 18; *P. G.*, vii. 1024.
[7] Pfaffian fragment, Irenæi *Opp.*, ed. W. W. Harvey, Fragm. 36, tom. ii. p. 502.
[8] Cyprian, *Ep.* 63, § 5; *P. L.*, iv. 389.
[9] Acts of Apollonius, ed. F. C. Conybeare, p. 39.

the Eucharist. St. Clement of Alexandria, contrasting the sumptuous sacrifices offered by the heathen to their gods with the sacrifice offered by Christians, identifies the Christian sacrifice with prayer generally; no doubt, not excluding, yet not specially naming, the Eucharistic sacrifice. He says—

'For the sacrifice of the Church is prayer which is offered by holy souls, when the whole mind is opened and offered in sacrifice to God,' etc.[1]

(*d*) *The Lord's Feast.*[2]
(*e*) *The Spiritual and Heavenly Sacrament.*[3]

The title of 'Εφόδιον, or Viaticum, for a death-bed communion occurs in the thirteenth Canon of the Council of Nice, but we have not found any instance of an Ante-Nicene use of this word with an exclusively or necessarily Eucharistic meaning.[4]

Time of Celebration.—The earliest records which we possess of the celebration of the Holy Eucharist outside the pages of Holy Scripture itself, speak of the early, and for the most part of the very early, morning.

Pliny in his letter to Trajan, *c.* A.D. 112, describes Christians as 'persons who met together early in the morning, and bound themselves with a sacrament,' etc.[5]

---

[1] *Stromata*, lib. vii. cap. 6; *P. G.*, ix. 443.
[2] Tertullian, *Ad Uxorem*, lib. ii. cap. 4; *P. L.*, i. 1294.
[3] Cyprian, *Ep.* 63, § 13; *P. L.*, iv. 396.
[4] The word occurs in the *Stromata* of St. Clement of Alexandria, lib. i. cap. 1.; *P. G.*, viii. 691, but not in reference to the Eucharist.
[5] Or 'by an oath.' See page 51, note 1.

Justin Martyr, though he gives clear information on other points, is silent as to the hour of the day. Tertullian speaks plainly about it. He says—

'The Sacrament of the Eucharist, though it was commanded by our Lord at meal-time and to all, we take in assemblies before daybreak (*antelucanis cœtibus*), and from the hands of no others except our presidents.'[1]

Again, when dissuading a Christian woman from marriage with a heathen man, he says—

'Your husband will not know what you are tasting secretly before all other food.'[2]

He refers also to the custom of a midnight celebration of the Easter Eucharist, the attendance at which will constitute another of the difficulties which await a Christian wife allied to a heathen husband.[3]

St. Cyprian thus explains and defends morning as against evening celebrations of the Eucharist. He is answering the argument which might be brought forward, that because Christ instituted the Eucharist after supper, therefore our celebration thereof ought to be after supper likewise, and he says—

'It behoved Christ to offer about eventide, that the hour itself of sacrifice might betoken the setting and evening of the world, as it is written in the Book of Exodus, "And the whole assembly of the congregation of Israel shall kill in the evening."[4] And again in the Psalms, "Let the lifting up

---

[1] *De Corona Militis*, cap. 3 ; *P. L.*, ii. 79.
[2] *Ad Uxorem*, lib. ii. cap. 5 ; *P. L.*, i. 1296. The reference here is to the reserved Sacrament.
[3] *Ibid.*, cap. 4 ; *ibid.*, 1294.   [4] Exod. xii. 6.

of my hands be an evening sacrifice." [1] But we celebrate the resurrection of the Lord in the morning.' [2]

Tertullian refers to the celebration of the Eucharist in connection with a wedding in these words—

'How may we suffice to describe the happiness of that marriage in which the Church unites, and which the oblation confirms, and the benediction seals?' [3]

Frequency of Celebration. The earliest evidence which is forthcoming points to a celebration of the Eucharist on one day in each week, that day being Sunday.

The stated day of the week referred to in Pliny's letter to Trajan [4] may be concluded with moral certainty to have been the first day of the week, if we bear Acts xx. 7 in mind, and weigh the fact that we have contemporary or earlier evidence of a definite kind about the Sunday worship of the primitive Church. In the *Didaché* there is this order—

'And on the Lord's day of the Lord come together and break bread, and give thanks, after confessing your transgressions, that your sacrifice may be pure.' [5]

After describing the Eucharistic Service, Justin Martyr mentions Sunday as the day on which all met for worship.[6]

In the Acts of Eugenia, which date from the third century, though they have not reached us without later additions, we read how her mother Clodia—

---

[1] Ps. cxli. 2.   [2] *Ep.* 63, p. 109.
[3] *Ad Uxorem*, lib. ii. cap. 9; *P. L.*, i. 1302.
[4] Page 51.   [5] Cap. xiv. § 1.   [6] *Apol.* i. 67. See p 53.

'on the Lord's day, at the hour of the completion of the sacrament, while she was in church and was offering prayer, gave up her spirit into the hands of Christ, the Lord of all spirits.'[1]

Other days which were specially marked by a celebration of the Eucharist, besides Sundays, were the festivals or anniversaries of martyrs;[2] also the two station days in each week, Wednesday and Friday;[3] and probably the fifty days from Easter to Pentecost, known as Quinquagesima, or Pentecostes, or Quinquagesima Paschalis, which Tertullian describes as one continuous festival.[4]

According to the Canons of Hippolytus the Eucharist was to be celebrated on Sundays, and on other days when the bishop wished, and also before the commemoration of the dead.[5]

But by the beginning of the third century we have evidence that a daily celebration had become, at least in Africa, an established custom. Tertullian, describing a certain class of unworthy clergy, says—

'The Jews once laid their hands on Christ; they daily harass His body. O hands which should be cut off! Let them see to it now whether it was said in a parable, "If thy hand offend thee cut it off." What hands should be cut off

---

[1] Conybeare (F. C.), *Monuments of Early Christianity* (London, 1894), p. 187.
[2] Tertullian, *De Corona Militis*, cap. 3; *P. L.*, ii. 79; Cyprian, *Epp.*, 34, 37; *P. L.*, iv. 323, 328.
[3] Tertullian, *De Oratione*, cap. 19; *P. L.*, i. 1181.
[4] *De Corona Militis*, cap. iii.; *De Idololatria*, cap. xiv.; *De Jejuniis*, cap. xiv.; *P. L.*, ii. 80; i. 682; ii. 973.
[5] Canon xxxiii. § 169, p. 106.

more than those in which the body of our Lord receives offence?'[1]

He gives a Eucharistic as well as a literal interpretation of the clause in the Lord's Prayer, 'Give us this day our daily bread.'[2]

St. Cyprian and other African bishops say in the Synodical Epistle of the Second Council of Carthage in 252—

'As priests who daily celebrate the sacrifices of God, let us prepare [men to become by martyrdom] offerings and victims to God.'[3]

St. Cyprian also says—

'A more serious and a more fierce contest awaits them, for which the soldiers of Christ ought to prepare themselves with unsullied faith and stout valour, considering that for this reason they daily drink the chalice of the blood of Christ, that they may have power themselves to shed their blood for Christ.'[4]

Commenting on the Lord's Prayer, he says—

'But we pray that this bread may be given to us daily, lest we who are in Christ, and receive the Eucharist daily as the food of salvation, should, while we are kept away and prevented from receiving the heavenly bread through the intervention of some very grave fault, be separated from the body of Christ.'[5]

Communion in both kinds.—It is unnecessary to produce evidence to prove the undisputed fact that

---

[1] *De Idololatria*, cap. vii. ; *P. L.*, i. 669.
[2] *De Oratione*, cap. vi. ; *P. L.*, i. 1160.
[3] *Ep.* liv., p. 78.   [4] *Ep.* lvi., p. 90.
[5] *Lib. de Oratione Dominica*, p. 209.

ordinarily the Eucharistic elements were administered to the communicants in both kinds; but an argument which is based exclusively on the administration of the cup, and which would have to be abandoned or altered in that part of Christendom where the cup is now withheld from all save the celebrant, deserves to be quoted and remembered.

In the synodical Epistle addressed to Cornelius, Bishop of Rome, after the second Council of Carthage in 252, St. Cyprian and his colleagues say—

'How do we teach or encourage men to shed their blood in the confession of His Name, if as they are about to start on their warfare we deny to them the blood of Christ? Or how do we fit them to drink the cup of martyrdom if we do not first admit them with the right of communicants, to drink the cup of the Lord in church?'[1]

The Prayer of Consecration.—The text of no ante-Nicene Liturgy having come down to us, we do not, and cannot, know with precision the exact formula of consecration, but we can infer something of its character from the titles by which it is described.

In the first place, it was a prayer, that is to say, it was not merely a recital of the words of institution, or of any other words in the shape of a formula, incantation, or charm. Origen says—

'Let Celsus, then, as an agnostic, tender his thanks to demons; while we, giving thanks to the Maker of the universe, eat also, with prayer and thanksgiving for blessings

---

[1] *Ep.* 54, p. 78. See also St. Cyprian's words just previously quoted on p. 117.

received, our oblations of bread, which, through the prayer [of consecration, διὰ τὴν εὐχήν], becomes a certain holy body, which makes those holy who partake of it with right dispositions.'[1]

The nature of this prayer is further defined in a difficult passage which occurs in the earlier writings of Justin Martyr, who says that—

'As Jesus Christ our Saviour was incarnate by the Word of God, and assumed flesh and blood for our salvation, so we have been taught that the food, from which our flesh and blood derive nourishment by assimilation, having been blessed [or made the Eucharist] by prayer of the word which is from Him,[2] is both the flesh and blood of that same Jesus who was made flesh.'[3]

The expression 'prayer of the word which is from Him' is difficult to interpret. It has by some been taken to refer to the words of institution, by others to mean the Lord's Prayer,[4] by others to mean the invocation of the Holy Ghost.[5] It must remain sufficient here to have pointed out the chief varieties of interpretation, without discussing them at length, or attempting to decide between them.

The Latin equivalent of εὐχή is 'prex' or 'prex Domini,' as in the following passage from St. Cyprian, where 'prex Domini' evidently denotes the Eucharistic consecration prayer, though 'prex'

---

[1] *Contra Celsum*, lib. viii. p. 33, tom. i. p. 766.
[2] Εὐχαριστηθεῖσαν δι' εὐχῆς λόγου τοῦ παρ' αὐτοῦ.
[3] *Apol.*, i. cap. 66. See p. 52 for a slightly varying translation.
[4] Wordsworth, J. (Bp. of Salisbury), *The Holy Communion* (Oxford, 1891), p. 62.
[5] Ffoulkes (E. S.), *Primitive Consecration*, p. 54.

is elsewhere used by St. Cyprian of prayer in a general sense:—

'How does he think that his hand can be transferred to the sacrifice and to the prayer of the Lord, which has been held in captivity to sacrilege and crime?'[1]

Another expression for the consecrating formula is 'the Word of God.' Irenæus says—

'When therefore the mixed cup and the natural bread receive the word of God (τὸν λόγον τοῦ Θεοῦ) it becomes the Eucharist of the blood and body of Christ.'[2]

A more frequent phrase is 'the word of invocation,' or the invocation of God (ἐπίκλησις Θεοῦ). Irenæus says again—

'As the bread which is from the earth, after receiving the invocation of God upon it, is no longer common bread, but the Eucharist, consisting of two things, an earthly and a heavenly, so our bodies after partaking of the Eucharist are no longer destructible, having hope of the resurrection that is for ever.'[3]

Describing the proceedings of a certain heretical Marcus, he reports how—

'Pretending to consecrate the Eucharist with a chalice of wine and water mixed, and making the word [or address, τὸν λόγον τῆς ἐπικλήσεως] of the invocation unusually long, he contrived that they should appear purple and red, as though the grace which is from the powers on high dropped its own blood into those chalices at his invocation.'[4]

---

[1] *Ep.* lxiv. p. 111.
[2] *Contra Hæres*, lib. v. cap. 2 ; *P. G.*, vii. 1125.
[3] *Ibid.*, lib. x. cap. 18 ; *P. G.*, vii. 1028.
[4] *Ibid.*, lib. i. cap. 13 ; *P. G.*, vii. 579. See also Fragm. xxxviii. Benedict ed., p. 26.

Origen says that it is sanctified by the word of God and by prayer.[1]

St. Firmilian describes a female religious impostor, who not only baptized people, but also dared to consecrate bread by a not contemptible [form of] invocation, and to pretend to offer the Eucharist.[2]

There is a difficult passage in Tertullian, where he connects the words of institution with the prayer of consecration. He says that our Lord—

'Took bread, and distributed it, and made it His body, by saying, "This is My body," that is to say, a figure of My body. But it would not have been a figure unless there had been a true body [for it to be a figure of].'[3]

The primitive consecration prayer, then, may be taken to have included an invocation, and the repetition of the words of institution. We do not know, because we are not told in what order they came, or of what words they consisted; but probably the order and the wording are those preserved in the Clementine Liturgy. With regard to words, there is one small point as to which we have information. There was a concluding 'Amen' uttered by the congregation. Tertullian asks how the mouth which has repeated 'Amen' at the holy service[4] can shout approval at a gladiatorial combat.[5] Cornelius,

[1] 'Per verbum Dei et orationem,' Hom. *in Matt.* xi. tom. iii. p. 499.
[2] St. Cyprian's *Epistles*, No. 75, p. 146 ; *P. L.*, iii. 1165.
[3] *Adv. Marcionem*, lib. iv. cap. 40 ; *P. L.*, ii. 460.
[4] 'In sanctum,' which some persons would translate 'at the reception of the Holy gift.'
[5] *De Spectaculis*, cap. 25 ; *P. L.*, i. 657.

Bishop of Rome, describes how the schismatic Novatian, in administering the Eucharist, compelled the communicants to substitute a formula of allegiance to himself for the 'Amen' wont to be said immediately after reception.[1]

The Mixed Chalice.—The mixed cup of wine and water is mentioned in Justin Martyr's description of the Eucharistic Service.[2] Irenæus mentions and condemns the Ebionites for rejecting the mixed chalice, and employing water only in the Eucharist,[3] and says that when the mixed cup and broken (MS. ὁ γεγόνως, factus) bread receive the word of God, they become the Eucharist of the blood and body of Christ.[4]

The mixed cup is mentioned in the epitaph of Abercius (Avircius Marcellus), a supposed successor of Papias in the see of Hierapolis in Phrygia, c. A.D. 160.[5] This epitaph is so important, as well as interesting, and at the same time is so little known, that we do not hesitate to print it in full, appending brief, but not always certain, explanations of difficult phrases in the footnotes.[6]

[1] Routh (J. M.), *Reliquiæ Sacræ*, 2nd ed. vol. iii. p. 27.
[2] *Apol.* i. cap. lxv. See p. 52.
[3] *Contra Hæres*, lib. v. cap. 1. Later on St. Augustine mentions the Aquarii, a sect who adopted the same practice (*De Hæres*, cap. 64; (Ehler, *Corpus Hæresiologicum*, tom. i. p. 215).
[4] *Contra Hæres*, lib. v. cap. 2 ; *P. G.*, vii. 1125.
[5] But see p. 123, note 10.
[6] The translation and notes are mainly those of Bp. Lightfoot. The original Greek is printed by De Rossi, *Inscriptiones Christianæ urbis Romæ*, vol. ii. pt. i., Introd. pp. xii.-xxiv., and by Bp. Lightfoot, *The Apostolic Fathers* (London, 1885), pt. ii. vol. i. pp. 476-485.

'The citizen of an elect [1] city, I made this [tomb] in my lifetime, that in due season I might have a resting-place for my body. Abercius by name, I am a disciple of the pure Shepherd, who feedeth His flocks of sheep on mountains and plains, who hath great eyes looking on all sides; for He taught me the faithful writings [of life]. He also sent me to royal Rome to behold it, and to see the golden-robed, golden-sandalled Queen.[2] And there I saw a people bearing the splendid seal,[3] and I saw the plain of Syria, and all the cities, even Nisibis, crossing over the Euphrates. And everywhere I had associates.[4] In company with Paul,[5] I followed, and everywhere Faith led the way, and set before me the Fish[6] from the fountain, mighty and stainless, whom a pure Virgin[7] clasped, and gave this to friends to eat always, having good wine, and giving the mixture[8] with bread. These words I, Abercius, standing by, ordered to be inscribed. In sooth, I was in the course of my seventy-second year. Let every one who considers my meaning and thinks with me pray for Abercius.[9] But no man shall place another tomb above mine. If otherwise, then he shall pay two thousand pieces of gold to the treasury of the Romans, and a thousand pieces of gold to my good fatherland, Hieropolis.'[10]

St. Cyprian is positive and vehement on the subject of the mixed chalice. He calls it a tradition from

[1] Ἐκλεκτῆς, *i.e.* Christian.
[2] Either the Empress Faustina or the Church.
[3] Probably the sign of the cross, especially as impressed at baptism and confirmation.
[4] *E.g.* fellow-Christians.
[5] Having St. Paul's writings with him, or being a traveller like St. Paul.
[6] The well-known emblem of our Lord found in the earliest paintings in the Catacombs.
[7] The B. V. M., or allegorically of the Church.
[8] Κέρασμα, the mixed chalice.
[9] Early testimony to the practice of prayer for the departed.
[10] Near Symnada, not Hierapolis on the Mæander.

our Lord (*Dominica traditio*), and urges that we ought to do nothing else than that which in the first instance our Lord did for us, viz. that the cup which is offered in commemoration of Him should be a mixed one.[1] He quotes, in support of it, the text, 'Come, eat of my bread, and drink of the cup which I have mingled.'[2] He then goes on, after adducing an extremely fanciful interpretation of the reason of the mixed chalice, to assert that it is necessary for the validity of the Eucharist, neither water alone nor wine alone being sufficient. He says—

'We see that people are to be understood by the water, and that the blood of Christ is exhibited in the wine. When water is mixed with wine in the chalice, the people is united to Christ and the multitude of believers is coupled and joined to Him in Whom they have believed; while coupling and joining of water and wine is thus made in the cup of the Lord as an inseparable commixture. . . . Thus, in consecrating the chalice of the Lord, water alone cannot be offered, just as wine alone cannot be offered. For if any one offer wine only, the blood of Christ begins to be in existence without us. If, however, there be water only, the people begin to be in existence without Christ. But when both are mixed and joined in mutually confused union, then the spiritual and heavenly sacrament is perfected.'[3]

This curious and inconclusive argument occurs in a letter intended to confute a practice introduced by some persons of consecrating water only for the Eucharist. So far as the invalidity of the use of

[1] *Ep.* 63, p. 104.   [2] Prov. ix. 5 ; *Ep.* 63, p. 105.
[3] *Ep.* 63, p. 108.

water only is concerned, St. Cyprian has been supported by the voice of the universal Church ; so far as the invalidity of the use of wine only is concerned, he has been overruled.

Origen stands alone among the Fathers in asserting that our Lord used pure unmixed wine at the Paschal Supper.[1]

Mr. F. C. Conybeare thinks that he has got proof that in the primitive Eucharist water only was used ; but the passages which he prints and adduces in support of such a view from the Acts of Paul and Thecla, and from the Acts of Callistratus, appear to contain no reference whatever to the Eucharist.[2]

One fact may be mentioned with reference to the chalice in early times. Tertullian informs us that it sometimes had the figure of the Good Shepherd painted on it.[3]

Reservation. We find traces of this custom for at least three purposes—

(*a*) *For sending to the absent, or for the communion of the sick.* Justin Martyr, in his account of the Eucharistic service, describes how, after those present had been communicated, the deacons bore away from the church portions of the consecrated elements for those who were absent.[4]

---

[1] *In Jeremiam,* Hom. xii. § 2, tom. iii. 194. The fact seems to be stated to enable a far-fetched allegorical interpretation to be worked out consistently.

[2] *Monuments of Early Christianity* (London, 1894), pp. 75, 292. See also p. 275.

[3] *De Pudicitia,* vol. ii. p. 645.

[4] *Apol.* i. cap. 65 ; see p. 52. For evidence of this practice in the fourth century, see St. Basil, *Ep.* 93 ; *P. G.*, xxxii. 485.

(*b*) *For private use.* St. Cyprian, writing against the custom of some Christians to frequent heathen games and shows, in spite of the immoralities and indecencies connected with them, denounces the profanity of the Christian worshipper, fresh dismissed from church, hastening at once to the play, and still carrying along with him, in accordance with custom, the Eucharist.[1] It was carried in a small basket or box (*arca*). St. Cyprian tells a story of a woman who tried to open her box which contained the holy gift of the Lord (*sanctum Domini*), but who desisted, being terrified by the fire which rose from the box.[2]

Tertullian advised scrupulous persons who would not receive at the three p.m. celebration of the Holy Eucharist on fast days, for fear of breaking their fast thereby, to attend the service, but to reserve their portion of the consecrated elements for reception at home in the evening, *i.e.* till the conclusion of the fast.[3]

He dissuades people from mixed marriages, because the heathen husband will get to know what is the food which the Christian wife tastes secretly before any other food,[4] referring evidently to the consecrated portion reserved for consumption at home.

(*c*) *For despatch to strangers as a token of amity.* We have already referred to the letter from Irenæus to Victor, Bishop of Rome, in which the former tells the latter that his predecessors in the Roman see sent the Eucharist to other bishops who disagreed

---

[1] *De Spectaculis*, p. 381.   [2] *De Lapsis*, p. 189.
[3] *Ad Uxorem*, lib. ii. cap. 5.   [4] *Ibid.*, cap. 4.

with them as to the proper day for the observance of Easter; and how Bishop Anicetus and Polycarp, on the occasion of the visit of the latter to Rome, agreed to differ on this point without any breach of intercommunion.[1]

Origen, in one passage, lays stress on the fact that at the institution of the Eucharist the bread was given to the disciples for immediate consumption, and not to be reserved for the morrow; but the context shows that he is arguing, not against the reservation of the material elements, but, metaphorically, against anything like staleness in offering the sacrifice of praise and thanksgiving.[2]

Mode of Reception.—Many details have not come down to us, but there is trace of a custom at Alexandria—a custom not universally followed even there —of permitting the communicants to approach the holy table, and to take, each for themselves, a portion of the consecrated Eucharist.[3] The same custom seems to be referred to in a letter from Dionysius of Alexandria to Xystus II., Bishop of Rome, preserved by Eusebius.[4]

Fasting Reception.—The fasting reception of the Eucharist by the newly baptized is ordered in the Canons of Hippolytus,[5] and also more generally for all the faithful; but in language which half suggests that fasting reception was not then the universal and

---

[1] See p. 111.   [2] Hom. v. in *Levit.* § 8; *P. G.*, xii. 453, 454.
[3] *Stromata*, lib. i. cap. i.; *P. G.*, viii. 691.   [4] See p. 81.
[5] Canon xix. §§ 150-153, pp. 101, 102. These passages are bracketed by the editors as probably an interpolation, but not as a later addition.

compulsory rule at all times, but that it was rigidly enforced on Good Friday.

'Let not any of the faithful taste anything before he has partaken of the mysteries, especially on the day of the holy fast.'[1]

We must again call attention to the passage in which Tertullian warns the Christian wife of a heathen husband that one of the difficulties of her situation will be that her husband will not know, and if he knows will not understand, what it is that she eats secretly before all other food.[2]

These are the only references which we have found in ante-Nicene writings to this subject. This is the more remarkable, because there is plentiful evidence for the fasting reception of the other great sacrament of the gospel.[3]

Infant Communion.—This is necessarily involved in the fact that infants were baptized, and that baptism was always immediately followed, if possible, by confirmation and first communion. St. Cyprian incidentally refers to the custom in his story about a child, who, unknown to its Christian mother, had been permitted by its nurse to taste food offered to idols, and who afterwards in church frantically refused to taste the contents of the consecrated

---

[1] Canon xxviii. § 205, p. 119. The same direction appears in the somewhat later *Egyptian Church Order*, with the enlargement that no deadly gift shall be able to injure the faithful recipient of the Eucharist (*ibid.*). This is evidently an allusion to St. Mark xvi. 17.

[2] See p. 114. For a curious translation and interpretation of 'ante omnem cibum' (*i.e.* before every meal), see F. T. Kingdon, *Fasting Communion* (London, 1875), p. 203.

[3] See p. 72.

chalice, and vomited when forced to do so.[1] On the other hand, a passage may be quoted from Origen to prove that infants were not communicants.[2] The reconciliation of the two passages lies in this: infants received the Eucharistic elements, probably, once in close connection with their baptism, but did not become regular communicants till they were more advanced in years.

HOLY DAYS. See SAINTS' DAYS.

§ 11. IMPOSITION OF HANDS.—We find reference to a fourfold usage and meaning of the ceremony of imposition of hands—

(*a*) In Absolution. See p. 56.

(*b*) In Confirmation. See p. 91.

(*c*) In Ordination. See p. 139.

(*d*) In Benediction. Several instances of this occur in the Acts of Thomas,[3] and probably elsewhere. Directions are given in the Apostolic Constitutions.[4]

§ 12. INCENSE.—There is no evidence for the use of incense in Christian worship during the first three centuries.[5] The offering of incense was so intimately associated with the worship of idols, and with the early persecutions of the Christian religion, that we

---

[1] *Lib. de Lapsis*, cap. xxv. p. 189.

[2] 'Antequam panis cœlestis consequamur annonam, et carnibus agni immaculati satiemur, antequam veræ vitis quæ ascendit de radice David sanguine inebriemur, donec parvuli sumus et lacte alimur,' etc. (*In Lib. Judicum*, Hom. vi. § 2).

[3] Cap. 10, *ad finem*, p. 10; cap. 29, p. 22; cap 46, p. 35.

[4] Lib. viii. cap. 37. See also cap. 38.

[5] A passage in Origen (Hom. iii., *In Lib. Judicum*, § 2), where he uses the words 'de altari Domini quod deberet incensi suavitate fragrare,' is plainly metaphorical.

K

may well conjecture, though we have no proof, that it was the association of incense with idolatry, and with suffering for the truth, which accounts for its non-use in the earlier days of Christianity.

The famous prophecy of Malachi [1] was frequently commented upon in early Christian literature; but though its Eucharistic reference is nearly always maintained, the allusion to incense is either passed over in silence or explained as referring to prayer in connection with Rev. v. 8.[2]

The following words, used by Tertullian, may be evidence that incense was not used in Christian worship in his time. He says that—

'as a Christian, he offers to God the rich and better offering which he himself has commanded, namely, prayer proceeding from a chaste body and an innocent mind, inspired by the Holy Spirit; not grains of incense of the value of one as, not the exudations of an Arabian shrub, not two drops of wine,' etc.[3]

It is possible that this, being a rhetorical passage, should not be pressed to prove the non-use of incense any more than it can be pressed to prove the non-use of Eucharistic wine.

Arnobius speaks of idol-worship and of the use of incense in terms which make it morally certain that he had no knowledge of any custom of using incense in Christian worship.[4]

[1] Mal. i. 11.
[2] *Didaché*, cap. xiv.; Justin Martyr, *Dialogus cum Tryphone*, capp. 28, 41, 116, 117; Irenæus, *Contra Hæres*, lib. iv. capp. 17, 18; Tertullian, *Adv. Judæos*, cap. 5; *Adv. Marcionem*, lib. iii. cap. 22.
[3] *Apol.*, cap. xxx.; *P. L.*, i. 444.
[4] *Adversus Gentes*, lib. vii. caps. 26-28; *P. L.*, v. 1135-1145.

Lactantius, in a very fine passage on 'the true worship and sacrifice due to God,' speaks of the uselessness of external offerings of victims, vestments, gold, silver, incense, etc., in language which seems to imply, though it does not directly state, that none of those things formed part of Christian worship in his time.[1]

Incense is first ordered for use in the Apostolic Canons,[2] and in the writings of Dionysius the Areopagite,[3] both post-Nicene authorities. See List of Authorities, pp. xii, xiv.

§ 13. KISS OF PEACE.—The kiss of peace (*Osculum*, *Pax*) was a recognized Christian custom throughout the period with which we are dealing. In the Passion or Acts of St. Perpetua we are told how the martyrs first kissed each other that they might complete their martyrdom with the solemnity of the kiss.[4] It formed part of the ritual of every Eucharistic celebration, its position being after the dismissal of the Catechumens and before or at the commencement of the Anaphora, or Mass of the Faithful. This is plain from the account of the service given by Justin Martyr,[5] and from the Canons of Hippolytus,[6] as well as from its position in the Clementine Liturgy.[7]

Tertullian refers with disapproval to a custom of omitting 'the kiss' on fast-days generally, though

---

[1] *Epitome Div. Institt.*, cap. lviii.; *P. L.*, v. 1135-1145. Origen has a fine passage to the same effect (*Contra Celsum*, lib. viii. capp. 17-19).
[2] Canon 3.
[3] *De Eccles. Hierarch.*, cap. iii. § 2; *P. G.*, iii. 426.
[4] Cap. xxi.   [5] *Apol.* i. cap. 65. See p. 52.
[6] Canon iii. § 19, p. 48.   [7] H., p. 11. See p. 289.

he would retain its omission on the greatest of all fast-days, Good Friday.¹

Origen, in his *Commentary on the Song of Solomon*, refers to that kiss which we give to each other in church at the time of the Mysteries,² and in his *Commentary on the Epistle to the Romans*, said that it was a traditional custom in the Church for brethren to salute each other with the kiss of peace after prayers.³

But the kiss was not only Eucharistic in its association. It was given at baptism to the newly baptized. Some people shrank from kissing an infant only a few days old, as an impure thing, but St. Cyprian thus argues with them in favour of the baptismal kiss—

'No one ought to shudder at that which God hath condescended to make. For although the infant is still fresh from its birth, yet it is not just that any one should shudder at kissing it, in giving grace and making peace; since in kissing the infant, every one of us ought, for his very religion's sake, to bethink him of the hands of God themselves, still fresh, which in some sort we are kissing in the man lately formed and freshly born, when embracing that which God hath made.' ⁴

A kiss of peace, which may be described as partly baptismal, partly Eucharistic, is mentioned in the Canons of Hippolytus, where, as the priest gives the kiss to the newly baptized, he says, 'The Lord

---
¹ *De Oratione*, cap. xviii. ; *P. L.*, i. 1176.
² Lib. i. tom. iii. p. 37.
³ Lib. x. § 33 ; *P. G.*, xiv. 1282. ⁴ *Ep.* 59, p. 98.

be with you,' and then the administration of the Holy Eucharist to them forthwith follows.[1]

As to the Ordination Service, the Canons of Hippolytus direct that the newly consecrated bishop shall receive the kiss of peace from all.[2] In later times it was ordered that the newly ordained presbyter should receive the kiss from the bishop and the rest of the clergy.[3]

Tertullian mentions the kiss at marriage as an old heathen custom, but he does not expressly say whether it was retained or not in the Christian marriage ceremonial of his day.[4]

§ 14. THE LOVE-FEAST, OR AGAPÉ.—The agapé was a feast or meal, of which in the earliest times all the members of the Christian Church partook in common as a token of brotherhood. It was an ordinary meal of a quasi-religious character.

In St. Paul's time, A.D. 57-8, the Eucharist and the agapé were closely connected, the latter apparently preceding the former. This is an inference from Acts xx. 7; and still more from the profane and scandalous behaviour condemned by St. Paul in I Cor. xi. 17-34. The title 'The Lord's Supper,' in I Cor. xi. 20, was originally applied to the combined agapé and Eucharist, and after the two had become dissociated, and after the former had become obsolete,

---
[1] Canon xix. § 139, p. 99. Fuller details are found in the Apostolic Constitutions, lib. viii. cap. 5.
[2] Canon iii. § 19, p. 48.
[3] Dionysius Pseudo-Areop., *De Eccles. Hierarch.*, cap. 5, § 7; *P G.*, iii. 510.
[4] *De Velandis Virginibus*, cap. xi.; *P. L.*, 904, 905.

was retained as a title for the Eucharist only. We do not know the exact date at which the dissociation took place. Probably it was very soon after St. Paul's time, and in order to avoid the possibility of such scandals as that which the Apostle had to condemn at Corinth.

It is a fair inference, from the language of Pliny's letter to Trajan,[1] that in Bithynia, in A.D. 112, the severance had already taken place, and that the Eucharist was then celebrated by itself at an early hour in the morning. The laws of imperial Rome were very strict against anything in the nature of a *sodalitas* or guild for social or other non-religious purposes, which involved a number of people meeting together. In order to avoid falling under this law, the agapæ were abandoned in the province of Bithynia-Pontus, ruled over by Pliny, and probably elsewhere as well.[2]

It is also inferred that in Justin Martyr's time at Rome (*c.* A.D. 140) the Eucharist was celebrated by itself at an early hour in the morning.[3]

On the other hand, there is an expression in the Epistle of St. Ignatius to the Smyrnæans which has been taken to imply that the dissociation had not taken place at Antioch or at Smyrna *c.* A.D. 110. Ignatius tells the Smyrnæans that it is not lawful to baptize or to celebrate the agapé apart from the bishop.[4] There would be incongruity in this

---

[1] Page 51.
[2] Ramsay (W. M.), *The Church in the Roman Empire before A.D. 170*, pp. 206, 215, 219, 358.
[3] *Apol.* i. capp. 65, 67, pp. 51-53.   [4] *Ad Smyrnæos*, cap. viii.

juxtaposition unless the other great sacrament was intended or included; and it seems impossible to resist the inference that the Eucharist and love-feast were still so closely united together, that the expression 'to celebrate the agapé' denoted or connoted to celebrate the Eucharist as well.[1]

This close connection between the love-feast and the Eucharist makes it sometimes difficult to decide whether passages and expressions in the earliest writings refer to the love-feast separately, or to the Eucharist separately, or to both conjointly. This difficulty arises with regard to the interpretation of the ninth and tenth chapters of the *Didaché*, which will be quoted at length and described hereafter.[2]

The following passage from Tertullian gives a graphic description of the love-feast in the earlier part of the third century:—

'Yet about the modest supper-room of the Christians alone a great ado is made. Our feast explains itself by its name. The Greeks call it love [*Agapé*]. Whatever it costs our outlay in the name of piety is gain, since with the good things of the feast we benefit the needy. Parasites do not, as with you, aspire to the glory of satisfying their licentious propensities, selling themselves for a belly feast to all disgraceful treatment; but, as it is with God Himself, a peculiar respect is shown to the lowly. If the object of our feast be good, in the light of that consider its further regulations. As it is an act of religious service, it permits no vileness or immodesty. The participants, before

---

[1] This is Bp. Lightfoot's conclusion. See his note in *Apostolic Fathers* (London, 1885), pt. ii. vol. ii. sect. i. p. 312.

[2] Chap. iii. § 3. See p. 172.

reclining, taste first of prayer to God. As much is eaten as satisfies the cravings of hunger; as much is drunk as befits the chaste. They say it is enough, as those who remember that even during the night they have to worship God; they talk as those who know that the Lord is one of their auditors. After manual ablution, and the bringing in of lights, each is asked to stand forth and sing, as he can, a hymn to God, either one from the Holy Scriptures or one of his own composing. This is a proof of the measure of our drinking. As the feast commenced with prayer, so it is closed with prayer. We go from it, not like troops of mischief-doers, nor bands of roamers, nor to break out into licentious acts, but to have as much care of our modesty and chastity as if we had been to a school of virtue rather than a banquet. Give the meeting of Christians its due, and hold it unlawful if it is like assemblies of the illicit sort, by all means let it be condemned if any complaint can be validly laid against it, such as is laid against secret factions. But who has ever suffered harm from our assemblies? We are in our meetings just what we are when we are separated from each other; we are as a community what we are as individuals; we injure nobody; we trouble nobody. When the upright, when the virtuous meet together, when the pious, when the pure assemble in congregation, you ought not to call that "a faction," but "a curia"—that is, "a sacred meeting."[1]

St. Clement of Alexandria alludes to the love-feast, warning his readers that the love-feast itself is not charity, but that it is a sign of that social benevolence which willingly imparts to others of its own abundance.[2]

In the Canons of Hippolytus it is implied that

[1] *Apol.*, cap. xxxix.; *P. L.*, i. 468.
[2] *Pædagog.*, lib. ii. p. 166.

the regular love-feast will take place on Sunday evening at the time of the lighting of the lamps.[1]

Some of the glass cups and plates found in the Roman catacombs, decorated with sacred figures and memorial inscriptions, may be dated back as far as the third century, and were probably in use at agapæ.[2]

The love-feast was celebrated by the Christians of the Thebaid on the sabbath (Saturday) as late as the time of Socrates.[3]

§ 15. MARRIAGE.—From the earliest days marriage has been regarded as a religious act, and solemnized with religious ceremonial. St. Ignatius of Antioch wrote—

'It is fitting for men and women who marry to form this union with the approval of the bishop, that their union may be according to the will of God, and not according to the dictates of concupiscence.'[4]

We have seen from Tertullian that the marriage itself was accompanied by a celebration of the Eucharist.[5]

A marriage so entered upon was regarded as indissoluble, except by death. Even in the case of a wife's unfaithfulness, though the innocent party might obtain a divorce, he might not marry again while his divorced wife was alive.

'What then, sir, say I, shall the husband do, if the wife continue in this case? Let him divorce her, saith he, and let the husband abide alone; but, if after divorcing his wife,

---

[1] Canons xxxii. § 164; xxxiii. § 172. There are other interesting details about the agapé in these Canons.
[2] Smith and Cheetham, *Dict. of Christian Antiqq.*, i. 734.
[3] *i.e.* in the fifth century (*Hist. Eccles.*, v. 22; *P. G.*, lxvii. 635).
[4] *Epist. ad Polycarpum*, cap. 5.   [5] Page 115.

he shall marry another, he likewise committeth adultery. If then, sir, say I, after the wife is divorced she repent and desire to return to her own husband, shall she not be received? Certainly, saith he. If the husband receiveth her not, he sinneth and bringeth great sin upon himself; nay, one who hath sinned and repented must be received, yet not often; for there is but one repentance for the servants of God. For the sake of her repentance, therefore, the husband ought not to marry. This is the manner of acting enjoined on husband and wife.'[1]

As to ceremonial details, we gather that the bride was usually dressed in white and veiled,[2] and that joining of hands and the kiss of peace were part of the Marriage Service.[3] The use of the ring at espousals was a part both of heathen and of Jewish nuptial ceremonial. It is alluded to more than once by Tertullian, who does not, however, expressly state that Christians used it. But St. Clement of Alexandria speaks of its Christian use in his time, saying that the ring is given to the woman, not as an ornament, but as a seal to signify the woman's duty in preserving the goods of her husband, because the care of the house belongs to her.[4] The bride and bridegroom were not crowned.[5]

---

[1] *Shepherd* of Hermas, Mandate iv. § 1. See Tertullian, *Adv. Marcionem*, lib. iv. cap. 34 ; *P. L.*, ii. 441 ; Clem. Alex., *Stromata*, lib. iii. cap. 23 ; *P. G.*, viii. 1096.

[2] Hermas, Vision iv. § 1 ; Clem. Alex., *Pædagog.*, lib. iii. cap. 11 ; *P. G.*, viii. 627, 657.

[3] Tertullian, *De Virginibus Velandis*, cap. xi. ; *P. L.*, ii. 904.

[4] *Pædagog.*, lib. iii. cap. 11 ; *P. G.*, viii. 632.

[5] *Ibid.*, lib. ii. cap. 8. Crowns were forbidden at first as a heathen custom (Justin Martyr, *Apol.*, i. 89 ; *P. G.*, vi. 339 ; Tertullian, *Apol.*, cap. 42 ; *P. L.*, i. 492). Their introduction is post-Nicene.

The marriage of the clergy of all grades was recognized throughout the primitive Church. The Apostolic Constitutions ordained that bishops, priests, and deacons should be only married once.[1]

§ 16. ORDINATION, HOLY ORDERS.—No extant office for the ordination or consecration of bishops, priests, or deacons is ante-Nicene in date; but we find allusions to the imposition of hands as forming the essential external act of ordination in primitive times.

Cornelius, Bishop of Rome (A.D. 251-2), writing to Fabian, Bishop of Antioch, describes the consecration of the schismatic Novatian to the episcopate, as performed by three Italian bishops by the imposition of hands.[2] That was evidently regarded as the essential outward sign. Had any other ceremony been regarded as essential we may be sure that Novatian would not have weakened his position by disregarding it, and that its use would have been recorded. In this same letter Cornelius incidentally mentions the number of the Roman clergy in his time. They were—46 presbyters, 7 deacons, 7 sub-deacons, 42 acolytes, 52 exorcists, readers, and doorkeepers; and there were 1500 widows and distressed persons supported by the Church.

In the Canons of Hippolytus the imposition of hands is prescribed at the ordination of bishops, priests, and deacons, without further ceremonial.[3]

---

[1] Lib. vi. cap. 17.
[2] Χειρεπιθεσία, Routh (J. M.), *Reliquiæ Sacræ*, 2nd ed. vol. iii. p. 23.
[3] Canons iii., iv., v., §§ 10, 30, 38. The imposition of hands is the only ceremony mentioned in the *Egyptian Church Order* and in the Apostolic Constitutions.

The following titles are found of persons in various grades of holy orders :—

Degree.	Title.	Authority.
Bishop	Ἐπίσκοπος	*Patres Apostolici, passim*, etc. ; Clementine Homilies, lib. iii. cap. 67, etc.
,,	Προκαθεζόμενος...	Clementine Homilies, lib. iii. cap. 72.
,,	Προηγούμενος	Clement of Rome, *Ep. to Cor.*, cap. xxi. ; *Shepherd* of Hermas, Vision iii. § 9.
,,	Ἄρχων ἐκκλησίας	Origen, *C. Celsum*, lib. iii. cap. 30, tom. i. p. 466.
,,	Ἀρχιερεύς [1]	Clem. Rom., *Ep. ad Cor.*, cap. xl.
,,	Episcopus	Canons of Hippolytus, xxxvi. § 186, p. 112, etc. ; Tertullian, *De Præscript. Hæret.*, cap. xvi., etc. ; Cyprian, *Ep.* 68, etc.
,,	Antistes	Cyprian. See *P. L.*, tom. iv. index.
,,	Præpositus	Firmilian, *Ep. ad Cyprianum;* Cyprian, *Opera;* *P. L.*, iii. 1158.
,,	Pontifex	Origen, in Levit., Hom. iv. § 6.
,,	Sacerdos	Cyprian most frequently uses this word for *episcopus*, but sometimes for 'presbyter ;' Canons of Hippolytus, xxxvi. §§ 186-188, p. 112.[2]
,,	Princeps sacerdotum	Canons of Hippolytus, xxiv. § 200, p. 117.
,,	Summus sacerdos	Tertullian, *De Bapt.*, cap. xvii.[3]
Priest	Προεστώς	Justin Martyr, *Apol.*, i. cap. 67. Comp. I Tim. v. 17.
,,	Πρεσβύτερος	Clem. Rom., *Ep. ad Cor.*, capp. xxi., xlvii., etc.; Clementine Homilies, lib. iii. cap. 67, etc.
,,	Ἱερεύς	Clem. Rom., *Ep. ad Cor.*, cap. xl. ; Ignatius, *Ad Philadelph.*, cap. ix. p. 126 ; [4] Canons of Hippolytus, xxxvii. § 201,

[1] But possibly the reference in this word is to Christ.

[2] It is not quite clear whether the *sacerdos* in this passage is the same as the *episcopus* or different.

[3] We may add that in the oldest Roman Sacramentary (*Sacramentarium Leonianum*), in seven masses for St. Xystus, ii. (Aug. 6), he is seven times entitled *sacerdos* (including once *præcipuus sacerdos* and once *sedis apostolicæ sacerdos*), once *præsul apostolicus*, once *pontifex*.

[4] The context renders it uncertain whether this word is applied to the Jewish or the Christian priesthood.

Degree.	Title.		Authority.
Priest	'Επίσκοπος	...	p. 118, etc.; Polycrates, in Euseb. *Hist. Eccles.*, lib. v. cap. 24.[1] Clem. Rom., *Ep. ad Cor.*, cap. xlii.; *Didaché*, cap. xv.
,,	Presbyter	...	Tertullian, *De Præscript. Hæret.*, cap. xli., etc.; Cyprian, *Ep.*, 36, etc.; Origen, *In Lib. Jesu Nave*, Hom. xvi. § 1.
,,	Senior ...	...	Tertullian, *Apol.*, cap. 39; Firmilian, *Ep. ad Cyprianum*; Origen, *In Lib. Jesu Nave*, Hom. xvi. § 1.
,,	Sacerdos	...	Cyprian, *Ep.* 68, etc.; Origen, in Genesim, Hom. xvi. § 5; Origen, in Levit., Hom. v. § 12, etc.
Deacon	Διάκονος	...	Clem. Rom., *Ep. ad Cor.*, cap. xlii.; *Didaché*, cap. xv.; *Patres Apostolici*, passim.
,,	Diaconus	...	Tertullian, *De Præscript. Hæret.*, cap. xli., etc.; Cyprian, *Ep.* 68, etc.; Canons of Hippolytus, xxxvii. § 201, p. 118..
,,	Levita ...	...	Clem. Rom., *Ep. ad Cor.*, cap. xl.; Origen, Hom. ii. *In Librum Jesu Nave*, § 1; Origen, Hom. xii. in Jeremiam, § 3; Apostol. Constit., lib. ii. cap. 25.[2]

§ 17. PRAYER.—(*a*) *Attitude*. The posture ordinarily assumed by the earliest Christians while engaged in the act of prayer was that of standing. This may be seen in the representations of the *orantes* in the paintings of the Roman catacombs. The figures are (it is believed always) there depicted as standing, with arms extended outwards and upwards.

[1] The word usually employed in the Clementine Liturgy is πρεσβύτερος, but ἱερεύς occurs once.

[2] Episcopi, Presbyteri, and Diaconi are mentioned together in one sentence by Origen in his *Selecta in Psalmos*, Hom. i. in Ps. xxxvii. § 2; tom. ii. p. 681.

Minucius Felix saw in these hands extended the sign of the cross.[1]

Tertullian condemns the hands extended to a strange heaven and another god.[2] Elsewhere he says—

'Gazing up heavenward, we Christians pray with hands extended because they are innocent; with the head uncovered, because we are not ashamed; finally, without a guide, because we pray from the heart.'[3]

The last expression points to the use, but not necessarily to the exclusive use, of extempore prayer. The same practice may be also implied in an expression used by Justin Martyr in his description of Sunday worship in his first *Apology*.[4]

In another place he mentions standing as an attitude for prayer, to be adopted on Sundays and during the period which extends from Easter to Pentecost.[5] So also does Irenæus. St. Peter of Alexandria speaks of standing as the Sunday attitude of prayer.

'We keep the Lord's Day as a day of gladness, because on it he rose again, and on it, according to tradition, we do not even kneel.'[6]

St. Cyprian exhorts that 'when we stand to pray, we should watch and join in the prayers with our whole heart.'[7]

---

[1] See p. 100.   [2] *Adv. Marcionem*, lib. i. cap. 23; *P. L.*, ii. 274.
[3] *Apol.*, cap. xxx.; *P. L.*, i. 442.   [4] See p. 53, note 1.
[5] The Quinquagesima Paschalia, *De Corona*, cap. 3; *P. L.*, ii. 79.
[6] Routh (J. M.), *Reliquiæ Sacræ*, 2nd ed. vol. iv. p. 45.
[7] *De Oratione Domini*, p. 213.

Origen says beautifully—

'Before a man stretches out his hands to heaven he must lift up his soul heavenward. Before he raises up his eyes he must lift his spirit to God. For there can be no doubt that among a thousand possible positions of the body, outstretched hands and uplifted eyes are to be preferred above all others, so imaging forth in the body those directions of the soul which are fitting in prayer. We are of opinion that this posture should be preferred, where there is nothing to forbid it, for there are certain circumstances, such as sickness, where we may pray even sitting or lying,' etc.[1]

But from the first, side by side with standing, kneeling or prostration was also adopted as an attitude of prayer.

With the example of our Lord Himself,[2] as well as of St. Stephen, St. Peter, and St. Paul,[3] on record, independently of the innate appropriateness of such a posture, it could hardly have been otherwise.

St. Clement of Rome, in a general exhortation to repentance from schism, says—

'Let us therefore root this out quickly, and let us fall down before the Master, and entreat Him with tears,' etc.[4]

When St. Ignatius, before his martyrdom, prayed for all the churches, he is represented to have been joined by all the brethren kneeling.[5]

In his first Vision, Hermas thus describes his locality and position—

[1] *De Oratione*, cap. 31, tom. i. p. 267.   [2] St. Luke xxii. 41.
[3] Acts vii. 60; ix. 40; xx. 36; xxi. 5.
[4] *Ep. to the Corinthians*, cap. 48, p. 77.
[5] *S. Ignatii Martyrium*, cap. vi. p. 571.

'When then I had crossed the river, I came into the level country, and knelt down and began to pray to the Lord and to confess my sins.'[1]

Hegesippus relates of St. James the Just, that he used to enter the temple alone, and to be found on his knees, which from continuous kneeling became as callous as the knees of a camel.[2]

Tertullian, referring to the miracle of the rain sent in answer to Christian prayers in the case of the Melitine legion in the Marcomannic war, c. 174, asks—

'When have not even droughts been driven away by our kneelings and fastings?'[3]

Eusebius, afterwards, in describing that incident, narrates how the Christian soldiers 'put their knees on the ground as our custom is in prayer.'[4]

Origen says that the posture of kneeling is necessary in confession of sin to God.

'It should be known that bending of the knees is necessary when any one is about in supplication to confess (*accusaturus*) his sins before God, that they may be forgiven and that he may be healed from them.'[5]

St. Cyprian, on his way to martyrdom, is narrated to have knelt on the ground and prayed.[6] St. Fructuosus and his companions knelt in prayer while

---

[1] *The Shepherd*, Vision i. § 1, p. 405.
[2] Eusebius, *Hist. Eccles.*, lib. ii. cap. 23.
[3] *Ad Scapulam*, cap. iv. tom. i. p. 155.
[4] *Hist. Eccles.*, lib. v. cap. 5.
[5] *De Oratione*, § 31, tom. i. p. 267.
[6] *Acta Proconsularia*, prefixed to St. Cypriani *Opera*, col. cxlvii.

they were being burned to death.¹ In the Acts of Paul and Thecla prayer is called a bending of the knees.²

From these and other passages which might be quoted it appears that the recognized attitude for prayer, liturgically speaking, was standing, but that kneeling was early introduced for penitential, and perhaps ordinary ferial, seasons, and was frequently, though not necessarily always, adopted in private prayer.

(*b*) *The eastward position.* The eastward position in prayer seems to have been usual from the earliest times. Tertullian refers to the suspicion of the heathen, that the Christians were worshippers of the sun, not only because Sunday (*Dies Solis*) was their holy day, and because they prayed at sunrise, but also because of their well-known custom of turning to the East in prayer.³

St. Clement of Alexandria said that—

'Prayers are made looking towards the sunrise in the East, and that because the East is the image of our spiritual nativity, and from thence the light first arises and shines out of darkness, and the day of true knowledge, after the manner of the sun, arises upon those who lie buried in ignorance.' ⁴

Origen, in his work on Prayer, devotes a short chapter to explaining and defending the eastward

---

¹ *Fructuosi, etc., Acta,* p. 340.
² Κλίσις γονάτων, Grabe, *Spicilegium* (Oxford, 1698), tom. i. p. 96.
³ *Apol.,* cap. xvi. ; *P. L.,* i. 369. See also *Adv. Valentinianos,* cap. iii.
⁴ *Stromata,* lib. vii. cap. 7 ; *P. G.,* ix. 462.

position as the usual and most appropriate position for prayer.[1]

At an early, but post-Nicene, date the candidate for baptism turned to the East to profess his belief in the Holy Trinity.[2] The Apostolic Constitutions are no doubt referring to a long-established custom when they direct that the whole congregation shall pray eastwards, in churches built eastward, and give various reasons for the direction.[3]

(c) *Prayer for the dead.* With regard to the subject matter of prayer there is only one point as to which it may be desirable to produce evidence, because there has been much popular misapprehension with regard to it. We refer to prayer for the departed. This was a recognized practice from the second century onwards. On this, as on most points, it is impossible, from dearth of material, to produce extra-Scriptural evidence of the first century, either for or against this kind of devotion.

The epitaph of Abercius, as has been seen, closes with this request—

'Let every one who considers my meaning, and thinks with me, pray for Abercius.'[4]

Tertullian says plainly—

'We offer oblations for the dead on the anniversary of their birth.'[5]

---

[1] *De Oratione*, cap. 32, tom. i. p. 270.
[2] St. Cyril of Jerusalem, *Catecheses*, 1, § 16, delivered in A.D. 347.
[3] Lib. ii. cap. 57.   [4] See p. 123.
[5] *De Corona*, cap. iii. ; *P. L.*, ii. 79.

Denouncing second marriages, he describes the true Christian widow as one who—

'prays for his [*i.e.* her husband's] soul, and requests refreshment for him in the meanwhile, and fellowship in the first resurrection, and she offers [sacrifice] on the anniversaries of his falling asleep.'[1]

As an argument against being married more than once, he denounces the praying constantly, and annually offering [sacrifice] for two wives.[2]

St. Cyprian, in a letter addressed to the clergy and laity of Carthage, announcing the appointment of the confessor Celerinus to the office of reader, reminds them how many martyrs the family of Celerinus had produced, viz. his grandmother Celerina, his uncles Laurentius and Egnatius, the one on his father's side, the other on his mother's side, and then adds—

'You remember we always offer sacrifices for them as often as with annual commemoration we celebrate the passions and days of the martyrs.'[3]

Origen says that—

'We devoutly make memorial [memories] of thy saints, and of our parents and friends, who die in the faith, as well as to rejoice in their refreshment, as to desire for ourselves a pious consummation in the faith.'[4]

---

[1] *De Monogamia*, tom. ii. p. 636. The Montanism of this fragment does not interfere with its genuineness, or with the value of the evidence of the passage quoted.
[2] *Lib. de Exhortatione Castitatis*, cap. xi. ; *P. L.*, ii. 926.
[3] *Ep.* xxxiv. § 3 ; *P. L.*, iv. 319.
[4] Lib. iii. *in Job*, tom. ii. p. 902, col. 1.

And again—

'It seems fitting and convenient to make remembrance of the saints in our solemn assemblies, in order that we may benefit ourselves by the recollection of their doings.'[1]

In the Canons of Hippolytus it is ordered that—

'If a memorial is celebrated for those who are departed, before people sit down [to the feast], let them partake of the Mysteries, but not on the first day of the week. After the oblation let there be distributed to them the bread of exorcism before they sit down.'[2]

Arnobius, referring to the destruction of Christian churches in the Diocletian persecutions, asks—

'What have our conventicles done that they should be ruthlessly destroyed, places in which God most High is prayed to, peace and pardon are asked for all men, for magistrates, armies, kings, friends, and foes, for persons still living, and for persons delivered from the bondage of the flesh?'[3]

In the Passion of St. Perpetua that saint in the second vision sees her brother Dinocrates, who had died of gangrene in the face at the age of seven years, in a dark place, dirty and pale, and with the wound still in his face. He is hot and thirsty, and vainly trying to get at the water of a font, the rim of which is above his head. In a later vision she sees him, in answer to her prayers, cleansed, well clad, and refreshed; only the scar of the old wound is to be seen; the rim of the font is lowered to the

---

[1] Lib. ix. in Rom. xii. § 12; *P. G.*, xiv. 1220.
[2] Canon xxxiii. §§ 169, 170, p. 106.
[3] *Adversus Gentes*, lib. iv. cap. 36; *P. L.*, v. 1076.

boy's waist; he gets as much water out of it as he wants, drinking out of a golden goblet which never fails. When his need was thus supplied, he departed from the water to play after the manner of children with great delight. 'Then,' adds Perpetua, 'I understood that he was released from punishment.'[1]

In the Acts of Paul and Thecla it is recorded that—

'after the beasts had been shown, Trifina took Thecla home with her, and they went to bed; and behold the daughter of Trifina, who was dead, appeared to her mother and said, "Mother, let the young woman Thecla be reputed by you as your daughter in my stead; and desire her, that she should pray for me, that I may be translated to a place of refreshment."'

Thecla complied with the request, and offered this short prayer—

'O Lord God of heaven and earth, Jesus Christ, Son of the most High, grant that her daughter Falconilla may live for ever.'[2]

The evidence yielded by early Christian inscriptions in the catacombs is of the same character. Many of them merely state or imply that the soul of the departed Christian is in peace, others are cast in the shape of prayer for the peace and refreshment of the soul of the departed; *e.g.*—

'Hilaris, may you live happily with your friends; may you be refreshed in the peace of God.'[3]

---

[1] Capp. vii., viii., pp. 29, 72-75.
[2] Cap. viii.; Grabe, *Spicilegium* (Oxford, 1714), pp. 108, 109.
[3] The original Latin or Greek of this and the following inscriptions, together with the cemetery in which the inscription is found, is given in

'Kalemeros, may God refresh thy spirit, together with that of thy sister Hilara.'[1]
'Timothea, mayest thou have eternal light in Christ.'[2]
'Irenæa, mayest thou live in God, Alpha and Omega.'[3]
'Marius Vitellianus to his most faithful wife Primitiva. Hail, innocent soul, dear wife, mayest thou live in Christ.'[4]
'Mayest thou live among the saints in peace.'[5]

The names of the departed for whom prayer was specially desired were mentioned by the priest in the course of divine service, being probably placed before him in some convenient form, such as the diptychs of later days.

St. Cyprian mentions that at Carthage no one was allowed, on dying, to nominate a cleric as executor or guardian, and that if any one did so, no offering was to be made for him, and no sacrifice celebrated for his repose (*pro dormitione ejus*).

'For that man does not deserve to be named at the altar in the prayer of the priests, who was ready to call away priests and ministers from the altar.'[6]

A few lines further on we learn that the particular prayer in which the name of the deceased was mentioned was called 'deprecatio' (aut deprecatio aliqua nomine ejus in ecclesia frequentetur). This is interesting, because we know that a similar usage

---

Dr. H. M. Luckock's *After Death*, 8th ed. (London, 1890), p. 94. They are a sample selected out of some six thousand extant epitaphs, about half of which may be ante-Nicene, and many of which might be quoted to the same effect.

[1] *Ibid.*, p. 94.   [2] *Ibid.*, p. 95.   [3] *Ibid.*, p. 95.
[4] *Ibid.*, p. 96.   [5] *Ibid.*, p. 97.   [6] *Ep.*, lxvi. p. 114.

and a similar use of the term 'deprecatio' prevailed afterwards in both the Gallican and Celtic churches.[1]

These prayers for the departed always referred to the peace and happiness of their souls, and contained no reference to the doctrine of a purgatorial fire, which was evolved in later times, and formulated in the Council of Trent.[2]

Nor did they imply that the eternal destiny of the soul of man could be altered by human intercession. Such a supposition is rendered impossible by such language as the following:—

'While we are on earth, then, let us repent; for we are clay under the craftsman's hand. For in like manner as the potter, if he is making a vessel, and it get twisted or crushed in his hands, re-shapeth it again; but if he have once put it into the fiery oven, he shall no longer mend it. So also let us, while we are in this world, repent with our whole heart of the evil things which we have done in the flesh, that we may be saved by the Lord, while we have yet time for repentance. For after that we have departed out of the world, we can no more make confession then, or repent any more.'[3]

'Once gone forth from hence there is no more place for repentance; no satisfaction can be accomplished. It is here that life is lost or saved; it is here that eternal salvation is provided for by the worship of God, and the fruits of faith.'[4]

---

[1] *Liturgy and Ritual of the Celtic Church*, pp. 105, 106.
[2] 'Præterea est purgatorius ignis, quo piorum animæ ad definitum tempus cruciatæ expiantur, ut eis in æternam patriam ingressus patere possit' (*Catechismus Concil. Trident.*, Pars prima, Art. v. § 5).
[3] *Second Epistle of St. Clement to the Corinthians*, § 8, p. 89.
[4] St. Cyprian, *Lib. ad Demetrianum*, ad finem, p. 224.

(d) *Prayer to the departed.* While there is abundant evidence for the practice of prayer for the departed from the earliest times, there is not a single genuine passage which can be quoted from any ante-Nicene Father in favour of the practice of prayer to the departed.

One ambiguous passage is sometimes quoted from Origen,[1] which may quite as well refer to prayer to living saints as to departed saints, and which, we may say, certainly does so in face of the absolute statement made by Origen elsewhere to this effect.

'For every prayer, and supplication, and intercession, and thanksgiving is to be sent up to the supreme God, through the High Priest, who is above all the angels, the living Word and God'[2]

Still, departed saints were held by him to be assisting those on earth. He says—

'I think that all those fathers who have fallen asleep before us, are fighting with us and helping us with their prayers.'[3]

There are, however, a considerable number of inscriptions in the catacombs, which contain invocations of departed saints. They are mostly post-Nicene in date; but a few may be assigned to the third century, or at least to a date before A.D. 325. Out of the thirty-five dated inscriptions, which are earlier than A.D. 325 (inclusive), only one contains

---

[1] *De Oratione*, § 14, tom. i. p. 221. The Greek original and a translation are printed by Dr. Luckock, *ut supra*, p. 175. See also pp. 187, 188.

[2] *Contra Celsum*, lib. v. § 4, tom. i. p. 580.

[3] Hom. xvi. in *Lib. Jesu Nave*, § 4, tom. ii. p. 437.

an address to the departed, and that this very simple one—

'Mayest thou live among the saints!'[1]

But among undated inscriptions we find such as the following:—

'Matronata Matrona, who lived for a year and fifty-two days. Pray for thy parents!'[2]

'Anatolius made this for his well-deserving son, who lived seven years, seven months, and twenty days. May thy spirit rest well in God. Pray for thy sister.'[3]

Are these epitaphs ante-Nicene or post-Nicene? It is impossible to decide. But, whatever their date, they are more like pious ejaculations than formal prayers. They do not involve more than 'ora pro nobis.' They fall far short of the strong appeals made to the departed saints for help of all kinds, and of the extravagant language in which these appeals were, and are frequently clothed, in mediæval and modern times. They are a testimony to the very early date at which a desire to appeal to departed saints began to take possession of men's minds. They are to be regretted, not as demonstrably wrong in themselves, but as unwise in the absence of any revelation as to whether departed saints can or cannot hear and give effect to our prayers to them, and as dangerous

[1] De Rossi, *Inscriptiones Christianæ Urbis Romæ* (Rome, 1857-61), p. 16. It is referred to the date 268 or 269.

[2] Northcote (J. S.), *Epitaphs of the Catacombs* (London, 1878), p. 81, No. 5.

[3] *Ibid.*, No. 6. It may be of interest to add that of the few early-dated epitaphs only one occurs in the first century; two occur in the second century; twenty-three or twenty-four in the third century.

in view of the extravagant character which prayer to departed saints assumed in after centuries.[1]

(e) *Times of prayer.* See SAINTS' DAYS (p. 155), SUNDAY (p. 157).

As to hours of prayer, there was probably no settled order of services corresponding to the night and day hours of the later Breviaries. The Christian Church was in too inchoate a condition, and too much harassed by heathen persecution, to admit of its elaborating such a scheme of worship as that known to us by the name of the 'Divine Office;' but allusions to prayers in the morning, in the evening, at night, at the third, sixth, and ninth hours of the day (*i.e.* Terce, Sext, and None) are found in the writings of Tertullian, St. Clement of Alexandria, and Origen.[2] Even if they refer primarily to private prayer, they foreshadow the Divine Office of later times. Terce, Sext, None, sunset (*vespere*, λυχνίκῳ, candle-light), midnight, and cock-crow are mentioned in the Canons of Hippolytus.[3] An early daily public service is described in the following canon :—

'Let presbyters, subdeacons, and readers, and all the people assemble daily in the church at time of cock-crow (*gallicinium*), and betake themselves to prayer, to psalms, and to the reading of the Scriptures, according to the

---

[1] Littledale (R. F.), *Plain Reasons*, etc. (S.P.C.K., London, 1886), p. 30, etc.

[2] The passages are given at length by Dom S. Baeumer, *Geschichte des Breviers* (Freiburg in Breisgau, 1895), pp. 42–49. Origen's references, which are less explicit, will be found on pp. 50, 51.

[3] Canons xxv. p. 127 ; xxvii. pp. 131, 133.

command of the Apostles, "Until I come attend to reading."'[1]

This passage is interesting as proving that the Divine Office was not exclusively monastic in its origin, or intended for the use of the clergy or of the cloister only. Other canons in the same collection are devoted to urging people to frequent the church on all days on which there are prayers, unless business prevents them from hearing the word of God; on those days on which there is not a service in church they are to read the Bible at home. On such days—

'Let the sun in the morning see the Scripture upon thy knees.'[2]

§ 18. SAINTS' DAYS.—Saints' days, so far as martyrs are concerned, began to be kept at a very early date. In the letter of the Smyrnæans, describing the martyrdom of St. Polycarp, we are told how the Christians, after he had been burned to death, gathered together his bones—

'and laid them in a suitable place, where the Lord will permit us to gather ourselves together, as we are able, in gladness and joy, and to celebrate the birthday of his martyrdom, for the commemoration of those who have already fought in the contest, and for the training and preparation of those who shall do so hereafter.'[3]

---

[1] Canon xxi. § 217, p. 122.
[2] Canons xxvi., xxvii. pp. 125, 126. These Canons deserve special notice. There is nothing corresponding to them in the Apostolic Constitutions. One would have thought that in the third century there could not have been sufficient copies of Holy Scripture in circulation to make the last-quoted direction capable of general observance.
[3] Cap. 18. Bp. Lightfoot, *The Apostolic Fathers*, 1891, p. 209.

St. Cyprian enjoins the presbyters and deacons—

'to note down the days of the deaths of the confessors, that the commemoration of them might be celebrated among the memorials of martyrs.'[1]

In another place he says—

'We always offer sacrifices for them, as often as we annually celebrate and commemorate the passions and death-days of the martyrs.'[2]

In A.D. 258, after the Decian persecution, when St. Gregory Thaumaturgus, Bishop of Neocæsarea, returned to his diocese, he ordered annual feasts in commemoration of the martyrs who had been faithful unto death.[3]

It will be noticed that, although St. Cyprian mentions confessors, yet it is martyrs who are specially referred to in all these cases. The commemoration of martyrs preceded all other commemorations. Those of other classes of saints, confessors, virgins, etc., were added afterwards. Even for the Blessed Virgin Mary no festival or commemoration was appointed in the first three centuries.

The following is the list of festivals and fasts enumerated in the Apostolic Constitutions :—Christmas Day ; the Epiphany ; Lent, consisting of the week before Easter, including Maundy Thursday, Good Friday, and Easter Even ; Easter Day ; Low Sunday ; the forty days of Eastertide ; the Feast of

---

[1] *Ep.* xxxvii. p. 50. [2] *Ep.* xxxiv. p. 47.
[3] Smith and Wace, *Dict. of Christian Biography*, vol. ii. p. 735. A panegyric on martyrs by him may be read in *P. G.*, x. 1199-1202.

Pentecost, with the week after it; all Sundays in the year; all Saturdays in the year are feasts, except Easter Even; and all Wednesdays and Fridays are fasts.[1]

SIGN OF THE CROSS. See § 7, p. 98.

§ 19. SUNDAY.—St. Ignatius describes Christians as no longer keeping the sabbath (Saturday), but as 'living after the Lord's day,'[2] that is to say, not only observing the first day of the week instead of the seventh, but thereby also showing their belief in a risen Saviour, and their acceptance of all which that belief involves. This is probably the first extra-scriptural allusion to the Christian Sunday.

In the *Didaché*, people are enjoined thus—

'And on the Lord's own day, gather yourselves together, and break bread, and give thanks, first confessing your transgressions, that your sacrifice may be pure.'[3]

The same title, Κυριακή, or the Lord's day, for Sunday, occurs in the recently discovered fragment of the Gospel of St. Peter, which probably belongs to the second century.[4]

In the Epistle of Barnabas the author writes—

'Wherefore we keep the eighth day as a day of gladness, on which also Jesus rose from the dead, and after He had appeared, ascended into heaven.'[5]

---

[1] Lib. v. capp. 13, 20. We have employed the modern nomenclature in writing down this list.

[2] Κατὰ κυριακὴν ζῶντες, *Ep. to the Magnesians*, cap. ix. pp. 114, 145.

[3] Cap. xiv. pp. 223, 234.

[4] Salmon (G.), *Introd. to the New Testament*, 7th ed., p. 584.

[5] Cap. xv. p. 261.

Justin Martyr explained the selection of the first day as being that on which God destroyed darkness and chaos, and created the world, and because Jesus Christ our Saviour on the same day rose from the dead.[1] He also declares Sunday to be the first and chiefest of all days, and refers to circumcision on the eighth day as a type of it.[2]

Irenæus, referring to the paschal controversy, in a letter to Victor, Bishop of Rome, said that the mystery of the Lord's resurrection ought to be celebrated only on the Lord's day.[3]

Origen ingeniously argued that manna was rained down from heaven on the Lord's day, and not on the sabbath day, to show the Jews that even in the time of Moses the former was preferred before the latter.[4]

Melito of Sardis wrote a treatise about the Lord's day, which, unfortunately, has not come down to us.[5]

St. Clement of Alexandria says that—

'Man thoroughly keeps the command in the Gospel, and makes that day the Lord's day, when he abandons an evil disposition, and assumes that of the gnostic, glorifying the Lord's resurrection in himself.'[6]

Dionysius, Bishop of Corinth, mentions the Lord's day as holy.[7]

---

[1] *Apol.* i., cap. 67. See p. 54.
[2] *Dial. cum Tryphone*, § 41 ; *P. G.*, vi. 564.
[3] Eusebius, *Hist. Eccles.*, lib., iv. cap. 26.
[4] Hom. ii. *in Exod.* § 5, tom. ii. p. 151.
[5] Eusebius, *Hist. Eccles.*, lib. iv. cap. 26.
[6] *Stromata*, lib. vii. cap. 12 ; *P. G.*, ix. 506.
[7] Quoted by Eusebius, *Hist. Eccles.*, iv. 23. 8.

Tertullian tells us that it was unlawful to fast on the Lord's day.[1]

We have already quoted the prohibition against kneeling on the Lord's day.[2] The attitude of standing in prayer on that day was explained as symbolical of the resurrection, through which, by the grace of Christ, we were saved from sin and death.[3]

In the Apostolic Constitutions, after double daily prayer has been ordered, it is added—

'And on the day of our Lord's resurrection, which is the Lord's Day, meet more diligently, sending praise to God that made the universe by Jesus, and sent Him to us, and condescended to let Him suffer, and raised Him from the dead. Otherwise what apology will he make to God who does not assemble on that day to hear the saving word concerning the resurrection? On that day we pray, standing thrice, in memory of Him who arose after three days, and on that day there is performed the reading of the prophets, and the preaching of the gospel, the oblation of the sacrifice, and the gift of the holy food.'[4]

And again—

'Every sabbath day, excepting one [*i.e.* Easter Even], and every Lord's day, hold your solemn assemblies and rejoice.'[5]

§ 20. UNCTION.—Most of what has to be said about Unction has already been said in connection

---
[1] *De Corona*, cap. 3; *P. L.*, ii. 79.   [2] Page 142.
[3] Irenæus, Gr. Fragm. vii., W. W. Harvey's ed. (Cambridge, 1857), vol. ii. p. 478.
[4] Lib. ii. cap. 58.
[5] Lib. v. cap. 20. A mine of information on the subject of Sunday will be found in Dr. G. A. Hessey's *Bampton Lectures*, 5th ed. (London, 1889), p. 279, etc.

with Baptism¹ and Confirmation.² One or two passages of a general character remain to be quoted.

Theophilus, sixth or seventh Bishop of Antioch, writing *c.* 180, thus defends himself against the taunt still levelled against the name of Christian by the heathen—

'When you laugh at me, calling me a Christian, you do not know what you are saying. First, that which is anointed is sweet and serviceable, and ought not to be laughed at.³ What ship can be serviceable and seaworthy unless it be first anointed? Or what tower or house is sightly or serviceable when it has not been anointed? What man, on entering into this life, or when contending in the games, is not anointed with oil? What work can be comely and sightly if it be not anointed and polished? Then even the air and all that is under heaven is, in a kind of way, anointed with light and spirit, and do you not wish to be anointed with the oil of God? We, therefore, are called Christians on this account, because we are anointed with the oil of God.'⁴

Origen mentions unction once, but incidentally, and without detail; though it is plain, from the context, that it was post-baptismal—

'If God have washed thee [in baptism], and the word of the law and the unction of the chrism have made thee clean, and then if the grace of baptism have remained uncontaminated in thee,' etc.

—in a fine passage comparing the dress and the

---

[1] Pages 68, 70.   [2] Pages 89, 98.
[3] This is a play upon the words χριστός (anointed) and χρηστός (serviceable).
[4] *Apologia ad Autolycum*, lib. i. § 12; *P. G.*, vi. 1042.

ornaments of the Levitical priesthood to the virtues which should adorn a Christian.[1]

Sometimes unction is metaphorically referred to, as when Tertullian tells the martyrs that Christ their Master has anointed them with His Spirit.[2]

We have already seen that there were two separate rites of unction, the one immediately before and preparatory to baptism, the other immediately after baptism, and so closely connected with confirmation, that in the East, at least from the earlier part of the fourth century, it has entirely superseded the action of laying on of hands. In the West, the same supersession was more gradual, and not universal till a much later date. Both baptismal unctions are mentioned in the Canons of Hippolytus. At the second unction with the chrisma (εὐχαριστίας), the formula to be used by the presbyter is, 'I anoint thee in the name of the Father, and of the Son, and of the Holy Ghost.'[3] They are both described in the Apostolic Constitutions with much fuller detail.[4] There the unction after baptism (μύρον) is called laying on of hands (χειροθεσία), and is thereby identified with confirmation, and is made an essential complement or accompaniment of baptism.

There is no allusion to unction of the sick or

[1] Hom. vi. *in Levit.*, § 5, tom. ii. p. 218.
[2] *Ad Martyres*, cap. iii. tom. i. p. 258. The passage is a vigorous piece of Latin: 'Bonum agonem subituri estis, in quo agonothetes Deus vivus est, xystarches Spiritus Sanctus. Corona æternitatis, brabium angelicæ substantiæ, politia in cælis, gloria in sæcula sæculorum. Itaque epistates vester Christus Jesus, qui vos Spiritu unxit,' etc.
[3] Canon xix. § 134, p. 98.
[4] Lib. vii. caps. 42-44, pp. 184, 185.

'extreme unction' in ante-Nicene literature. Origen is sometimes referred to in connection with this subject, but if readers will refer to the passage adduced, they will find a rhetorical sentence in which St. James v. 14 is quoted, but not in such a way as to make it fair or possible to quote Origen as an authority for the practice of unction of the sick.[1]

§ 21. VESTMENTS.—If we except one recently discovered passage quoted below, there is no evidence that any distinctive kind of dress was worn by the clergy in the first three centuries, either in ordinary life or at any time of their ministrations. On the contrary, there are plain statements in later writers that special vestments were unknown to the primitive Church. We will quote two sentences from mediæval ritualists of recognized authority.

Walafrid Strabo, writing in the ninth century, says—

'In primitive times priests used to celebrate mass clothed in their ordinary dress, as some of the Orientals are reported to do even to the present day.' [2]

Beleth of Paris, writing in the twelfth century, says—

'Formerly the [Eucharistic] Sacrifice was celebrated by the Apostles and by Apostolic men in the primitive Church with vessels of wood, and in common dress.' [3]

The earliest reference to a special vestment appears

[1] Hom. ii. in *Levit.*, § 4, tom. ii. 191.
[2] *De Rebus Eccles.*, cap. 24; *P. L.*, cxiv. 952.
[3] *Divinorum Officiorum Explicatio*, cap. xlii. (Naples, 1859), p. 778.

to be in the Canons of Hippolytus, which lay down directions for a white ministerial dress:—

'As soon as the bishop wishes to celebrate the mysteries, let the deacons and presbyters come together to him, clad in white vestments more beautiful than all the people, and as splendid as possible. But good work excels all vestments. Let the readers also have festival garments. . . . The readers also are to wear festal dresses.'[1]

Afterwards, in the Apostolic Constitutions, the celebrant is described as standing at the altar clad in a shining garment.[2]

The golden plate or fillet or mitre (τὸ πέταλον) which Polycrates informs us was worn by St. John the Divine,[3] and which a later authority, Epiphanius, tells us was worn by St. James the Less,[4] seems to have been something quite exceptional in its character, and cannot be referred to as an instance of settled ministerial dress.

Origen has a long disquisition on the vestments of the Jewish priesthood, and with his usual ingenuity calls attention to their counterpart in the various virtues which should adorn and clothe the Christian; but he nowhere makes any allusion to their finding a material counterpart in any article or articles of Christian ministerial dress.[5]

The 'poderis,' 'rationale,' and 'tiara sacerdotalis,'

---

[1] Canon xxxvii. §§ 201, 203, pp. 118, 119.

[2] Λαμπρὰν ἐσθῆτα μετενδύς, lib. viii. cap. 12, § 3, see p. 290.

[3] In his letter to Victor, Bishop of Rome, preserved by Eusebius, *Hist. Eccles.*, lib. v. cap. 24.

[4] *Hæres.*, xxix. 4 (ed. Œhler, tom. ii., pars prior), p. 232.

[5] Hom. vi. in *Levit.*, tom. ii. p. 215.

mentioned by him in his Commentary on Psalm xxxiv. 2,[1] are, we imagine, Jewish, and not Christian, vestments. There are frequent references to them in the Old Testament. All three words are found as the names of Christian vestments in mediæval writers.[2]

§ 22. VULGAR TONGUE, USE OF THE.—There is no trace of the use of a dead language in the services of the early Church. It would seem to be inconsistent with the line of argument used by St. Paul in 1 Cor. xiv., as well as with the dictates of common sense.

Justin Martyr describes the reading of the Holy Scriptures in the Christian assemblies, and then the founding of a discourse thereon by the president in a way which plainly indicates that all was conducted in intelligible language, and that there was no need of an interpreter.[3]

Origen says, in answer to a charge of the unintelligibility of Christian worship brought by Celsus—

'The Grecians use the Greek language in their prayers, and the Romans the Roman, and so every one in his own dialect prays to God, and the God of all languages hears them that pray in all dialects, understanding their different languages as well as if they spake with one tongue.'[4]

§ 23 (a). WASHING OF HANDS.—The custom of washing the hands before prayer is referred to by Tertullian, who appends a caution when he asks—

[1] Tom. ii. p. 650. [2] See Du Cange, *Glossarium*.
[3] Apol. cap. 67. See p. 53.
[4] *Contra Celsum*, lib. viii. § 37 ; *P. G.*, xl. 1574.

'What is the use of entering on prayer with the hands washed indeed, but with the spirit defiled?'[1]

A reference to the ablution of the hands at the love-feast has already been quoted from the same writer.[2]

In the Canons of Hippolytus the Christian is directed to wash his hands whenever he prays.[3]

Ablution of hands, no doubt, preceded every act of worship, and may have originated in a natural instinct of cleanliness, before it was crystallized into the ceremonial lavabo of later times.

(*b*) WASHING OF FEET.—The washing of feet was ceremonially practised in the week before Easter in the mediæval Church, as it is still practised in some places in imitation of our Lord washing the feet of His Apostles in the upper chamber on the first Maundy Thursday. But there is no evidence for its practice by the earliest Christians. Indeed, Origen, commenting at length on the scriptural feet-washing, as described in St. John's Gospel,[4] decides that it is not to be perpetuated literally.[5]

The curious custom of a baptismal *pedilavium*, or washing of the feet of the newly baptized after their baptism, as found in some of the baptismal offices of Spain, Gaul, Milan, and Ireland, or as referred to in

---

[1] *De Oratione*, cap. xi. tom. i. p. 250.
[2] Page 136.
[3] 'Christianus lavet manus omni tempore quo orat,' Canon xxv. § 224, p. 124, and Canon xxviii. § 241, p. 130.
[4] Cap. xiii. 2-30.
[5] *P. G.*, xiv. 773, 774.

writings or canons connected with those places, may have stretched back into the third century, for we find it prohibited by the 48th Canon of the Council of Elvira, A.D. 306.[1]

[1] Hefele, *History of the Christian Councils*, 2nd ed. (Edinburgh, 1872), vol. i. p. 157. See p. 49.

CHAPTER III.

ANTE-NICENE LITURGICAL REMAINS.

§ 1. A Prayer from the Epistle of St. Clement—§ 2. Extract from the Epistle of St. Clement—§ 3. Prayers from the *Didaché*—§ 4. A Prayer of the Scillitan Martyrs—§ 5. Prayers of Origen—§ 6. Forms of Creed—§ 7. A Hymn to Christ—§ 8. The Virgins' Song—§ 9. An Evening Hymn—§ 10. Prayers and Thanksgivings from the Canons of Hippolytus—§ 11. Anthems, etc., of uncertain date—§ 12. Ancient Liturgies.

It is proposed in this chapter to collect together and lay before the reader such devotional formulæ, prayers, hymns, etc., as can with certainty be assigned to the ante-Nicene period of the Christian Church. Though not all strictly liturgical, they may be ranged under the head of liturgical remains, if we interpret the epithet 'liturgical' in the general sense which it has gradually acquired, and in which it is now frequently, though not with technical correctness, used.

§ 1. A Prayer of the Christian Church of the First Century, taken from Chapters LIX., LX., LXI. of the [first] Epistle of St. Clement of Rome to the Corinthians.—The references in the notes seem to justify the conclusion that we have here preserved to us a piece of the Roman Liturgy of the first century.[1]

59. 'Grant unto us, Lord, that we may set our hope on Thy Name, which is the primal source of all creation, and open the eyes of our hearts, that we may know Thee, who alone abidest *Highest in the high, Holy in the holy;*[2] who *layest low the insolence of the proud*,[3] who *scatterest the imaginings of nations;*[4] who *settest the lowly on high;*[5] who *makest rich and makest poor;*[6] who *killest and makest alive;*[7] who alone art the Benefactor of spirits and the God of all flesh; who *lookest into the abysses*,[8] who scannest the works of man; the succour of them that are in peril, the *Saviour of them that are in despair*,[9] the Creator and Overseer of every spirit;[10] who multipliest the nations upon earth, and hast chosen out from all men those that love Thee, through Jesus Christ, Thy beloved Son, through whom Thou didst instruct us, didst sanctify us, didst honour us. We beseech Thee, Lord and Master, to be our *help and succour*.[11] Save those among us who are in tribulation; have mercy on the lowly; lift up the fallen; show Thyself unto the needy; heal the ungodly; convert the wanderers of Thy people; feed the hungry; release our prisoners;[12] raise up the

---

[1] Lightfoot (J. B.), *The Apostolic Fathers* (London, 1890), Part I., vol. ii., whence the following notes are mainly taken.

[2] Isa. lvii. 15. This and the following references are to the LXX.

[3] Isa. xiii. 11.   [4] Ps. xxxii. 10.   [5] Ezek. xxi. 26.

[6] I Kings ii. 7.   [7] Deut. xxxii. 39.

[8] Suggested by Ecclus. xvi. 18, 19. In the preface of the Liturgy of St. Basil, God is addressed as ὁ καθημένος ἐπὶ θρόνου δόξης καὶ ἐπιβλέπων ἀβύσσους (H., p. 106).

[9] Judith ix. 11. The phrase also occurs with variation and amplification in the Great Intercession in the Liturgy of St. Mark (H., p. 181), and in the same part of the Liturgy of St. Basil (H., p. 122).

[10] Adapted from Job x. 12. Compare ἐπίσκοπε πάσης σαρκός in the Great Intercession in the Liturgy of St. Mark (H., p. 181).

[11] Ps. cxviii. 114. The phrase occurs in the Prayer of Humble Access in the Clementine Liturgy (H., p. 20).

[12] A similar petition occurs in the Clementine Liturgy (H., p. 9),

meek; comfort the faint-hearted. *Let all the Gentiles know that Thou art God alone,*[1] and Jesus Christ is Thy Son,[2] and *we are Thy people and the sheep of Thy pasture.*[3]

60. Thou through Thine operations didst make manifest the everlasting fabric of the world.[4] Thou, Lord, didst create the earth. Thou that art faithful throughout all generations, righteous in Thy judgments, marvellous in strength and excellence, Thou that art wise in creating and prudent in establishing that which Thou hast made, that art good in the things which are seen, and faithful with them that trust on Thee, *pitiful and compassionate,*[5] forgive us our iniquities, and our unrighteousness, and our transgressions and shortcomings. Lay not to our account every sin of Thy servants and of Thine handmaids, but cleanse us with the cleansing of Thy truth, and *guide our steps to walk in holiness,*[6] and righteousness, and singleness of *heart,*[7] and *to do such things as are good and well-pleasing in Thy sight,*[8] and in the sight of our rulers. Yea, Lord, *make Thy face to shine upon us in peace for our good,*[9] that we may be sheltered *by Thy right hand,*[10] and delivered from every sin *by Thine uplifted arm.*[10] And deliver us from them that hate us wrongfully. Give

and in many of the ancient Liturgies; Liturgy of St. Mark (H., p. 181); Liturgy of St. James (H., p. 44). In the West we find similar allusions in some of the ancient Gallican Liturgies, which form a strong proof of their great antiquity, as in the Missale Gothicum : 'Domini misericordiam deprecemur pro fratribus et sororibus nostris captivitatibus elongatis, carceribus detentis, metallis deputatis,' a præfatio among the Orationes Paschales (No. xxxiii.).

[1] 1 Kings viii. 60.
[2] This word (παῖς) is twice applied to Christ in the Clementine Liturgy (H., pp. 20, 23).
[3] Ps. xcix. 3.
[4] Part of this sentence, partly based on Wisdom vii. 17, is borrowed in the Apostolic Constitutions, lib. viii. cap. 22.
[5] Ps. cii. 8, and frequently.
[6] Ps. xxxix. 2; cxviii. 133.
[7] 2 Kings ix. 4.
[8] Deut. xiii. 18.
[9] Suggested by Jer. xxi. 10.
[10] Exod. vi. 1, and frequently.

concord and peace to us and to all that dwell on the earth as Thou gavest to our fathers, *when they called on Thee in faith and truth*,[1] with holiness, [that we may be saved] while we render obedience to Thine almighty and most excellent Name, and to our rulers and governors upon the earth.

61. Thou,[2] Lord and Master, hast given them the power of sovereignty through Thine excellent and unspeakable might, that we, knowing the glory and honour which Thou hast given them, may submit ourselves unto them, in nothing resisting Thy will. Grant unto them therefore, O Lord, health, peace, concord, stability, that they may administer the government which Thou hast given them without failure. For Thou, O Heavenly Master, King of the ages, givest to the sons of men glory and power over all things that are upon the earth. Do Thou, Lord, direct their counsel, according to that which is good and well pleasing in Thy sight; that, administering in peace and gentleness with godliness, the power which Thou hast given them, they may obtain Thy favour. O Thou, who alone art able to do these things, and things far more exceeding good than these for us, we praise Thee through the High Priest and Guardian [3] of our souls, Jesus Christ, through whom be the glory and the majesty unto Thee both now and for all generations, and for ever and ever. Amen.'

§ 2. EXTRACT FROM THE EPISTLE OF ST. CLEMENT.—The following passage occurs in the

---

[1] Ps. cxliv. 18.

[2] Prayers for earthly rulers, resembling this, are a common and conspicuous feature in ancient Liturgies. See Clementine Liturgy, II., p. 18. They reflect the teaching of St. Paul (1 Tim. ii. 42; Rom. xiii. 1-7), and St. Peter (1 Pet. ii. 17), and form an eloquent testimony to the law-abiding spirit and loyalty of the early Christians, sometimes under the most trying and adverse conditions.

[3] These two titles, ἀρχιερεύς and προστάτης, are both applied to Christ in the Clementine Liturgy, the former twice (II., pp. 12, 16), the latter once (*Ibid.*, p. 10).

thirty-fourth chapter of St. Clement's [first] Epistle to the Corinthians:—[1]

'Let us submit ourselves to His (God's) will; let us mark the whole host of His angels how they stand by and minister (λειτουργουσιν) unto His will. For the Scripture saith, " *Ten thousand times ten thousand stood by Him, and thousands of thousands ministered unto Him : and they cried aloud, Holy, holy, holy, is the Lord of Sabaoth : all creation is full of His glory.*"[2] Yea, and let us ourselves then, being gathered together into one place [3] with intentness of heart,[4] cry unto Him as from one mouth earnestly, that we may be made partakers of His great and glorious promises. For he saith, "*Eye hath not seen, nor ear heard, and it hath not entered into the heart of man what great things He hath prepared for them that patiently await Him.*"'[5]

The liturgical cast of this passage has been frequently noticed. We infer from it that the Triumphal Hymn, commonly called the 'Tersanctus,' formed part of the Roman Liturgy at the close of the first century, and that the scriptural quotation, 'Eye hath not seen,' etc., was likewise embedded in it.

The Triumphal Hymn formed a part of every known ancient Liturgy, and in the following Liturgies there occurs the two-fold reference to Isa. vi. 3 as well as to Dan. vii. 10 :—The Clementine Liturgy,[6]

---

[1] Lightfoot (J. B.), *The Apostolic Fathers* (London, 1891), pp. 23, 71.

[2] Dan. vii. 10 (but mark the liturgical term ἐλειτούργουν substituted by Clement for the LXX. ἐθεράπευον) and Is. vi. 3.

[3] 'Επὶ τὸ αὐτό. Bp. Lightfoot translates it 'in concord.'

[4] Or 'with a lively conscience.' The Greek words both for this phrase and for 'earnestly' are of common occurrence in the ancient Liturgies.

[5] Is. lxiv. 4, as quoted by St. Paul in 1 Cor. ii. 9. [6] II., p. 16.

the Liturgy of St. Chrysostom,[1] St. Mark,[2] Coptic St. Cyril,[3] Ethiopic,[4] SS. Adæus and Maris,[5] Greek St. James,[6] Syriac St. James;[7] but in the last two named Liturgies the reference to Dan. vii. 10 has got transplaced into the Preface to the Lord's Prayer. There does not appear to be any such quotation in Western Liturgies, Roman, Ambrosian, Mozarabic, or Gallican.

The text from 1 Cor. ii. 9, 'Eye hath not seen,' etc., is found in various positions in Liturgies, both Eastern and Western, *e.g.* in the Great Oblation in the Liturgy of Greek St. James;[8] in the Diptychs of the Dead in the Liturgy of St. Mark;[9] in a Preface in the Gallican Liturgy;[10] in a Capitulum in the Mozarabic Breviary, in Festo S. Torquati.[11]

Chapters xl. and xli. of the same Epistle imply the existence of a settled Christian Liturgy, though they do not throw any further light upon its language or contents.

§ 3. PRAYERS FROM THE 'DIDACHÉ.'—The following forms of thanksgiving are found in the *Didaché*, or the Teaching of the Twelve Apostles :—[12]

CHAPTER 9.

'But as touching the eucharistic thanksgiving, give ye thanks thus. First, as regards the cup—

---

[1] H., pp. 107, 108.   [2] *Ibid.*, p. 185.   [3] *Ibid.*, p. 218.
[4] *Ibid.*, p. 257.   [5] *Ibid.*, p. 273.   [6] *Ibid.*, pp. 40, 47.
[7] *Ibid.*, pp. 69, 78.   [8] *Ibid.*, p. 42.   [9] *Ibid.*, p. 183.
[10] *Sacramentarium Gallicanum*, Mabillon's ed., p. 361.
[11] Migne's ed. ; *P. L.*, tom. lxxxvi. col. 1115.
[12] See list of authorities, p. xiv.

"We give Thee thanks, O our Father, for the holy vine of Thy son David, which Thou madest known unto us through Thy Son Jesus; Thine is the glory for ever and ever."

Then as regards the broken bread—

"We give Thee thanks, O our Father, for the life and knowledge which Thou didst make known unto us, through Thy Son Jesus; Thine is the glory for ever and ever. As this broken bread was scattered upon the mountains, and being gathered together became one, so may Thy Church be gathered together from the ends of the earth into Thy kingdom; for Thine is the glory and the power through Jesus Christ, for ever and ever."

But let no one eat or drink of this eucharistic thanksgiving, but they that have been baptized into the Name of the Lord; for concerning this also the Lord hath said, "Give not that which is holy to the dogs." [1]

CHAPTER 10.

And after ye are satisfied,[2] thus give ye thanks—

"We give Thee thanks, Holy Father, for Thy holy Name which Thou hast made to tabernacle in our hearts, and for the knowledge and faith and immortality, which Thou hast made known unto us through Thy Son Jesus; Thine is the glory for ever and ever. Thou, Almighty Master, didst create all things for Thy Name's sake, and didst give food and drink unto men for enjoyment, that they might render thanks to Thee; but didst bestow upon us spiritual food and drink and eternal life through Thy Son. Before all things we give Thee thanks that Thou art powerful. Thine is the glory for ever and ever. Remember, Lord, Thy Church to deliver it from all evil, and to perfect it in Thy love, and gather it from the four winds,[3] even the Church

---

[1] St. Matt. vii. 6.　　[2] Μετὰ τὸ ἐμπλησθῆναι.
[3] St. Matt. xxiv. 31.

which has been sanctified, into Thy kingdom which Thou hast prepared for it; for Thine is the power and the glory for ever and ever. May grace come, and may this world pass away. Hosanna to the Son of David. If any man is holy let him come; if any man is not, let him repent. Maranatha. Amen."

But permit the prophets to offer thanksgiving as much as they desire.'[1]

It has been debated whether the above thanksgivings are connected with the Sacrament of the Eucharist, or with the agapé, or love-feast. There are the following reasons for thinking that the former connection is impossible:—

(a) The thanksgiving connected with the cup precedes the thanksgiving connected with the broken bread.

(b) No traces of these thanksgivings have been found in any existing Liturgies, Eastern or Western.

(c) The Eucharist is separately treated of later on in the *Didaché* (cap. 14).

(d) Such an expression as μετὰ τὸ ἐμπλησθῆναι, though it might be paralleled in rhetorical passages of such a writer as Bishop Jeremy Taylor, or in the enraptured devotions of mediæval or modern saints, could hardly be used in a direction resembling a rubric in such a formal document as the *Didaché*.

§ 4. PRAYER OF THE SCILLITAN MARTYRS.—A prayer which the earliest extant Greek Version (A.D. 890) puts into the mouths of the Scillitan martyrs,

---

[1] This allusion to the existence of a class of persons exercising the function of prophets, and still called by that name, is one of the proofs of the very early date of the *Didaché*.

III.] *ANTE-NICENE LITURGICAL REMAINS.* 175

who suffered death by the sword for the faith in Africa, on July 17 (A.D. 180).[1] Their names were Speratus, Nartzalus, Cittinus, Veturius, Felix, Aquilinus, Celestinus [in the Latin text, Lætantius], Januaria, Generosa, Vestia, Donata, Secunda.

'We give thanks to Thee, thrice-holy Lord, and we magnify Thee because Thou hast mercifully completed the conflict of our confession, and Thy kingdom endureth for ever and ever. Amen.'

§ 5. PRAYERS OF ORIGEN.—Origen quotes the following short prayer as in constant use in church in his time :—

'Grant us, O Almighty God, grant us a part with Thy prophets; grant us a part with the Apostles of Thy Christ; grant that we may be found at the feet of Thy only-begotten Son.'[2]

The following prayers also occur in his writings :—

'Almighty Lord God, may it never happen to us that Jesus Christ, after He is risen from the dead, should again die in us. For what doth it profit me if He liveth in others from their virtue, while He dieth in me from the infirmity of sin? What doth it profit me if He doth live in me and in my heart, and doth not work out in me the works of life ? What doth it profit me if in another He is born and made again from good desires, good faith, and good works,

---

[1] The original Latin version, contained in a ninth-century MS. in the British Museum (Addit. MS. No. 11880), shortens this prayer to two words, 'Deo gratias' (Appendix to J. A. Robinson's edition of the *Passion of St. Perpetua*, p. 116 ; *A. C. L.*, vol. for 1897, p. 283).

[2] Hom. xiv. in Jerem, § 14, *Opera*, tom. iii. p. 217. This prayer occurs in substance, though abbreviated, in the Diptychs of the dead in the centre of the Preface, Liturgy of St. Mark : 'Grant unto us to have part and lot with all Thy saints' (H., p. 183).

while in me and in my heart He is, as it were, strangled and put to death by evil thoughts, unlawful desires, and most evil imaginations.'[1]

'O Lord Jesu, Son of David, come, I pray Thee, lay aside from Thee the nature wherewith Thou hast clothed Thyself on my account, and gird Thyself for my sake, and pour water into a bason, and wash the feet of Thy servants, and cleanse away the filth of Thy sons and of Thy daughters. Wash Thou the feet of our mind, that we, imitating and following Thee, may put off from us our old garments, and may say, "By night I have put off my coat; how shall I put it on? I have washed my feet; how shall I defile them?"[2] For as soon as Thou shalt have washed my feet, make me to recline with Thee, that I may hear Thy words, "Ye call me Master and Lord: and ye say well; for so I am. If I then, your Lord and Master, have washed your feet; ye also ought to wash one another's feet."[3] I too, therefore, am willing to wash the feet of my brethren, to wash the feet of my fellow disciples. And, therefore, I take water, and I draw from the fountains of Israel that which I wring out of the Israelitish fleece. For at one time I wring water out of the fleece of the Book of Judges, and at another time water from the fleece of kingdoms, and water from the fleece of Isaiah or Jeremiah; and I pour it into the bason of my mind, conceiving the sense in my heart; and I take the feet of those who offer themselves, and prepare themselves for supper; and, in so far as the power lies in me, I desire to wash the feet of my brethren, and to fulfil the commandment of the Lord, that through the word of teaching the hearers may be purged from the contamination of their sins, and may cast away from themselves all the uncleanness of their vices, and may have clean feet wherewith they may rightly walk towards

---

[1] *In Lib. Judicum*, Hom. ii. § 2, tom. ii. p. 461.
[2] Cant. v. 3. [3] St. John xiii. 13, 14.

the preparation of the gospel of peace; so that all of us, purified together in Christ Jesus by the Word, may not be rejected from the Bridegroom's chamber, because of our unclean garments; but that with shining vesture, and washed feet, and clean heart, we may recline at the banquet of the Bridegroom, our Lord Himself, Jesus Christ, to whom be glory and dominion for ever and ever. Amen.'[1]

'Haste Thee to help me, [O Lord God of my salvation], for the battle is great and the adversaries are powerful. The enemy is hostile, the invisible foe fighting through visible forms. Haste Thee, therefore, to help us, and assist us through Thy holy Son, our Lord Jesus Christ, through whom Thou hast redeemed us all, through whom be glory and power to Thee for ever and ever. Amen.'[2]

§ 6. FORMS OF CREED.—The following creeds, or fragments of creeds, have been put together from writers of the pre-Nicene period:—

(*a*) From the *Apology* of Aristides, written in the reign of Antoninus Pius, A.D. 138–161:—

> 'We believe in one God, Almighty,
> Maker of heaven and earth;
> And in Jesus Christ His Son,
> Born of the Virgin Mary;
> He was pierced by the Jews;
> He died, and was buried;
> The third day He rose again;
> He ascended into heaven;
> He is about to come to judge.'[3]

---

[1] *In Lib. Judicum*, Hom. viii. § 5, tom. ii. 476. The whole prayer is proof that Origen did not interpret the command as to the 'Pedilavium' literally.

[2] *Select. in Psalmos*, in Ps. xxxvii., Hom. ii. § 9, tom. ii. p. 689.

[3] *The Apology of Aristides*, edited by J. R. Harris, with an appendix by J. A. Robinson, being vol. i. of *Texts and Studies* (Cambridge, 1891), p. 25.

(*b*) From the *Apology* of Athenagoras, presented to the emperors Aurelius and Commodus, *c.* A.D. 177—

'We acknowledge one uncreated, and eternal, and invisible, and impassible, and incomprehensible, and illimitable God. . . . By whom, through His word, the universe has been created and adorned, and is preserved.

We acknowledge the Son of God. . . . The Son of God is the Word of the Father, in form and efficacy; for according to Him, and by Him, have all things been made, since the Father and the Son are one,'[1] etc.

(*c*) From the writings of St. Irenæus, A.D. 170-180—

'We believe in one God, the Father Almighty,
Who made heaven, and earth, and the seas, and all that in them is.
And in one Jesus Christ, the Son of God,
Who was made flesh for our salvation.

And in the Holy Ghost,
Who preached through the prophets.

And the birth [of Jesus Christ] of a Virgin,
And His passion,
And His resurrection from the dead,
And the ascension into heaven in the flesh, of the beloved Christ Jesus our Lord,
And His coming from heaven in the glory of the Father, to gather up again all things unto Himself,
And to raise up all flesh of the human race.'[2]

---

[1] *Supplicatio* [see *Legatio*] *pro Christianis*, cap. x.; *P. G.*, tom. vi. col. 908.

[2] Irenæus, *Adv. Hæres.*, lib. i. cap. x. § 1; *P. G.*, tom. vii. col. 549; Heurtley (C. A.), *A History of Earlier Formularies of the Faith* (Oxford, 1893), p. 20.

III.] *ANTE-NICENE LITURGICAL REMAINS.* 179

(*d*) From the writings of Tertullian—
'[I believe in] one God Almighty, the Creator of the world :
And in His Son, Jesus Christ,
Born of the Virgin Mary,
Crucified under Pontius Pilate ;
On the third day He rose from the dead,
He was received into heaven,
He is now seated at the right hand of the Father.
He will come to judge the quick and the dead,
Through the resurrection also of the flesh.'[1]

(*e*) From the writings of St. Cyprian—
'I believe in God the Father,
In Christ the Son,
In the Holy Spirit :
I believe in the remission of sins,
And life eternal,
Through the Holy Church.'[2]

(*f*) The Confessio fidei of Hippolytus, printed by Bunsen, is rather a treatise than a creed.[3]

(*g*) The Creed of Novatian, *c.* 260, the ringleader of a schism at Rome which hinged on a point not of doctrine but of discipline, was similar to the above, as may be gathered from St. Cyprian's allusions to Novatian and his teaching in his Epistle to Magnus.[4]

(*h*) Creed of St. Gregory Thaumaturgus, produced between A.D. 260–265.

[1] *Liber de Virginibus Velandis*, cap. i.; *P. L.*, tom. ii. col. 889; Heurtley (C. A.), *ut supra*, p. 22.
[2] This is put together from S. Cypriani, *Ep.* lxxvi. (al. 69), ad Magnum (*Opera omnia*, ed. Baluz, Paris, 1726, p. 154), and *Ep.* lxx. ad Januarium et ceteros episcopos Numidas (ed. *ut supra*, p. 125).
[3] *Analecta ante-Nicæna*, vol. ii. p. 383. [4] See note 2.

'There is one God, Father of Him who is the Living Word, subsisting Wisdom, and Power, and eternal Impress, Perfect Begetter of the Perfect, Father of the Only-Begotten Son.

There is one Lord, Alone of the Alone, God of God, Impress and Image of the Godhead, the operative Word; Wisdom comprehensive of the system of the universe, and Power productive of the whole creation; true Son of true Father, Invisible of Invisible, and Incorruptible of Incorruptible, and Immortal of Immortal, and Eternal of Eternal.

And there is one Holy Ghost, who hath His being of God, who hath appeared, that is to mankind,[1] through the Son, Image of the Son, Perfect of the Perfect; Life, the cause of all them that live; Holy Fountain, Holiness, the Bestower of sanctification, in whom is manifested God the Father, who is over all and in all, and God the Son, who is through all. A perfect Trinity, not divided nor alien in glory and eternity and dominion.'[2]

(*h*) An early instance of the expansion of the Creed is found in the letter sent by Hymenæus, Bishop of Jerusalem, who died in A.D. 273, and his colleagues to Paul of Samosata. The faith which has been handed down from the beginning was—

'That God is unbegotten, One without beginning, unseen, unchangeable, whom no man hath seen or can see, whose glory and greatness it is impossible for human nature to conceive or to trace out adequately . . . but we must be content to have a moderate conception of Him. . . . His Son reveals Him. . . . as He Himself says, "No man knoweth the Father, save the Son, and he to whomsoever the Son revealeth Him." We confess and proclaim His Begotten

---

[1] These four words are of doubtful authority.

[2] Smith and Wace, *Dictionary of Christian Biography*, vol. ii. p. 733, where the authorities for and against the genuineness of this passage are set forth.

Son, the only-begotten, the Image of the invisible God, the Firstborn of every creature, the Wisdom and Word and Power of God, being before the worlds God, not by foreknowledge, but by essence and substance,' etc.[1]

(*i*) The following interrogative form of creed is put to the candidate for baptism in the Canons of Hippolytus :—

'Dost thou believe in God the Father Almighty?
℟. I do believe.
Dost thou believe in Jesus Christ, the Son of God, whom the Virgin Mary begat of the Holy Ghost, who came to save the human race, who was crucified [for us] under Pontius Pilate, who died, and rose from the dead on the third day, and ascended into heaven, and sitteth at the right hand of the Father, and shall come again to judge the quick and the dead?
℟. I do believe.
Dost thou believe in the Holy Ghost [the Paraclete, proceeding from the Father and the Son]?
℟. I do believe.'

After each response the candidate is directed to be immersed beneath the water, and the baptismal formula is repeated at each of the trine immersions.[2]

A much fuller form of Baptismal Creed will be found in the Apostolic Constitutions.[3]

§ 7. A HYMN TO CHRIST.—The following hymn to Christ was composed by St. Clement of Alexandria (A.D. 170–220). The original Greek is given in Daniel's *Thesaurus Hymnologicus*, tom. iii. p. 3.

[1] Routh (J. M.), *Rel. Sac.*, 2nd ed. vol. iii. p. 290.
[2] The words within brackets are later additions. Canon xix. §§ 112–133, pp. 94–97.
[3] Lib. vii. cap. 41. See p. 272.

Further information about its authorship and character will be found in Julian's *Dictionary of Hymnology*, pp. 238, 456.

The present translation is taken from *A. C. L.*, iv. 345,[1] where also a metrical, but necessarily less literal version is given.

'Bridle of untamed colts, Wing of unwandering birds, Sure helm of babes, Shepherd of royal lambs, assemble Thy simple children to praise holily, to hymn guilelessly, with innocent mouths, Christ, the Guide of children.

O King of Saints, all-subduing Word of the most high Father, Ruler of wisdom, Support of sorrows, rejoicing in eternity, Jesus, Saviour of the human race, Shepherd, Husbandman, Helm, Bridle, Heavenly Wing of the all-holy flock, Fisher of men who are saved, catching the chaste fishes with sweet life from the hateful wave of a sea of vices ;—

Guide us, Shepherd of rational sheep ; guide, O holy King, Thy children safely along the footsteps of Christ ; O heavenly Way, perennial Word, immeasurable Age, eternal Light ; Fount of mercy, Performer of virtue.

Noble is the life of those who hymn God, O Christ Jesus, heavenly Milk of the sweet breasts of the graces of the Bride, pressed out of Thy Wisdom. Babes nourished with tender mouths, filled with the dewy spirit of the rational pap, let us sing together simple praises, true hymns to Christ our King, holy fee for the teaching of life, let us sing in simplicity the powerful Child. O choir of peace, ye Christ-begotten ones, O chaste people, let us sing together the God of peace.'

§ 8. THE VIRGINS' SONG ("Ανωθεν παρθένοι).— The following song was composed by Methodius,

[1] One slight alteration being introduced in the last sentence, and the readings in two notes preferred to those in the main text.

Bishop of Tyre (see List of Authorities, p. xv.). The original Greek is printed in *P. G.*, tom. xviii. coll. 207-214. The spirited translation given here was composed by the Rev. A. W. Chatfield, and is quoted from his *Songs and Hymns of the Earliest Greek Poets* (London, 1876), p. 141. Further information will be found in Julian's *Dictionary of Hymnology*, p. 458; *Greek Hymnody*, § x. 2, as well as in Mr. Chatfield's introduction.

1.

The Bridegroom cometh! Overhead
The shout descending wakes the dead!
   Go forth to meet the King,
   The gates just entering.
Virgins, white-robed, with lamps haste eastward forth to meet Him;
Haste ye, O haste ye to greet Him!

The Refrain.

With holy feet, and lamps bright burning,
I go to meet my Lord returning.

2.

Earth's mournful bliss I left, and toys
Of wanton life, and foolish joys:
   To Thee alone I cling:
   Thou art my Life, my King;
Grant that I may, O Blessed, ever close to Thee,
   Thy royal beauty see.

The Refrain.

With holy feet, and lamps bright burning,
I go to meet my Lord returning.

3.
Thou art my wealth : for Thee I fled
All worldly lure, and upward sped ;
 And come in spotless dress
 Of Thine own righteousness,
With Thee to enter in the bridal chamber gates,
 Where perfect bliss awaits.

The Refrain.
With holy feet, and lamps bright burning,
I go to meet my Lord returning.

4.
Saved from the dragon's myriad wiles,
By which the simple he beguiles,
 I bore the dreadful fire,
 And wild beast's savage ire ;
Waiting till Thou from heaven, O Hope of all creation,
 Shouldst come to my salvation !

The Refrain.
With holy feet, and lamps bright burning,
I go to meet my Lord returning.

5.
My home and country for Thy sake,
And maiden dance, I did forsake,
 And mother's pride and race,
 And thoughts of rank and place ;
For Thou, O Christ the Word, art all in all to me,
 I long for naught save Thee.

The Refrain.
With holy feet, and lamps bright burning,
I go to meet my Lord returning.

6.

Hail! Christ the Life, unchanging Day,
Accept this humble virgin lay;
 To Thee our song of praise
 With heart and voice we raise!
In Thee, O Thou perfection's flower, O Word Divine,
 Love, joy, mind, wisdom shine.

The Refrain.

With holy feet, and lamps bright burning,
I go to meet my Lord returning.

7.

O Bride, triumphant now in light,
And clad in robes of purest white,
 Sweet breathing, sinless, free,
 Ope wide the gates to me:
Sit we in self-same company near Christ above,
 And sing Thy marriage, Love!

The Refrain.

With holy feet, and lamps bright burning,
I go to meet my Lord returning.

8.

Ah me! some virgins vainly pour
Their sobs and cries outside the door:
 Their lamps are quenched, and they
 No burning light display:
Their error they would mend; but ah! they come too late,
 And closèd is the gate.

The Refrain.

With holy feet, and lamps bright burning,
I go to meet my Lord returning.

9.

For they a foolish part had played,
And from the sacred pathway strayed ;
Oil, they had purchased none :
Ah ! wretched and undone !
Forbidden with dead lamps the home of bliss to see,
They wail their misery.

The Refrain.

With holy feet, and lamps bright burning,
I go to meet my Lord returning.

10.

Lo ! goblet filled with sweetest wine ;
Drink we, O virgins, 'tis Divine,
And forth-set for our need :
Lo ! this is drink indeed ;
This for the guests, who to the marriage bidden are,
The Bridegroom doth prepare.

The Refrain.

With holy feet, and lamps bright burning,
I go to meet my Lord returning.

11.

First type, O Blessèd One, of Thee
In Abel shining bright we see :
To Heaven he lifts his eyes,
Blood-dripping, and thus cries :
' Me, by my cruel brother slain, receive, O Lord,
O Thou the Eternal Word.'

The Refrain.

With holy feet, and lamps bright burning,
I go to meet my Lord returning.

12.

Joseph, another type of Thee,
Won highest prize of purity:
  Whom Thou wouldst own Thy child,
  He scorned to be beguiled
By shameless woman; stripped, he yet her wrath defied,
  And straight to Thee he cried.

The Refrain.

With holy feet, and lamps bright burning,
I go to meet my Lord returning.

13.

A lamb for sacrifice is sought:
A lamb-like victim Jephthah brought:
  For rash-made vow he cared,
  Nor virgin daughter spared:
A type, O Blessèd One, of Thy humanity,
  She poured her soul to Thee.

The Refrain.

With holy feet, and lamps bright burning,
I go to meet my Lord returning.

14.

In valour Judith holds high post:
The leader of the oppressing host,
  She smote by beauty's lure,
  Herself a type all pure:
He headless lay; and unto Thee the conquering maid
  Her love in song displayed.

The Refrain.

With holy feet, and lamps bright burning,
I go to meet my Lord returning.

15.

The judges twain, by passion's flame
Enkindled, and all dead to shame,
   Would chaste Susannah bind
   To their unhallowed mind:
To their proposals base, she gave a just reply,
   And raised her voice on high:

The Refrain.

With holy feet, and lamps bright burning,
I go to meet my Lord returning.

16.

' 'Twere better far that I should die,
Than traitress be to marriage tie,
   And, yielding to your will,
   Both soul and body kill:
Base men! God's fire of wrath eternal would me seize.
   Save me, O Christ, from these.'

The Refrain.

With holy feet, and lamps bright burning,
I go to meet my Lord returning.

17.

And he who thousands washed from sin,
Of Thy true light the bringer-in,
   For Virtue's cause alone
   Is into prison thrown
By wicked king, and staining now the ground with gore,
   He cried to Thee the more.

The Refrain.

With holy feet, and lamps bright burning,
I go to meet my Lord returning.

18.
And Thy blest mother, spotless maid,
Was thought her vows to have betrayed,
  When travailing with Thee,
  O Lord of purity:
And found with child of transcendental heavenly birth,
  She raised her voice from earth.

The Refrain.
With holy feet, and lamps bright burning,
I go to meet my Lord returning.

19.
Thy saints, all eager that they may
Behold the glories of the day
  Of Thine espousals high,
  With holy gifts draw nigh:
For Thou, O Word, hast called them, Thou the angel's King,
  White-robed to Thee they sing.

The Refrain.
With holy feet, and lamps bright burning,
I go to meet my Lord returning.

20.
O holy Church, O heavenly Bride,
With hymns, attending at Thy side,
  We yet on earth below
  Thine honour thus forth-show:
All snow-white thou, all beauteous spouse of Christ above,
  All purity, all love.

The Refrain.
With holy feet, and lamps bright burning,
I go to meet my Lord returning.

21.

Past are corruption, sickness, pain,
Nor tears shall ever flow again;
   For troubles all have fled,
   And death itself is dead:
And sin and folly with dark dismal train are gone,
   Since grace in glory shone.

The Refrain.

With holy feet, and lamps bright burning,
I go to meet my Lord returning.

22.

No longer Paradise of men
Is void; for *there* God wills again
   That man should safely dwell;
   Yea, man the same who fell
Beneath the serpent's wiles: now in the promised rest,
   Immortal, fearless, blest.

The Refrain.

With holy feet, and lamps bright burning,
I go to meet my Lord returning.

23.

Thou now to heavenly places raised,
By all the virgin choir art praised,
   O Bride of heavenly King,
   And song all new we sing:
With lighted torch in hand, with snow-white lilies crowned,
   Thy praise in Christ we sound.

The Refrain.

With holy feet, and lamps bright burning,
I go to meet my Lord returning.

24.

Father of Heaven, supreme in might,
Dwelling in pure eternal light
  With Thine own Son most dear,
  Admit—for we are here—
E'en us within the gates of life, to sing Thy love
  In Thy blest courts above.

The Refrain.
With holy feet, and lamps bright burning,
I go to meet my Lord returning.

§ 9. AN EVENING HYMN.—The following evening hymn of the Greek Church may be referred to an earlier date than A.D. 300. St. Basil the Great, writing in the 4th century, alludes to it as an ancient composition of unknown authorship.[1] It was sung in the ancient Church at the lighting of the lamps, and hence is known as 'The Lamp-light, or Candle-light Hymn' (ἐπιλύχνιος εὐχαριστία). The original Greek may be seen, with further authorities and details, in Julian's *Dictionary of Hymnology*, p. 894.

The translation here appended is taken from Rev. A. W. Chatfield's *Songs and Hymns of the Greek Christian Poets* (London, 1876), p. 176. A less literal but more familiar translation occurs in *Hymns Ancient and Modern*, No. 18.

  'Propitious light of holy glory,
  Of the immortal heavenly Father,
  Holy, blessed,
  O Jesu Christ,

[1] *De Spiritu Sancto*, cap. 29.

Having come to the setting of the sun,
Having seen the evening light,
We hymn the Father, the Son,
And the Holy Spirit, God.
Thou art worthy at all times
To be hymned with thankful voices,
O Son of God, Who givest life,
Wherefore the world glorifieth Thee.'

§ 10. PRAYERS AND THANKSGIVINGS FROM THE CANONS OF HIPPOLYTUS.

(*a*) A Prayer to be said by the Bishop at the Imposition of Hands on the newly baptized, as prescribed in the Canons of Hippolytus.

'We bless Thee, O Lord God, who hast rendered these persons worthy of being born again, and over whom Thou pourest out Thy Holy Spirit, that those who have been united to the body of the Church may never be separated from it by wicked works. Grant rather to those, to whom Thou hast already given the remission of sins, the pledge also of Thy kingdom, through our Lord Jesus Christ, through whom to Thee, with Himself and with the Holy Ghost, be glory for ever and ever. Amen.'[1]

(*b*) Form of 'Gloria Patri' to be said after the Benediction of each of the Offerings of Firstfruits by the Celebrant in the Holy Eucharist.

'Glory be to Thee, to the Father, and to the Son, and to the Holy Ghost, world without end. Amen.'[2]

(*c*) Form of Prayer at the Reception and Blessing of the Firstfruits.

---

[1] Canon xix. §§ 137, 138, p. 98.   [2] Canon iii. § 29, p. 56.

'We give thanks to Thee, Almighty Lord God, for that Thou hast made us worthy to see these fruits which the earth hath this year produced. Bless them, O Lord, as the crown of the year, according to Thy lovingkindness, and let them be for the satisfying of the poor among Thy people; and bless Thy servant N. who hath offered these [firstfruits] out of Thy gifts, because he feareth Thee. Bless him from Thy holy heaven, together with his household and his sons, and pour upon them Thy mercy and Thy holy grace, that he may know Thy will in all things, and cause him to inherit that which is in heaven, through our Lord Jesus Christ, Thy beloved Son, and the Holy Ghost, for ever and ever. Amen.'[1]

(d) A Prayer to be used at the Consecration of a Bishop.

'O God, the Father of our Lord Jesus Christ, Father of mercies and God of all consolation, who dwellest [*habitat*] in high places, and beholdest the lowly, and knowest all things before they happen. Thou, who hast fixed the bounds of Thy Church, by whose command it takes place, that the race of the just should continue from Adam by reason of this Bishop who is the great Abraham,[2] who hast constituted prelacy and princedom,[3] look upon Thy servant N., giving him Thy strength, and the spirit of power, which Thou gavest unto Thy holy Apostles, through our Lord Jesus Christ, Thine only Son; to them who have founded the Church in every place to the honour and glory of Thy holy Name. Because Thou hast known the heart of each, grant unto him that he may behold Thy people without sin, that he may be worthy to feed Thy great and holy

---

[1] Canon xxvi. §§ 189-193, pp. 112, 113.

[2] 'Ratione hujus episcopi, qui est magnus Abraham.' This is unintelligible. The words do not occur in the later forms of the prayer found in the *Egyptian Church Order* and in the Apostolic Constitutions.

[3] 'Prælaturas et principatus.'

flock. Grant also that his manner of life [*mores*] may be superior to that of all the people, without any falling away. Grant also that on account of his excellence he may be envied by all; and accept his prayers and oblations, which he shall offer by day and night, and let them be unto Thee a sweet-smelling savour. Give unto him, O Lord, the office of bishop, and the spirit of clemency, and the power of remitting sins; and endue him with the power of breaking all the chains of wickedness of devils, and of healing all diseases; and tread down Satan under his feet swiftly, through our Lord Jesus Christ, through whom to Thee be glory with Him and with the Holy Ghost for ever and ever. Amen.'[1]

In Canon iv. § 31, this same prayer is directed to be used at the ordination of a presbyter, the word 'presbyter' being substituted for the word 'bishop.'

(*e*) Prayer to be said at the Ordination of a Deacon, as the Bishop lays his hands upon him.

'O God, the Father of our Lord Jesus Christ, we earnestly beseech Thee that Thou wouldest pour Thy Holy Spirit upon Thy servant N., and prepare him a place with those who serve Thee according to Thy good pleasure, as Stephen, and that Thou wouldest grant unto him the strength to conquer all the power of the crafty one by the sign of Thy Cross, wherewith he himself is signed; and that Thou wouldest grant unto him a manner of life without sin in the presence of all men, and teaching on behalf of many, whereby he may lead a numerous people into the holy Church, unto salvation, without scandal. Accept all his service through our Lord Jesus Christ, through whom to Thee with Himself, and with the Holy Ghost be glory for ever and ever. Amen.'[2]

---

[1] Canon iii. §§ 11–18, pp. 42–47.
[2] Canon v. §§ 39–42, pp. 66, 67.

§ 11. ANTHEMS, ETC., OF UNCERTAIN DATE.—The foregoing, we believe, exhaust the list of formulæ of Christian devotion, to which an ante-Nicene date can be assigned with certainty.

There are other ancient devotional forms which may possibly or even probably be of ante-Nicene antiquity, but we have no certain evidence of the fact, and the documents in which they first reach us are not themselves of an ante-Nicene date.

Such are the hymn 'Gloria in Excelsis,' of which the earliest known forms are found in chaps. 47–49 of Book iii. of the Apostolic Constitutions, and in the *Codex Alexandrinus* of the Bible, a fifth-century MS. now in the British Museum; the Triumphal Hymn, or Tersanctus, which is found in the Clementine Liturgy, in the eighth book of the Apostolic Constitutions; numerous prayers, thanksgivings, benedictions, etc., in the Apostolic Constitutions, and more especially in the seventh and eighth books thereof.

§ 12. ANCIENT LITURGIES.—We must, however, say a few words about ancient Liturgies. In the last volume of their *Ante-Nicene Library*, Messrs. Roberts and Donaldson somewhat arbitrarily select and translate *in extenso* the following Liturgies and no others :—

(1) The Liturgy of St. James; (2) The Liturgy of St. Mark; (3) The Liturgy of the Holy Apostles (Adæus and Maris).

There are no very early MSS. of these Liturgies in

existence. They are not ante-Nicene in their present form, though much of their substance, no doubt— probably the greater part of it—springs from a date anterior to A.D. 325. But the same remark is true of many other Liturgies both Eastern and Western. Bunsen, in the third volume of his *Analecta Ante-Nicæna*, prints the whole or part of many of them, including even the Roman Canon of the Mass (St. Gregory's)[1] which is the one Liturgy of which it may be confidently asserted that it is not ante-Nicene.

If any one Liturgy has a claim above others to be ranked as ante-Nicene, it is the so-called Clementine Liturgy preserved in Book viii. of the Apostolic Constitutions, and which is given in its entirety in the Appendix, p. 278. Bunsen has printed this in the second volume of his *Analecta Ante-Nicæna*.[2] Its claim to antiquity rests not only on the place and mode of its preservation, but also on internal points of evidence in favour of a very early date, which, however, we must not attempt to produce and examine and discuss here.

It is not known in what Church it was in use, or whether it ever was actually in use in any Church. Internal evidence points to Antioch as the place of its composition; but it would hardly have been attributed to St. Clement unless it fairly represented the Liturgy of the Church of Rome during the first three centuries, while that Church was still a Greek-speaking community. It claims to be the composition of St. Clement, Bishop of Rome. But this claim

[1] Page 287.   [2] Page 380, etc.

cannot be substantiated. A great quantity of early Christian literature was labelled as Clementine. It is due to the highly inconvenient—we will not say dishonest, because it was not intended to be dishonest—but the highly inconvenient practice of attributing documents to some early Father, or to one of the Twelve Apostles themselves, in order to secure for them acceptance and respect.

There is, however, external testimony for assigning to the Clementine Liturgy the earliest date among all Liturgies in a statement made under the name of Proclus, Patriarch of Constantinople (434-446), in a tract attributed to him, about the 'handing down of the Divine Liturgy.'[1] This tract, even if not genuine, and in some respects not historical, is so important for other reasons besides its statement about the Clementine Liturgy, that it deserves to be translated and laid before our readers in full.

'Many other pastors and teachers of the Church who succeeded the Apostles have committed an edition of the mystic Liturgy to writing, and have handed it down to the Church; of whom these are the first and the most conspicuous, The blessed Clement : the disciple and successor

[1] Λόγος περὶ παραδόσεως τῆς θείας λειτουργίας, printed in *P. G.*, tom. lxv. col. 849. Its genuineness has been doubted by many writers, chiefly on internal evidence, *e.g.* because of the position of honour which it assigns to the Clementine Liturgy; because the Liturgy of St. Basil does not seem to be sufficiently abbreviated as compared with those of St. Clement and St. James to substantiate Proclus' assertion about St. Basil's action in this matter. In our opinion these objections, if of sufficient weight to disprove its genuineness, do not rob the anonymous document of its great interest and importance. The subject has been discussed at length by Rev. E. S. Ffoulkes, *Primitive Consecration*, etc. (London, 1885), p. 178, etc.

of the chief of the Apostles, at the dictation of the holy Apostles themselves, and the divine James, whose lot lay in the Church of Jerusalem, of which he was appointed the first bishop by the first and greatest High Priest, Christ our God. Then Basil the Great noticed the slothfulness and degeneracy of men, and that they were wearied by the length of the liturgy—not that he himself considered that there was anything too long or superfluous in it—and cut away the idle objections of those who prayed and those who heard, which in the course of long time had grown up, by abbreviating it.

After the ascension of our Saviour into heaven, the Apostles, before they were scattered over the whole world, met together and spent whole days in prayer, and found such consolation in the mystic sacrifice of the Lord's body, that they chanted it at very great length, and they considered it their chiefest duty to teach others to do the same.

They spent time over this Divine rite with happiness and with the greatest joy, remembering the word of the Lord when He said, "This is My body," and "Do this in remembrance of Me; he that eateth My flesh and drinketh my blood abideth in Me, and I in him." Therefore, with contrite hearts they chanted many prayers, imploring the Divine favour. They also accustomed the newly baptized converts both from the Jews and Gentiles to attend these mysteries of grace, piously teaching them and training them to desert the services which preceded the dispensation of grace; and which were a shadow of good things to come.

By such prayers, then, they besought and expected the descent of the Holy Ghost, in order that by His Divine Presence He might cause and make the bread and wine mingled with water, which were proposed for sacrifice, to become the very body and blood of our Saviour Jesus Christ. This is still done among us at the present day, and will be done till the end of the world. But their successors, losing the firmness and fervour of the first faith, and entangled with the business and cares of the world, became wearied, as I said above, with the length of the Liturgy, and were got with difficulty to come and hear the Master's words. Wherefore the Divine Basil, by way of medicinal remedy, shortened the Liturgy. Again, not long afterwards, our Father, John Chrysostom, like a good shepherd caring for the safety of his flock, contemplating the slothfulness of human nature, determined to cut off, root and branch, all the excuses suggested by Satan. Accordingly he cut off many things, and still further shortened the celebration of the holy rite, lest by degrees men, who most dearly love freedom and leisure, should become deceived by the fallacious reasonings of the adversary, and should hold aloof from the service of apostolic and Divine appointment; a defection which we have seen taking place by many people at many times and in many places, and which may be seen till the present day.'

But in spite of the certainty that part, and the possibility that the whole, of the Clementine Liturgy belongs to a date prior to the Council of Nice, we do not feel justified in printing it here, because the earliest document in which it has come down to us, viz. Book viii. of the Apostolic Constitutions, is a compilation of the second half of the fourth century, and it is impossible for us to say with certainty what additions or touches it may have received at the hands of the compiler of those Constitutions.[1]

[1] This compiler has been identified by Rev. F. E. Brightman (and others), with the pseudo-Ignatius, the interpolator of the seven genuine epistles and the forger of the remaining six of the long recension of the Ignatian Epistles (*Liturgies, Eastern and Western*, Oxford, 1896, vol. i. p. xliii.).

CHAPTER IV.

THE CONNECTION BETWEEN THE LITURGY AND RITUAL OF THE JEWISH AND CHRISTIAN CHURCHES.

§ 1. Introductory—§ 2. The Temple Services—§ 3. The Synagogue Services—§ 4. The Shema—§ 5. The Eighteen Benedictions—§ 6. The Kadish—§ 7. The Kedusha—§ 8. The Paschal Supper—§ 9. Vitringa's theory—§ 10. Bickell's theory. *Detailed resemblances in:* § 11. Baptism—§ 12. Bells—§ 13. Benedictions—§ 14. Colours—§ 15. Confirmation—§ 16. Churches, name of—§ 17. Silent Prayer—§ 18. Bowing at the Sacred Name—§ 19. Removal of shoes—§ 20. Bowing towards the altar—§ 21. Eastward position—§ 22. Washing of hands, etc.—§ 23. Standing up at the Gospel—§ 24. Procession of the Gospel—§ 25. Separation of the sexes—§ 26. Mode of singing—§ 27. Dedication of churches—§ 28. Festivals and Fasts—§ 29. Hebrew language, use of the—§ 30. The Eucharist—§ 31. Imposition of hands—§ 32. Holy orders—§ 33. Marriage—§ 34. Prayer, hours of—§ 35. Prayer, attitude at—§ 36. Prayer for the dead—§ 37. Vestments—§ 38. Jewish origin of certain Christian formulæ of devotion—§ 39. Gospel for the Tenth Sunday after Trinity—§ 40. Heathen worship suggested as the source of some Christian ritual.

§ 1. INTRODUCTORY.—It is proposed to bring before the reader in this chapter a difficult subject, on which different views have been held by various writers at various times; namely, the relationship, or absence of relationship, of the Liturgy and Ritual of the Christian Church to the Liturgy and Ritual of the Jewish Church which preceded it.

It must be allowed at starting that the following grounds constitute a strong, *à priori* ground for supposing that the Christian and Jewish organization, liturgy, and ritual would show at least some signs of connection and resemblance:—

(1) The Divine Founder of the Christian Church was Himself, in His human nature, of Jewish nationality.

(2) He lived throughout His life on earth as a loyal son of the Jewish Church, frequenting its services, and fulfilling all that the Levitical law enjoined.

(3) On the night before His death He was actually engaged in the solemnization of the Jewish Paschal Supper when He instituted the Christian Eucharist.

(4) The Apostles and the saints who founded the first Christian Churches were likewise Jews, and frequented the temple services, certainly at first, and probably as long as the temple stood.

The law of evolution would lead us to expect a natural continuity between Jewish and Christian worship. But when we come to details, to decide exactly what part of the temple service or of the synagogue service was the basis on which some apparently corresponding part of the Christian service was formed, to decide whether certain resemblances in points of ritual were and are intentional or accidental, then we are confronted with great difficulties. There is no direct statement upon the point in Holy Scripture, or in apostolic or sub-apostolic times. Mediæval writers have a good deal to tell us on this subject; but mediævalism was uncritical, and unless statements of this sort made by mediæval writers are supported by evidence, they cannot be relied upon as necessarily true.

Then, unfortunately, there are not extant sufficient authentic Jewish liturgical remains of the first century A.D., for us to base an independent conclusion upon them with certainty. Such early remains as do exist come to us through the *Mischna*, of the second century after Christ, yet containing documents of an earlier date; the *Tosiphtha*, a little later than the *Mischna;* and the two *Gemaras*, that of Jerusalem (4th century), and that of Babylon (5th century). All these are included in the corpus of the Jewish documents known as the Talmud.

Perhaps the most helpful plan will be to lay before the reader the main facts about the services of the temple and the synagogue, together with an account of the Paschal Supper, giving *in extenso* the few portions of the Jewish Liturgy which are by general consent as old as the time of our Saviour. We will then call attention to points of similarity in the Jewish and Christian services, and shall have to decide how far such similarities are accidental, or due to a connection between the former and the latter.

§ 2. THE TEMPLE SERVICES.—These included the daily offering of a lamb on the altar of burnt offering, in the morning and at even, accompanied with a meat offering (flour and oil), and a drink offering (wine). On the sabbath two lambs were offered instead of one. There was a daily offering of incense on the altar of incense in the morning before, and in the evening after the daily sacrifice. In connection with the offering of the burnt sacrifice, there was vocal and instrumental music; the priests blew silver trumpets, and the Levites played on various instruments. A special psalm was appointed for use on each day of the week, viz. on Sunday, Ps. xxiv.; on Monday, Ps. xlviii.; on Tuesday, Ps. lxxxii.; on Wednesday, Ps. xciv.; on Thursday, Ps. lxxxi.; on Friday, Ps. xciii.; on the sabbath, Ps. xcii. There were special sacrifices and services on the great festivals, which we will not describe here, though it will be necessary to speak later on about the Passover. In addition to these there were a multitude of private offerings and sacrifices, of which it is unnecessary to give any description here.

On the sabbath day the Song of Moses (Deut. xxxii.), divided into six portions for as many sabbaths, was sung after the morning sacrifice,[1] and the Song of Moses (Exod. xv.) was sung after the evening sacrifice.[2]

There is no early evidence forthcoming as to any scheme of the regular repetition of the Psalter corresponding to the use of the Psalter in the Divine Office of the Christian Church, either in the case of the temple or of the synagogue services.

---

[1] Deut. xxxii. 1-43 is used at Lauds, daily (Greek use), on some Sundays (Mozarabic), instead of Benedictus on Sundays in Advent, Christmas Day, Circumcision, Epiphany (Ambrosian), on Saturdays (Roman).

[2] Exod. xv. 1-19 is used at Lauds, daily (Greek use), Easter-tide (Mozarabic), Sundays (Ambrosian), Thursday (Roman).

The Talmud is our earliest extant authority for the character of services held originally in the temple, and afterwards transferred to the synagogue, viz. at morning (Shacharith), noon (Musaph), afternoon (Minchah), and evening (Arbith). The greater part of the Psalter was used, and is used still, at these and other services ; *e.g.* in the morning service of the London Synagogue of to-day the following Psalms are used on sabbaths and Holy Days : xix., xxxiv., xc., xci., cxxxv., cxxxvi., xxxiii., xcii., xciii. ; and on all days of the week, cxlv., cxlvi., cxlvii., cxlix., cxlviii., cl.[1] We need not go through the whole of the Jewish Prayer-book. If these services are as ancient as the time of Christ, and if they were held in the temple before being transferred to the synagogue, then it is impossible not to trace in them the origin, or at least the inspiring, idea of the Christian Divine Office. Can it be a mere coincidence that Psalms cxlviii.-cl., which formed an integral part of the daily Jewish morning service, have been found everywhere as an unvarying element in the daily morning Christian service of Lauds ?

§ 3. THE SYNAGOGUE SERVICES.—The chief parts of the service in the synagogue were, according to the Mischna,[2] (1) The recitation of the Shema ;[3] (2) prayer; (3) the reading of the Thorah (*i.e.* the Pentateuch) ; (4) the reading of the Prophets ; (5) the blessing ; to which was added a translation

---

[1] *The Authorized Daily Prayer-book of the United Hebrew Congregation of the British Empire*, 3rd ed. (London, 1892), pp. 20–33.
[2] Megilla, iv. 3.   [3] See § 4.

into the vernacular Aramaic of the lessons, read in the ancient Hebrew, and a discourse founded thereon.

It will be noticed that the recitation of the Psalter, which is the centre of the Christian Divine office, and round which everything else circles, is absent from the synagogue service as here described. Its main object appears to be instruction, whereas the main object of the Christian Divine office is worship.[1] We are inclined to extend to the whole Christian service a remark which Mons. E. de Pressensé makes with regard to sacred song—

'Its cradle was not the synagogue, where the frigid service consisted only of reading and prayer, without any intermingling songs of praise (Luke iv. 17; Acts xv. 21). Christian song comes directly from the temple, the offspring of that grand Hebrew poetry uttered by lips touched by the live coal from off the altar, the sublimest lyric expressions ever given to the griefs and yearnings of the human heart.'[2]

The mediæval Liturgy of the synagogue is full of blasphemies against Jesus Christ and the Blessed Virgin Mary,[3] which seem to be the outcome and the perpetuation of a deep-seated and long-standing hostility between the Jewish Synagogue and the Christian Church.

It should also be borne in mind that synagogues

---

[1] But see end of § 3. The translation of προσευχή, in Acts xvi. 13, 16, as 'a house of prayer' is untenable.

[2] *Christian Life and Practice in the Early Church* (London, 1877), p. 299.

[3] Streane (A. W.), *Jesus Christ in the Talmud*, etc. (Cambridge, 1893), pp. 21*, 27*.

in the first century A.D. were a comparatively modern institution, and had no hereditary claim on the reverence or affection of either Jews or Christians. The contrary has sometimes been inferred from the statement of St. James, in Acts xv. 21, but the words used there might mean anything from one thousand to one hundred years. As a matter of fact, the meaning must be near the latter and not the former limit. There is no reference to synagogues in the Old Testament. Ps. lxxiv. 8 is generally admitted to be a mistranslation;[1] nor can 3 Macc. vii. 20 be relied upon, although it is usually supposed to refer to the building of a synagogue at Alexandria, c. 217-215 B.C. There is really no evidence for the generally accepted theory and often-repeated statement that the foundation or re-foundation of synagogues took place in the days of Nehemiah or Ezra.[2]

Synagogues were village institutes and police courts as well as halls of worship. Within their precincts cases were tried, prisoners were sentenced, and the sentences were carried out.

Our Lord said—

'They shall lay their hands on you, and persecute you, delivering you up to the synagogues, and into prisons, being brought before kings and rulers for My Name's sake.'[3]

---

[1] If it is not a mistranslation, this Psalm is assigned to the period of the Maccabees in consequence of this verse (S. R. Driver, *Introduction to the Literature of the Old Testament*, 3rd ed. p. 364).

[2] The fact is doubtfully accepted in Smith's *Dictionary of the Bible*, vol. iii. p. 1398.

[3] St. Luke xxi. 12.

'Beware of men, for they will deliver you up to the councils, and they will scourge you in their synagogues.'[1]

St. Paul tells how—

'I imprisoned and beat in every synagogue them that believed. . . . I punished them oft in every synagogue, and compelled them to blaspheme; and being exceedingly mad against them, I persecuted them even unto strange cities.'[2]

In later times St. Paul was himself five times sentenced by his fellow-countrymen to undergo the penalty of the lash,[3] and the place where these scourgings were inflicted must have been the synagogue. Surely, with such painful and degrading associations and recollections, the synagogue would not have been the quarter to which the first Christians would have turned to find a model, either for their proceedings or their services.[4] Their thoughts would more naturally centre round the temple, which our Saviour, and His Apostles after Him, regularly frequented, and which was, *par excellence*, the house of God.

Yet some further information about the arrangements of the synagogue may be acceptable.

The building faced so that the worshippers might look towards the Holy City. The door for the entrance of the congregation was at one end of the building. At the further end—which we will call

---

[1] St. Matt. x. 17; xxiii. 3, 4; St. Luke xii. 11.
[2] Acts xxii. 19; xxvi. 11.   [3] 2 Cor. xi. 24.
[4] See King (R.), *The Ruling Elder* (Armagh, 1892—not published), capp. xxxii.-xxxiv.

the east end—elevated on steps, was an ark, or closet, over which a canopy was spread. This ark always contained the scrolls of the law, and sometimes the official garments of the officers of the community.

The desk for the leader of Divine worship was placed in front of the ark.

The rostrum, or bema, an elevated pulpit or platform, from which the lessons of the law were read and discourses were delivered, usually stood in the centre of the building.

In front of the ark there were armchairs, in which the elders of the synagogue and doctors of the law sat, facing the congregation.

A light was kept perpetually burning, in evident imitation of the temple light.[1]

Trombones were kept, to be blown on the first day of the year, and trumpets, to be blown on feast days.

The usual hours of daily worship in the synagogue were nine a.m., when the morning sacrifice was being offered in the temple, and three p.m., when the evening sacrifice was being offered in the temple, or rather, while the sacrifice in the temple was being burned, which was interpreted to mean any hour between dark and dawn.

It is not known with precision what the Jewish service was in the time of our Lord.

Dr. Ginsburg says—

'That the Jews in the time of Christ had a liturgical

[1] Exod. xxvii. 20.

service is certain; but it is equally certain that the present Liturgy of the synagogue embodies a large admixture of prayers which were compiled after the destruction of the second temple.'[1]

Dr. Schürer says—

'As the Shema undoubtedly belongs to the time of Christ, it is evident that certain established prayers were then already customary in public worship. It can, however, hardly be ascertained how much of the somewhat copiously developed Liturgy of post-Talmudic Judaism reaches back to that period.'[2]

It is of no use, therefore—or rather, it is worse than useless, because it would be misleading—to take up a Jewish Prayer-book of the present day, and, with that as an authority, to institute a comparison between the liturgical language and ritual of the Jewish and Christian Churches.

We will now quote those portions of the Jewish Liturgy, which, apart from, and in addition to, lections from Holy Scripture, are believed to be as old or older than Christianity, and to have been in use in the time of our Lord.

§ 4. THE SHEMA.—Two introductory benedictions, called the *Shema*, or *Keriath Shema*.

1. 'Blessed art Thou, O Lord our God, King of the universe, who createst light and formest darkness, who makest peace and createst all things. He in mercy causes the light to shine upon the earth and the inhabitants

[1] Article 'Synagogue,' in Kitto's *Cyclopædia of Biblical Literature*, iii. 905.
[2] *A History of the Jewish People*, div. ii. vol. ii. p. 77.

thereof, and in goodness (renews every day the work of creation. Blessed art Thou, the Creator of light.

2. With great love hast Thou loved us, O Lord our God. Thou hast shown us great and abundant mercy, O our Father and King, for the sake of our forefathers who trusted in Thee. Thou who didst teach them the love of life, have mercy upon us, and teach us also . . . to praise and acknowledge Thy unity in love. Blessed art Thou, O Lord, who in love hast chosen Thy people.'

[Recitation of the ten commandments. The Shema consisting of Deut. vi. 4-9; xi. 13-21; Numb. xv. 37-41.]

3. Concluding benediction—

'It is true and firmly established that Thou art the Lord our God, and the God of our forefathers; there is no God besides Thee. Blessed art Thou, O Lord, the Redeemer of Israel.'

It is to be noticed that, in the conversation between our Saviour and the lawyer who inquired, 'Master, what must I do to inherit eternal life?' the lawyer recited a verse of the Shema (Deut. vi. 4, 5; St. Luke x. 26, 27).

§ 5. THE EIGHTEEN BENEDICTIONS, OR THE PRAYER 'SHEMONAH ESRAH.'—These were recited in the temple daily; three of them were pronounced upon the people by the priests every day in the temple court. The sixteenth and seventeenth were used by the high priest on the Day of Atonement.

1. 'Blessed art Thou, O Lord our God, the God of our Fathers Abraham, Isaac, and Jacob, great, omnipotent, fearful, and most high God, who bountifully shewest mercy,

who art the possessor of all things, who rememberest the pious deeds of our fathers, and sendest the Redeemer to their children's children, for His mercy's sake in love, O our King, Defender, Saviour, and Shield. Blessed art Thou, O Lord, the Shield of Abraham!

2. Thou art powerful, O Lord, world without end. Thou bringest the dead to life in great compassion, Thou holdest up the falling, healest the sick, loosest the chained, and shewest Thy faithfulness to those that sleep in the dust. Who is like unto Thee, Lord of might? and who resembles Thee? a Sovereign killing and bringing to life again, and causing salvation to flourish, and Thou art sure to raise the dead. Blessed art Thou, O Lord, who raisest the dead.

3. Thou art Holy, and Thy Name is Holy, and the holy ones praise Thee every day continually. Blessed art Thou, O Lord the holy God.

4. Thou mercifully bestowest knowledge upon men, and teachest the mortal prudence. Mercifully bestow upon us from Thyself, knowledge, wisdom, and understanding. Blessed art Thou, O Lord, who mercifully bestowest knowledge.

5. Our Father, lead us back to Thy law. Bring us very near, O King, to Thy service, and cause us to return in sincere penitence into Thy presence. Blessed art Thou, O Lord, who delightest in repentence.

6. Our Father, forgive us, for we have sinned; our King pardon us, for we have trangressed; for Thou art forgiving and pardoning. Blessed art Thou, O Lord, merciful and plenteous in forgiveness.

7. Look at our misery, contend our cause, and deliver us speedily, for Thy Name's sake, for Thou art a mighty deliverer. Blessed art Thou, O Lord, the Deliverer of Israel.

8. Heal us, O Lord, and we shall be healed; save us,

and we shall be saved, for Thou art our boast; grant us a perfect cure for all our wounds, for Thou, O Lord our King, art a faithful and merciful physician. Blessed art Thou, O Lord, who healest the sick of Thy people Israel.

9. Bless to us, O Lord our God, for good this year, and all its kinds of produce. Send Thy blessing upon the face of the earth, satisfy us with Thy goodness, and bless this year as the years bygone. Blessed art Thou, O Lord, who blessest the seasons.

10. Cause the great trumpet to proclaim our liberty, raise the standard for the gathering of our captives, and bring us together from the four corners of the earth. Blessed art Thou, O Lord, who gatherest together the dispersed of Israel.

11. Reinstate our judges as of old, and our councillors as of yore; remove from us sorrow and sighing, and do Thou alone, O Lord, reign over us in mercy and love, and judge us in righteousness and justice. Blessed art Thou, O Lord the King, who lovest righteousness and justice.

12. Let the apostates have no hope, and let those who perpetrate wickedness speedily perish; let them all be suddenly cut off; let the proud speedily be uprooted, broken, crushed, and humbled speedily in our days. Blessed art Thou, O Lord, who breakest down the enemy, and humblest the proud.

13. On the righteous, on the pious, on the elders of Thy people, the House of Israel, on the remnant of the Scribes, on the pious proselytes, and on us bestow, O Lord our God, Thy mercy; give ample reward to all who trust in Thy name in sincerity, make our portion with them for ever, and let us not be ashamed, for we trust in Thee. Blessed art Thou, O Lord, the Support and Refuge of the righteous.

14a. To Jerusalem, Thy city, in mercy return, and dwell in it according to Thy promise; make it speedily in our day an everlasting building, and soon establish therein the throne of David. Blessed art Thou, O Lord, who buildest Jerusalem.

14*b*. The branch of David Thy servant speedily cause to flourish, and exalt his horn with Thy help, for we look to Thy help all day. Blessed art Thou, who causest to flourish the horn of David.

15. Hear our voice, O Lord our God, have pity and compassion on us, and receive with mercy and acceptance our prayers, for Thou art a God hearing prayer and supplication, our King; do not send us empty away from Thy presence, for Thou hearest the prayers of Thy people Israel in mercy. Blessed art Thou, O Lord, who hearest prayer.

16. Be favourable, O Lord our God, to Thy people Israel, and to their prayer; restore the worship to Thy sanctuary; receive lovingly the burnt sacrifice of Israel and their prayer, and let the service of Israel Thy people be always well-pleasing to Thee. May our eyes see Thee return to Israel in love. Blessed art Thou, O Lord, who restorest Thy Shechinah to Zion.

17. We thankfully confess before Thee that Thou art the Lord our God, and the God of our fathers, world without end, and that Thou art the Shepherd of our life, and the Rock of our salvation, from generation to generation; we render thanks unto Thee, and celebrate Thy praises. Blessed art Thou, O Lord, whose Name is goodness, and whom it becomes to praise.

18. Bestow peace, happiness, blessing, grace, mercy, and compassion upon us, and upon the whole of Israel Thy people. Our Father, bless us all unitedly with the light of Thy countenance, for in the light of Thy countenance didst Thou give to us, O Lord our God, the law of life, loving-kindness, justice, blessing, compassion, life, and peace. May it please Thee to bless Thy people Israel at all times, and in every moment with peace. Blessed

art Thou, O Lord, who blessest Thy people Israel with peace.'[1]

It will be evident from 14*a* and 16 that in this form, the earliest form known to us, the eighteen Benedictions are more recent than the destruction of Jerusalem, A.D. 70. They may be dated A.D. 70 to A.D. 100, but their groundwork is more ancient, and we have printed them as containing, for the most part, material as ancient or more ancient than the time of Christ.

§ 6. THE KADISH.—The Kadish was part of the morning service of the synagogue. It was in these words, the legate of the congregation speaking, the congregation taking up the responses—

1. 'Exalted and hallowed be His great Name in the world which He created according to His will; let His kingdom come in your lifetime, and in the lifetime of the whole House of Israel, very speedily.

R℣. Amen. Blessed be His great Name, world without end.

2. Blessed and praised, celebrated and exalted, extolled and adored, magnified and worshipped be Thy holy Name. Blessed be He far above all benedictions, hymns, thanks, praises, and consolations, which have been uttered in the world.

R℣. Amen.

3. May the prayers and supplications of all Israel be graciously received before their Father in heaven.

R℣. Amen.

4. May perfect peace descend from heaven, and life upon us and all Israel.

R℣. Amen.

[1] Kitto, *Cyclopædia of Biblical Literature*, vol. iii. p 907.

5. May He who makes peace in His heaven confer peace upon us and all Israel.

R̰. Amen.'[1]

Two petitions in the Lord's Prayer, as taught by our Saviour, seem to be based upon the first section of this *Kadish*.

§ 7. THE KEDUSHA. The following is the wording of the *Kedusha*, which was substituted in public worship for the third of the eighteen Benedictions. It is said in the same way as the *Kadish*.

'Hallowed be Thy Name on earth as it is hallowed in heaven above, as it is written by the prophet, And one calls to the other, and says—

R̰. Holy, holy, holy, is the Lord God of Sabaoth; the whole earth is filled with His glory.

Those who are opposite them respond—

R̰. Blessed be the glory of the eternal, each one in his station.

And in Thy Holy Word it is written, thus saying—

R̰. The Lord shall reign for ever and ever, Thy God, O Zion, from generation to generation. Hallelujah.

From generation to generation we will disclose Thy greatness, and for ever and ever celebrate Thy holiness, and Thy praise shall not cease in our mouth, world without end; for Thou, O Lord, art a great and holy King. Blessed art Thou, holy God and King.'[2]

It will be seen that the Triumphal Hymn, or Tersanctus, which is now part of the Christian Liturgy, had a position previously in the *Kedusha* of the Jewish Church. The first section of it is also suggestive of a petition in the Lord's Prayer.

[1] Kitto, *ut supra*.   [2] Kitto, *ut supra*, p. 908.

§ 8. THE PASCHAL SUPPER.—We proceed next to describe the order and ceremonial of the Paschal Supper.

'The company having assembled, after the lamps were lighted, arranged themselves in due order on couches, round the tables, reclining on their left sides. A cup of red wine mingled with water, was filled for every one, and drunk, after a benediction by the head man of the group. A basin of water was then brought in, that each might wash his hands, and then another blessing was pronounced. A table was then carried into the open space between the couches, and bitter herbs and unleavened bread, with a dish, made of dates, raisins, and other fruits mixed with vinegar to the consistency of lime, in commemoration of the mortar with which their fathers worked in Egypt, set on it, along with the paschal lamb. The head man then took some of the herbs, dipped them in the dish, and after giving thanks to God for creating the fruits of the earth, ate a small piece, and gave one to each of the company. A second cup of wine and water was then poured out, and the son of the house, or the youngest boy present, was asked the meaning of the feast. The questions to be put had been minutely fixed by the rabbis, and were as formally and minutely answered in appointed words, the whole story of deliverance from Egypt being thus repeated year after year, at each Passover table, in the same terms throughout all Israel.'

The first part of the great 'Hallel' or 'Hallelujah' (Psalms cxiii., cxiv.) was now chanted, introduced by the formula—

'Therefore it is our bounden duty to thank, praise, exalt, glorify, praise and celebrate Him who has done all these things for our fathers, and for us. He has led us out of bondage to freedom, out of misery to joy, out of mourning to rejoicing, out of darkness to great light, out of slavery to liberty. Therefore let us sing before Him a new song, Hallelujah.'

The resemblance of these words to the Preface in the Christian Eucharistic Service will be noticed at once.

Then followed a prayer, beginning—

'Blessed art Thou, O Lord our God, King of the universe, who hast redeemed us and our forefathers from Egypt.'

Upon which the blessing and the drinking of the second cup followed. This was followed by a second washing of hands. A third cup was now poured out, and then came the grace after meals. A fourth and last cup followed, and then Psalms cxv.–cxviii., which formed the rest of the 'Hallelujah;' and another prayer closed the feast. Ps. cxxxvi. was sung at the conclusion of the Hallel, and was itself called the Great Hallel.[1]

§ 9. VITRINGA'S THEORY.—The Dutch Protestant theologian, Vitringa,[2] whose voluminous writings on the subject have been conveniently translated by the Rev. J. L. Bernard,[3] maintained that the order, discipline, and ritual of the Christian Church were directly derived not from the Jewish temple, but from the Jewish synagogue. Whether the Christian Liturgy itself was derived from the same source, he

---

[1] The above account is mainly taken from Geikie (C.), *Life of Christ*, vol. i. p. 216.

[2] Vitringa, *De Synagoga Vetere* (Francquerae, 1696).

[3] *The Synagogue and the Church* (London, 1842).

held it to be impossible to decide in the absence of primitive Christian service books; but he illustrated his point by references, especially, to synagogical laws and practices in the matter of excommunication,[1] ordination,[2] preaching,[3] lections of Holy Scripture,[4] the use of lights,[5] of a pulpit, desk, etc.,[6] the prohibition of women from speaking in public,[7] the attitude of prayer,[8] etc. He says—

'In a word, if we attentively consider the laws made in the early ages respecting the Church and its furniture, the reverence and respect due to it, there is hardly a law to be found that is not derived from the canons of the synagogue.'[9]

We do not think that Vitringa established his point. Some of the above arrangements are based upon the ordinary requirements of convenience; a great part, and the more distinctive part, of the regulations which he adduces, were common to both the synagogue and the temple.[10]

§ 10. BICKELL'S THEORY.—Dr. G. Bickell,[11] followed by Dr. W. F. Skene,[12] has laboured to prove that the earlier part—the pre-anaphoral part—of the Christian Liturgy is based upon the Jewish Sabbath

---

[1] Bernard, *ut supra*, p. 61. [2] *Ibid.*, pp. 83, 145. [3] *Ibid.*, p. 93.
[4] *Ibid.*, p. 124. [5] *Ibid.*, p. 46. [6] *Ibid.*, p. 141.
[7] *Ibid.*, p. 206. [8] *Ibid.*, p. 203. [9] *Ibid.*, p. 144.
[10] But Vitringa has been largely followed. See Bingham, *Christian Antiqq.*, Bk. viii. cap. vi. § 10. Bingham mentions, without endorsing, the theory that the structural arrangements of the early Christian Churches were borrowed from the synagogue. In Smith's *Dictionary of the Bible*, under the article 'Synagogue,' Vitringa's position is substantially adopted.
[11] *Messe und Pascha* (Mainz, 1872).
[12] *The Lord's Supper and the Paschal Ritual* (Edinburgh, 1891).

Morning Prayer; and that the latter part of it—the anaphora, or canon—is based upon the language and ritual used in the Paschal Supper. The supposed similarity is exhibited in parallel columns,[1] the Clementine Liturgy being used as a basis, supplemented from other quarters, especially from the Syriac Liturgy of St. James. If any one will read through these parallel columns, he will probably come to the same conclusion as the present writer, viz. that the resemblance, though sometimes evident, is generally slight, in some cases fanciful, in other cases undiscernible, and that there is not, on the whole, sufficient similarity to establish or to disestablish the theory which has been built upon it.

There are, however, a considerable number of the ordinances of the Christian Church, and of points of order, ritual, and language, which find a counterpart in the worship and ceremonial of the Jewish Church.

We will enumerate and describe them, after which we shall be in a better position to decide whether the resemblances are the result of relationship or of chance.

§ 11. BAPTISM.—Baptism was used by the Jews for the admission of proselytes into the Jewish Church, in addition, no doubt, to certain other

---

[1] *Messe und Pascha*, pp. 100-104, 116-122. Bickell's view has been adopted and popularized in a series of interesting articles in the *Dawn of Day* (S.P.C.K., 1895-96). They are entitled, 'The Passover and the Holy Communion,' by E. M.

ceremonies which it would be beside our purpose to mention or describe here.[1]

Bathing, or washing with water, was also the appointed rite for the removal of certain Levitical defilements, and before the execution of priestly offices, such as entering the Holy Place, offering sacrifice, etc.[2]

It is quite possible that our Lord followed Jewish precedent in selecting and ordaining baptism as the rite of initiation into the Christian Church, the age at which it was administered being derived from the Jewish law and practice with regard to circumcision with which Christian baptism is expressly associated by St. Paul.[3] At least this seems more probable than that pagan rites for the purification of infants should have been copied, as has been suggested by one of the most eminent writers of the present day.[4]

The unction which accompanied baptism is expressly stated by Tertullian to have been borrowed from the practice of the Old Testament dispensation, and likewise the imposition of hands.[5]

§ 12. BELLS.—Bells form part of the ministration robes of priests in the Greek Church, and were occasionally found attached to sacerdotal vestments in the Western Church,[6] just as they formed part

---

[1] For proof of this statement, which has been sometimes doubted, see Schürer, *The Jewish People*, etc., Div. ii. vol. ii. pp. 319-324.

[2] Exod. xxix. 4; Levit. xvi. 4, etc. [3] Col. ii. 11, 12.

[4] Mr. Whitley Stokes. See correspondence in the *Academy* of Feb. 15 and Feb. 22, 1896.

[5] His words have been quoted in chap. ii. § 6, p. 90.

[6] Scudamore (W. E.), *Notitia Eucharistica*, 2nd ed. p. 89.

of the dress of the Jewish high priest as described in the Book of Exodus.[1]

§ 13. BENEDICTIONS AT LECTIONS.—Benedictions were pronounced before and after each of the lessons read out of the Old Testament in the Jewish sabbath morning prayers.[2] These apparently correspond to the benedictions and responsories connected with the lessons in Western Breviaries.

§ 14. COLOURS.—Various sequences of colours have grown up in course of time to be in use in the Christian Church. They were simple at first, but grew more complex as time went on. The following curious attempt to associate them with a Levitical origin is taken from a mediæval Irish tract preserved in the *Lebar Brecc*:—

'Query, by whom were your various colours first brought into the robe of offering?

Not hard to say: Moses, son of Amram, brought them into the robe of offering of Aaron, son of Amram, his own brother. He was the first priest in the law of Moses.

It is worth knowing how many colours were set by Moses in Aaron's robe.

Not hard to say: eight, to wit, yellow, blue, white, green, brown, red, black, purple. That, then, is the number of colours which every robe of offering is bound to have in it from that time to this.

It is worth knowing why that diversity was brought into the robe of offering, instead of its being one colour.

Not hard to say: through mystery and figure.

It is not fitting for any priest to approach Christ's body

[1] Chap. xxviii. 33-35.
[2] Skene (W. F.), *The Lord's Supper and the Paschal Ritual*, p. 146.

towards the offering, without a robe of shining satin around him, with the various colours therein,'[1] etc.

§ 15. CONFIRMATION.—There is something, at first sight, analogous to confirmation, at least as administered now in the Western Church, and especially in the Church of England, in the way in which a Jewish lad, when twelve years of age, was presented in the temple or the synagogue, and formally taking upon himself the obligations of the Jewish Church, was solemnly admitted into full membership. Yet the resemblance must be accidental. Confirmation was originally closely connected with baptism, and its ceremonial finds no counterpart in the Jewish reception of the twelve-year-old lad.[2]

§ 16. CHURCHES, NAME OF.—There are a considerable number of points connected with the structure and arrangement of churches, with their dedication, their decoration, and the reverence shown for them, on which comparisons might be drawn out at considerable length between Jewish and Christian customs; but the connection between them is of too unsubstantial and unproven a character to make it worth while to pursue the matter in detail. Probably similar comparisons might be worked out between the temples

---

[1] This document, with the original Irish, is printed by Mr. Whitley Stokes in his *Tripartite Life of St. Patrick*, Rolls Series (London, 1887), pt. i. p. clxxxvii.

[2] St. Luke ii. 42. See Norton (J. G.), *Worship in Heaven and on Earth* (London, not dated), pp. 477-479, where there is an interesting description of the Jewish ceremony.

IV.] JEWISH AND CHRISTIAN RITUALS. 223

and worship of the Christian and the Buddhist or almost any other religion. There is, however, one trace of a Jewish influence or connection to which attention may be drawn, namely, the use of the word 'synagogue,' as a kind of loan word to describe a Christian place of worship. We have already seen that it occurs in that sense in the New Testament.[1]

St. Ignatius, in his Epistle to Polycarp, says—

'Let Church assemblies (synagogæ) be held frequently.'[2]

In *The Shepherd* of Hermas we read—

'When a man having the Divine spirit comes into a synagogue of just men.'[3]

Theophilus of Antioch speaks of—

'The synagogues yet called the holy churches.'[4]

Theodotus (the Valentinian) calls—

'The Church, which is Christ's Body, the blessed synagogue.'[5]

The word is used by Firmilian of Cæsarea in his Epistle to St. Cyprian, in which he says—

'We do not share the same synagogue with heretics.'[6]

A Greek inscription over a Marcionite church on Mount Hermon, A.D. 308 or 318, runs thus—

---

[1] Page 45.   [2] Cap. iv.
[3] Mand. xi. § 9, p. 335. Συναγωγή is used more than once in this chapter.
[4] *Ad. Autol.* ii. 14.
[5] Inter *Opera* Clem. Alex., ed. 1715, p. 971.
[6] *Ep.* 75; Cypriani *Opera omnia*, ed. 1716, p. 147.

'Συναγωγὴ Μαρκιωνιστῶν κώμ[ης] Λεβάδων τοῦ κ[υρίο]υ καὶ Σ[ωτῆ]ρ[ος] Ἰησοῦ Χρηστοῦ προνοίᾳ Παυλου πρεσβ[υτέρου] τοῦ λχ ἔτους.'[1]

These are all instances of the perpetuation in Christian usage of a Jewish word.

The following modes or marks of Jewish reverence or devotion seem to correspond to similar characteristics in Christian worship:—

§ 17. SILENT PRAYER.—The silent prayer which accompanied the offering of incense[2] may have suggested the silent prayer in Eastern Liturgies,[3] and the *oratio secreta* said *super oblata*, as well as the canon now said *secreto* in the Roman rite.

§ 18. BOWING AT THE SACRED NAME.—When the name of Jehovah was mentioned, Jewish worshippers bowed down or prostrated themselves to the ground.[4] This is akin to the Christian custom of bowing at the ascription of praise to God or to the Holy Trinity, or at the mention of the Name of Jesus, though the latter is more likely to have arisen out of a misunderstanding of Phil. ii. 10.

§ 19. REMOVAL OF SHOES.—Jewish worshippers removed their shoes from their feet when they entered the temple, a custom connected with Exod. iii. 5 and Josh. v. 15. Sandals were worn

[1] *Inscriptions de la Syrie*, No. 2558; Smith and Wace, *Dictionary of Christian Biography*, iii. 819.
[2] Dr. Edersheim, *The Temple*, etc., p. 138.
[3] Brightman (F. E.), *Eastern Liturgies* (Oxford, 1896), p. 83, etc. Τῶν πιστῶν τρεῖς εὐχὰι πρώτην διὰ σιωπῆς, *Concil. Laod.*, Canon 19.
[4] Norton (J. G.), *Worship in Heaven and on Earth*, pp. 430, 447-448.

by Jewish priests in the temple, but they were barefooted while actually engaged in any ministration.[1] It is interesting to find traces of a similar custom in certain parts of the Christian Church. Irish ecclesiastics appear to have taken off their sandals at the chancel rail when they went to celebrate or to pray at the altar, and to have put them on again when they returned thence. This custom is implied in a story told of St. Columba and his attendant Scannlan in the *Book of Lismore*.[2] It is also an Eastern practice. Mr. Butler tells us that in the Coptic Church it is a rule for all who enter the haikal (= sanctuary) to put off their shoes at the door, and this applies even to the celebrant. This practice does not prevail in the Nestorian and Armenian Churches, though in the latter the priests wear special sandals or slippers.[3]

Cassian tells us of the Egyptian monks that they always wore sandals instead of shoes, and that they always put off their sandals when they went to celebrate or to receive the holy mysteries.[4]

§ 20. BOWING TOWARDS THE ALTAR.—On entering the temple all the congregation reverently bowed their heads. On leaving the vicinity of the altar both the priests and the worshippers were required to walk backward as far as the Gate of Nicanor, and there to stand, with their heads reverently bowed

[1] Dr. Edersheim, *The Temple*, etc., p. 117.
[2] *Lives of the Saints*, from the *Book of Lismore*, ed. by W. Stokes, p. 313.
[3] Butler (A. J.), *Ancient Coptic Churches*, vol. ii. p. 233.
[4] *Institt.*, lib. i. cap. 10.

towards the altar before withdrawing.[1] The mediæval and modern Christian custom of bowing towards the altar is an act of reverence of the same kind, but it is impossible to establish directly the derivation of the Christian from the Jewish custom, especially in the absence of any allusion to the practice in ante-Nicene times. Bingham follows Mede in thinking that it is highly probable that the Christian act of reverence is derived from the Jewish, though proof is wanting.[2]

§ 21. EASTWARD POSITION.—The Jewish worshipper always turned his face towards the Holy of Holies, *i.e.* towards Jerusalem. This would always involve, in European congregations, the orientation of synagogues, and the eastward position in prayer, which have prevailed so generally, though not universally, in Christendom.[3]

§ 22. ABLUTIONS.—The numerous ceremonial washings of hands or feet or body, prescribed to the Jewish priests in the Levitical code, bear a certain resemblance to the ceremonial ablution of the hands, known as the *lavabo*, which, either at the offertory or at some other point, forms a feature of most, if not all, Christian Liturgies, and also to the ceremonial washing of the feet, known as the *pedilavium*, on Maundy Thursday and at baptism.[4]

§ 23. STANDING AT THE GOSPEL.—The standing

[1] Norton (J. G.), *ut supra*, p. 432.
[2] *Antiqq. of the Christian Church*, Bk. viii. chap. x. § 7.
[3] Vitringa, *De Synagoga Vetere*, lib. i. pars. i. cap. 8, p. 178 ; lib. i. pars. iii. p. 457.
[4] See pp. 164-166.

up of the congregation in the synagogue at the reading of the law is analogous to the widely spread Christian custom of standing, as an act of reverence, during the reading of the liturgical gospel.[1]

§ 24. PROCESSION OF THE GOSPEL.—The solemn procession of the roll of the law to the reader's desk in the synagogue, resembles the ceremonial procession of the Holy Gospels in Eastern Liturgies, known as 'The Little,' or 'The Lesser Entrance.'[2]

§ 25. SEPARATION OF THE SEXES.—The separation of the sexes in the Jewish Church, the men occupying the body of the synagogue and the women the galleries, or the congregation being divided upon the ground floor, was adopted in the early Christian Church, and is, to some extent, retained still.

It might seem to be in the Christian Church merely the outcome of general Oriental sentiment as to the separation of the sexes, but a specially Jewish origin for it has been generally maintained.[3]

The separation of men and women in church was ordered in the Canons of Hippolytus,[4] which also directed that women were to be carefully veiled.[5]

In no case was a woman allowed to preach, except in certain heretical communities.[6]

---

[1] Norton (J. G.), *ut supra*, p. 458.
[2] Neale (J. M.), *Liturgies of St. Mark*, etc. (London, 1859), p. xii.
[3] Prideaux, *Connection*, etc., Pt. ii. Bk. v. p. 504; Schürer (E.), *The Jewish People*, etc. (Edinburgh, 1890), Div. ii. vol. ii. p. 75; Bingham, *Antiquities*, etc., Bk. viii. chap. v. § 6.
[4] Canon 97, p. 88.   [5] Canon 98, p. 88.
[6] Tertullian, *De Præscriptionibus*, cap. xli.; *P. L.*, tom. ii. col. 56; *De Virginibus Velandis*, *Ibid.*, col. 901; Apostolic Constitutions, lib. ii. cap. 57, p. 67.

§ 26. MODE OF SINGING.—The mode of singing in the Jewish Divine service—partly responsorial, partly antiphonal, and possibly the actual chants used—are believed by some persons to have passed on into the service of the Christian sanctuary. In a letter attributed to St. Germanus Parisiensis (sixth century, but probably of somewhat later date), the use of antiphons and of antiphonal singing is derived from King Solomon, and the use of responsorial chanting from Miriam.[1]

According to a modern authority, Jewish melodic recitation may be the basis of the mode of chanting the service in the Christian Church.[2]

§ 27. DEDICATION OF CHURCHES.—The solemn dedication of places of worship was observed throughout Jewish history, as in the case of the dedication of the tabernacle,[3] of Solomon's temple,[4] of the temple rebuilt under Zerubbabel,[5] of the building of the temple and rebuilding of the altar when Judas Maccabæus had driven out the Syrians,[6] of the temple as restored under Herod.[7] This practice of dedication passed on into the Christian Church. The rubrics in the earlier Latin Pontificals and Sacramentaries, which, however, do not date from further back than the eighth century, seem purposely to borrow their language from the Old Testament, and to copy details in the Levitical ritual. The expression, 'the

---

[1] Germani Parisiensis, *Ep.* ii. ; *P. L.*, tom. lxxii. col. 97.
[2] Nauman (E.), *History of Music* (London, not dated), vol. i. p. 84.
[3] Exod. xl. 1-11.   [4] 1 Kings viii.   [5] Ezra vi. 16, 17.
[6] 1 Macc. iv. ; 2 Macc. x.
[7] Josephus, *Antiqq. of the Jews*, Bk. xv. cap. xi. § vi.

horn,' or 'the horns of the altar,' is used to denote the corner or the corners of the altar.[1] This expression is evidently borrowed from Exod. xxvii. 2—

'And thou shalt make the horns of it upon the four corners thereof: his horns shall be of the same: and thou shalt overlay it with brass.'

The directions to employ hyssop for sprinkling, and the sevenfold perambulation round the altar,[2] seem to be based upon Exod. xxii. 22, etc., and Levit. iv. 17, etc. Any sprinkling water which remained was directed to be poured out at the base of the altar,[3] an expression drawn from Exod. xii. 29 and Levit. iv. 25, etc.

§ 28. FASTS AND FESTIVALS.—Dec. 25 (25th of Chislev) was the Jewish Feast of the Dedication.[4] It was adopted at a very early date by the Christian Church as the Feast of the Nativity of our Saviour, or Christmas-Day; but there is no proof that the identity of date is more than a coincidence, or that there was any connection between the Jewish and the Christian festival.

The four fasts observed annually by the Jews, and referred to in Zech. viii. 19, are stated to have suggested the institution of the four Ember seasons. The connection, as to number, is maintained in a

[1] *Sacramentarium Gelasianum*, Muratori's ed. col. 610; Ordo *Romanus*, ii., *Ibid.*, 1027.
[2] Both ordered in rubrics in the Order for Consecrating a Church in the Pontifical of Egbert and in that of Robert of Jumièges : Martene, *De Antiq. Eccles. Rit.* (Bassani, 1788), lib. ii. cap. xiii. Ordines ii., iii.
[3] 'Ad basim altaris,' *Ibid.*   [4] St. John x. 22.

passage in a treatise, 'De Hæresibus,' by Philaster, Bishop of Brixia, in the middle of the fourth century;[1] but the purposes for which these Jewish and Christian fasts were instituted were of a totally different character, and it is difficult to believe that there was any connection between them. There were two weekly Jewish fast-days, Monday and Thursday, for which the Christian Church at a very early date substituted Wednesday and Friday, commemorating the betrayal and the crucifixion of our Lord, but we have not met with any statement or allusion asserting or suggesting any connection between the two arrangements.

A high sabbath connected with a feast was the sabbath previous to it, not the sabbath after it, or the sabbath within the octave, as is usually the case in the Christian Church. The only similar arrangement which has come under our notice is in the case of the Eastern Church, where Quinquagesima week is the week before and not the week after Quinquagesima Sunday.[2]

§ 29. HEBREW LANGUAGE, USE OF THE.—It has been stated by Durandus that in the primitive Church the Divine Mysteries were celebrated in Hebrew,[3] and some Orientalists have expressed an opinion that the structure of certain liturgical sentences indicates a translation from a Semitic language.[4] But we have

---

[1] Cap. clxix. (Ehler, *Corpus Hæresiologicum*, tom. i. p. 167, referring not to Ember Days, but to Advent, Lent, Rogation Days (probably), and Pentecost. See Œhler's notes on a doubtful and difficult passage.
[2] *Studia Biblica* (Oxford, 1890), ii. 114.
[3] *Rationale*, lib. iv. cap. i. § 10.
[4] *Church Quarterly Review*, July, 1894, p. 350.

searched in vain for corroboration of Durandus' statement. Hebrew words occasionally occur in Latin Liturgies, but only in the case of such expressions as 'Amen,' 'Hallelujah,' 'Hosanna,' or of such titles of God as 'Hel,' 'Rucha.'[1] The alphabet inscribed by a bishop at the consecration of a church was once written in Greek, Latin, and Hebrew.[2]

§ 30. THE EUCHARIST.—(*a*) Dr. Edersheim thinks that the word 'Haggadah,' which means 'shewing forth,' and which was a Hebrew term for the Paschal Liturgy, suggested the language of St. Paul—

'As often as ye eat this bread, and drink this cup, ye do shew the Lord's death till He come.'[3]

(*b*) The washing of hands, which took place in the Paschal Supper after the partaking of the first and also of the second cup,[4] is suggestive of the Eucharistic lavabo.

(*c*) Only red wine was allowed to be used at the Paschal Supper, and it was always mixed with water, just as the mixed chalice has been almost universally used in the Christian Eucharist.

(*d*) Dr. Edersheim quotes a passage from the Mischna,[5] which looks as if the water thus used was warm water—

'If two companies eat [the Passover] in the same house,

[1] *Winchester Troper*, ed. by W. H. Frere (1894), p. 48, being vol. viii. of the publications of the Henry Bradshaw Society.
[2] Martene, *De Antiq. Eccles. Ritibus* (Bassani, 1788), tom. ii. p. 243.
[3] *The Temple*, etc., p. 199; but the word 'Haggadah' has a wider signification. Compare Exod. xiii. 8.
[4] *Ibid.*, pp. 205, 207.   [5] *Pes.* vii. 13.

the one turns its face to one side, the other to the other, and the kettle [warming kettle] stands between them.'[1]

This offers a curious parallel to the infusion of warm water into the chalice at the commixture in the Byzantine rite, for which, however, no very early authority can be produced, nor is the practice known in any other Liturgy, Eastern or Western.[2]

(*e*) The Paschal Supper was preceded by a fast. The evening sacrifice was ordinarily offered at 2.30 p.m. and slain at 3.30 p.m., but on the eve of the Passover these hours were put back to 1.30 p.m. and 2.30 p.m. No food was partaken of from that hour until the Paschal Supper,[3] and that was not commenced until dark. This may have suggested the practice of fasting reception of the Eucharist, which has been observed with rare exceptions from the earliest times.

§ 31. IMPOSITION OF HANDS.—This was not part of the prescribed Levitical ritual, but it was the recognized external sign accompanying benediction, and appointment to office.[4] There had been variation of practice in earlier times, but for some time before our Lord's day the appointment or ordination of a rabbi had come to be made or performed by the laying on of hands, and the presence of three ordained rabbis was required to make such an ordination

---

[1] *The Temple*, etc., p. 204.
[2] II., p. 123; 2nd ed. by F. E. Brightman, pp. 341, 394; but the words 'Irene da calda[m]' are inscribed over a figure in a representation of the agapé in the catacombs (W. E. Scudamore, *Notitia Eucharistica*, 2nd ed., p. 689).
[3] Dr. Edersheim, *The Temple*, etc., p. 203.
[4] Gen. xlviii. 14; Deut. xxxiv. 9.

valid.[1] This is suggestive of the only universally used external sign which has scriptural authority in connection with ordination in the Christian Church, and reminds us of the early Canons which made the presence and co-operation of three bishops necessary not to the validity, but to the regularity of a consecration.[2]

§ 32. HOLY ORDERS.—The conviction that the Christian ministry in its threefold form was evolved out of the ministerial organization of the Jewish Church, found support at an early date. It is suggested by the language of St. Clement of Rome, in a chapter in which he is evidently describing the office and work of the Christian ministry, wherein he says—

'For to the high-priest (τῷ ἀρχιερεῖ) are given certain functions, and to the priests (τοῖς ἱερεῦσιν) their proper place is assigned, and to the Levites (λευίταις) appertain their proper ministries, and the laymen (ὁ λαϊκὸς ἄνθρωπος) are confined within the bounds of what is commanded to laymen.'[3]

Later on St. Jerome said—

'What Aaron, and his sons, and the Levites were in the temple, the same bishops, priests, and deacons are in the Church.'[4]

The comparison is drawn out in still greater detail in the Apostolic Constitutions, where it is said that—

'The Jewish sacrifices are the Christian prayers and

---
[1] Dr. Edersheim, *The Life and Times of Jesus*, 2nd ed. ii. 382.
[2] Apostolic Canons, i.; Apostolic Constitutions, viii. 4, 27, etc.
[3] *Ep.* ad Cor. cap. xl. It has been considered by some to be uncertain whether St. Clement refers here to the Jewish or Christian ministry.
[4] *Ep.* xlvi.; *P. L.*, tom. xxii. col. 1195.

supplications and Eucharist. Jewish firstfruits and tithes, and offerings, and gifts, are the oblations offered by the holy bishops to the Lord God through Jesus Christ, who died for them. For the bishops are your high priests, and the presbyters are your priests, and the deacons of to-day are your Levites, and so on with your readers, and singers, and ostiarii, and with your deaconesses, and widows, and virgins, and orphans; and the bishop, who is above all these, is the high priest.'[1]

In its earliest form, in apostolic times, the threefold ministry of the Christian Church was differently constituted. It consisted of, firstly, Apostles; secondly, presbyters or bishops; thirdly, deacons. These gradations, according to a modern liturgical writer of eminence, had also their Jewish counterparts. The Apostles corresponded to ethnarchs; the presbyters to rulers of the synagogue; the deacons to the ὑπηρεταὶ.[2]

Mons. de Pressensé maintained that the two Christian orders of bishops, or elders, and deacons (the Apostles representing the first order, divinely appointed, and not intended to be perpetuated) were borrowed not from the temple worship, but from the synagogue, which had nothing priestly about it, and the very simple organization of which singularly adapted it to the needs of the new community.[3]

These connections and correspondences may be deemed unproven or even fanciful, but they are

---

[1] Apostolic Constitutions, lib. ii. cap. 25.
[2] Duchesne (L.), *Origines du Culte Chrétien* (Paris, 1889), p. 10.
[3] *Christian Life and Practice in the Early Church* (London, 1877), p. 39.

infinitely more probable than the theory put forward now in certain quarters that the Christian Church borrowed or adapted its ministerial organization from paganism.

§ 33. MARRIAGE.—Some of the ceremonies connected with the Christian marriage service were probably taken over from Judaism, though, as in the case of the ring and of the white dress, they may have prevailed far and wide outside and beyond the Jewish community.

The ring was recognized in the Old Testament, and used as a token of fidelity, and of reception into a family.[1]

The distinctive attire of the bride, including the white dress,[2] if she were not a widow, and the veil,[3] and the crown or chaplet,[4] were also Jewish usages to which reference is made in Holy Scripture. They have all been adopted into Christian marriage ritual; the crown especially in the Greek Church, where both bride and bridegroom are crowned, and where the whole service is known as 'the Service of the Coronation.'[5]

§ 34. PRAYER, HOURS OF.—In connection with Jewish devotion, we find in Holy Scripture references to various hours of prayer both by day and night, *e.g.*—

'And they stood up in their place, and read in the book of the law of the Lord their God, one fourth part of the

---

[1] Gen. xli. 42; St. Luke xv. 22.
[2] Rev. xix. 8.   [3] Gen. xxiv. 65.   [4] Cant. iii. 11.
[5] Ἀκολουθία τοῦ Στεφανώματος, *Euchologion*.

day, and another fourth part they confessed, and worshipped the Lord their God.'[1]

'In the evening, and morning, and at noon-day will I pray, and that instantly: and He shall hear my voice.'[2]

'At midnight I will rise to give thanks unto Thee, because of Thy righteous judgments.'[3]

'Seven times a day do I praise Thee, because of Thy righteous judgments.'[4]

'Arise, cry out in the night: in the beginning of the watches pour out thine heart like water before the face of the Lord.'[5]

'He kneeled upon his knees three times a day, and prayed, and gave thanks before his God, as he did aforetime.'[6]

'For these are not drunken, as ye suppose, seeing it is but the third hour of the day.'[7]

'Now Peter and John went up together into the temple at the hour of prayer, being the ninth hour.'[8]

'Peter went up upon the housetop to pray about the sixth hour.'[9]

There can be little doubt that the sevenfold division of the day services of the Christian Church into Lauds, Prime, Terce, Sext, None, Vespers, and Compline, and the lengthy night services called 'Nocturns' or 'vigiliæ nocturnæ,' owe their existence to the indications of Jewish customs contained in the

---

[1] Neh. ix. 3. The Vulgate text runs, 'Et consurrexerunt ad standum; et legerunt in volumine legis Domini Dei sui, quater in die, et quater confitebantur, et adorabant Dominum Deum suum (II. Lib. Esdræ ix. 3).

[2] Ps. lv. 18.   [3] Ps. cxix. 62.   [4] Ps. cxix. 164.

[5] Lam. ii. 19. 'Consurge, lauda in nocte in principio vigiliarum,' etc. (Vulgate).

[6] Dan. vi. 10.   [7] Acts ii. 15.   [8] Acts iii. 1. See also x. 3.

[9] Acts x. 9.

above verses. We do not mean that the arrangement was taken over at once from the Jewish temple, because we do not know that such a multiform arrangement of services ever existed there; but, that when, in the course of centuries, the Christian scheme of services was developed, it was very largely influenced by scriptural, that is, by Jewish, considerations.

§ 35. PRAYER, ATTITUDE AT.—The ordinary attitude in prayer among the Jews was standing,[1] though kneeling and prostration were also practised. We have described at length early Christian practice in this matter,[2] which, deliberately or otherwise, followed very closely upon Jewish precedent.

§ 36. PRAYER FOR THE DEAD.—There is no plain direction to pray for the departed either in the Old or the New Testament, nor is there any instance of such a prayer, if we except St. Paul's pious aspiration with regard to the probably deceased Onesiphorus—

'The Lord grant unto him that he may find mercy of the Lord in that day.'[3]

But there can be no doubt that such prayer was in use among the Jews before the time that our Lord was upon earth. A statement with reference to Judas Maccabæus, in the Second Book of Maccabees, puts this fact beyond all question—

'For if he had not hoped that they that were slain should have risen again, it had been superfluous and vain to pray for the dead.'

[1] Deut. x. 8; Neh. ix. 2-4; St. Matt. vi. 5.
[2] Chap. ii. § 17, p. 141.
[3] 2 Tim. i. 18.

And also in that he perceived that there was great favour laid up for those that died godly, it was an holy and good thought. Whereupon he made a reconciliation for the dead, that they might be delivered from sin.'[1]

Accordingly we are not surprised to find that the following prayer has formed part of the Jewish Liturgy. It was said in some congregations on each sabbath morning, in others on certain of the highest festivals, in others only on the Day of Atonement. We have not been able to ascertain the date of its composition, nor whether it existed in the time of our Lord. Neither this prayer, nor any other form of prayer for the dead, is found in the *Authorized Daily Prayer-book of the United Hebrew Congregations of the British Empire* (London, 1892).

A Prayer.

' May God remember the souls of my father and mother, my grandfather and grandmother, my uncles and aunts, my brothers and sisters, my relatives on the father's and mother's side, who have passed into their eternity. For the sake of the alms which I commend for them, may their souls be included in the bundle of life with the souls of Abraham, Isaac, and Jacob, Sarah, Rebecca, Rachel, Leah, and the other righteous men and women in Paradise; and let us say, Amen.'[2]

The evidence of early Jewish tombstones is in favour of the custom of prayer for the dead, but the date of these mortuary inscriptions has not been

---

[1] 2 Macc. xii. 44, 45.
[2] Bickell (G.), *Messe und Pascha* (Mainz, 1872), p. 69; Luckock (H. M.), *After Death*, 8th ed. (London, 1890), p. 58.

ascertained with sufficient certainty for any conclusive argument to be based upon them.[1]

We have already produced evidence as to the widespread practice of prayer for the departed in the early Christian Church.[2] In the silence of Holy Scripture on the subject, one naturally asks, 'Whence was the practice derived?' It may be a deep-seated instinct or craving in our spiritual and intellectual nature finding outward expression for itself in formal prayer. But, more probably, the practice was taken over from the Jewish Church, a transfer made more easy by the absence of any condemnation of it, on the part of our Lord or His Apostles, in the pages of the New Testament.

On the other hand, in the absence of certain proofs that prayer for the dead formed part of the Jewish Liturgy in our Lord's time, some modern writers have held that it was a later importation from Christianity into Judaism.[3] But, considering the conservatism of the Jews, and their hostility to the Christian Church, this seems to be improbable. M. Israel Lévi is conscious of this difficulty, but does not do much to meet it.[4]

§ 37. VESTMENTS.—We have seen that there is little proof of the existence of any distinctive dress of the Christian clergy during the first three centuries.[5] The first reference to a vestment is in the

---

[1] Luckock, *ut supra*, pp. 61–64.   [2] Chap. ii. § 17, p. 146.
[3] Article by M. Israel Lévi, *The Revue des Études Juives*, July-Sept. (Paris, 1894), tom. xxix. pp. 43–60.
[4] *Ibid.*, p. 59.   [5] Chap. ii. § 20.

Canons of Hippolytus (p. 163). The next is early in the fourth century, when the emperor Constantine gave to Macarius, Bishop of Jerusalem, a rich vestment embroidered in gold, to wear when administering baptism.[1] After that time varied and splendid vestments began to be worn by officiating clergy—bishops, priests, and deacons, having each their distinctive dress—and the common theory of the mediæval ritualists, in which they are largely followed by writers of the present day, is that these vestments were copied from those of the Levitical priesthood ; *e.g.* Rabanus Maurus, in the ninth century, asserts this of vestments in general, and of the amice, or superhumeral, in particular.[2] Durandus, writing in the thirteenth century, makes the same assertion, but in qualified terms, as to vestments generally.[3] The Levitical theory is incorporated in a rubric of a ninth-century Service Book of English Use, which runs thus—

'Incipiunt orationes ad vestimenta sacerdotalia seu levitica.'[4]

The Chasuble and Rationale are both described as of Jewish origin in a letter attributed to S. Germanus Parisiensis (A.D. 555–576), but probably of somewhat later date.[5]

---

[1] Theodoret, *Hist. Eccles.*, lib. ii. cap. 23 ; *P. G.*, tom. lxxxii. col. 1065.
[2] *De Institutione Clericorum*, lib. i. capp. 14, 15.
[3] *Rationale Divinorum Officiorum*, lib. iii. cap. 1, § 2.
[4] *Liber Pontificalis Gemmeticensis*, MS. 362 in the public library at Rouen, as quoted by Martene, *De Antiq. Eccles. Ritibus*, lib. ii. cap. x. ordo. iii. (ed. 1788), p. 252.
[5] *Ep.* ii. ; *P. L.*, tom. lxxii. col. 97.

Bishop Young, writing in the present day, says—

'If any one will compare the engravings of the vestments of the Jewish high priest, priest, and levite, as given by Calmet, with those now in use by the bishops, priests, and deacons of the Oriental Church, he will be struck with the resemblance between them, and the presumptive proof which the comparison affords that the latter were derived from the former.'[1]

But can this theory as to the origin of vestments be true? We think not; because considering the state of alienation and antipathy, which existed between Jews and Christians during the early and middle ages, it is an unlikely, though not an impossible, supposition that the latter should have directly borrowed their ministerial dress from the former; and there is a simpler theory of the origin of vestments, which has philological support, viz. that the Christian ministerial dress is a survival of the ordinary lay dress of the opening centuries of the Christian era. We repeat[2] that there is slight trace of special dress in use before the reign of Constantine; then if we examine the names which the clerical vestments now bear, and have borne from the first, we find that they denote ordinary articles of lay attire once in everyday use. Such names are—

Alba, the white undergarment, tunic, or shirt.

Capa, the cope, a late Latin word, denoting an article of dress corresponding to the toga, the ordinary outer garment of a Roman citizen. Another name for the

---

[1] Young (J. F.), *Papers on Liturgical Enrichment* (New York, 1883), p. 17.

[2] Chap. ii. § 21, p. 162.

cope was 'pluviale,' literally, that which protects a man's body from the rain.

Casula, the chasuble, a little hut, covering the whole body, corresponding to the 'pænula,' an outer garment or cloak.

Cingulum, the cincture or girdle with which the tunic was fastened.

Manipulus, the maniple, literally a handful, *i.e.* the handkerchief in the hand.

Stola, the stole. This word did not come into use to designate an article of ecclesiastical dress till the ninth century, and it probably has no connection with the classical stola. The earlier name for stole was 'orarium' or handkerchief.

A somewhat similar process has been going on in England, in another department of clerical dress, in recent times. The levée dress, in which clergy have to appear at court in 1897, including buckle-shoes, silk stockings, knee-breeches, and three-cornered hat, is the everyday dress of the clergy of two centuries ago, petrified for a particular purpose, and perpetuated in state ceremonial.

§ 38. JEWISH ORIGIN OF CHRISTIAN FORMULÆ OF DEVOTION.—It may be asked, Have any portions of Jewish liturgical language been transferred into the services of the Christian Church? and if so, to what extent? It is not easy to give a complete answer to these questions, but the answer must undoubtedly be, To a considerable extent. It is no matter of surprise that such a borrowing should have taken place in the case of New Testament Canticles, which were the devout outpourings of the minds of persons familiar with the devotions of the Jewish

Temple and synagogues from their childhood; but similarity of thought and language extends and is found beyond them, as may be seen by aid of the following parallel tables:—

St. Luke i.	*Magnificat.*	*The Eighteen Benedictions.*
49	He that is mighty hath done to me great things.	2. Thou art mighty, O Lord, world without end. . . . Who is like unto thee, Lord of might?
51	He hath scattered the proud in the imagination of their hearts.	12. Let the proud speedily be uprooted, broken, crushed and humbled speedily in our days. Blessed art Thou, O Lord, who breakest down the enemy, and humblest the proud.
52	He hath put down the mighty from their seats, and exalted them of low degree.	
54	He hath holpen His servant Israel, in remembrance of His mercy;	1. Blessed art Thou who rememberest the pious deeds of our fathers, and sendest the Redeemer to their children's children. Blessed art Thou, O Lord, the Shield of Abraham.
55	As He spake to our fathers, to Abraham, and to his seed for ever.	
	Benedictus.	*The Eighteen Benedictions.*
68	Blessed be the Lord God of Israel; for He hath visited and redeemed His people.	1. Blessed art Thou, O Lord our God, the God of our fathers Abraham, Isaac, and Jacob, who rememberest . . . and sendest the Redeemer to their children's children.
69	And hath raised up an horn of salvation for us in the house of His servant David.	14*b*. The branch of David Thy servant speedily cause to flourish, and exalt his horn with Thy help. . . . Blessed art Thou, O Lord, who causest to flourish the horn of David.
71	That we should be saved from our enemies, and from the hand of all that hate us;	See St. Luke i. 51, 52; Ben. 12.
72	To perform the mercy promised to our fathers and to remember His holy covenant;	See St. Luke i. 54; Ben. 1.
73	The oath which he sware to our father Abraham,	

St. Luke i.		
77	To give knowledge of salvation unto His people	4. Thou mercifully bestowest knowledge upon men, and teachest the mortal prudence. Mercifully bestow upon us from Thyself, knowledge, wisdom, and understanding.
	by the remission of their sins,	6. Our Father, forgive us, for we have sinned; our King, pardon us, for we have transgressed, for Thou art forgiving and pardoning.
78	Through the tender mercy of our God.	13. On us bestow, O Lord our God, Thy mercy. 18. Bestow . . . mercy, compassion upon us, and upon the whole of Israel Thy people.
79	To give light to them that sit in darkness and in the shadow of death, to guide our feet into the way of peace.	18. Bless us all unitedly with the light of Thy countenance; for in the light of Thy countenance didst Thou give to us the law of life, etc. May it please Thee to bless Thy people Israel at all times and in every moment with peace. Blessed art Thou, O Lord, who blessest Thy people Israel with peace.[1]
St. Luke ii.		
	Gloria in Excelsis.	*The Kadish.*
14	Glory to God in the highest, and on earth peace, good will toward men.	Blessed and praised, celebrated and exalted, . . . may perfect peace descend from heaven, and life upon us and all Israel.[2]
	Nunc Dimittis.	*The Eighteen Benedictions.*
29	Lord, now lettest Thou Thy servant depart in peace;	2. Thou loosest the chained, and shewest Thy faithfulness to those that sleep in the dust.
30	For mine eyes have seen Thy salvation.	16. May our eyes see Thee return to Israel in love. Blessed art Thou, O Lord, who restorest Thy Shechinah to Zion.[3]

[1] The contents of these parallel columns are borrowed largely from F. H. Chase, *The Lord's Prayer in the Early Church* (Cambridge, 1891), pp. 147-149.
[2] Page 214.　　　[3] Pages 211, 213.

The Lord's Prayer.	The Kedusha.
Hallowed be Thy Name.	Hallowed be Thy Name on earth, as it is hallowed in heaven above.[1]
The Triumphal Hymn.	*The Kedusha.*
Holy, holy, holy, Lord of Sabaoth; heaven and earth are full of His glory. Blessed be He for ever. Amen.[2]	Holy, holy, holy is the Lord God of Sabaoth; the whole earth is filled with His glory.[3]
The Eucharistic Preface.	*At the Paschal Supper.*
It is verily meet and right, holy and becoming, and advantageous, to our souls, Jehovah, Lord God, Father Almighty, to worship Thee, to hymn Thee, to give thanks to Thee, to return Thee praise, etc.[4]	Therefore it is our bounden duty to thank, praise, exalt, glorify, praise, and celebrate Him, etc.[5]

The 'Kyrie Eleyson,' preserved in its Greek form in Latin Liturgies, was probably in its origin a Greek-Jewish liturgical formula, derived from such Old Testament passages as the following:—Κύριε, ἐλέησον ἡμᾶς ;[6] Ἐλέησον ἡμᾶς, Κύριε, ἐλέησον ἡμᾶς ;[7] Ἐλέησον με, Κύριε.[8]

There is a curious addition to the text of 'Gloria in Excelsis' in several ancient Irish versions, consisting of the words 'et omnes dicimus Amen' ('and we all say, Amen'). It has also been found in the Armenian version of the Vespers evening hymn, 'Hail, gladdening light,' etc. There can be little doubt that this is an importation of the phrase וְנֹאמַר אָמֵן (= 'and say we, Amen') which occurs so

---

[1] Page 215. [2] From the Clementine Liturgy, p. 297.
[3] Page 215. [4] From the Liturgy of St. Mark.
[5] Page 216. [6] Isa. xxxiii. 2.
[7] Ps. cxxxii. 3. [8] Ps. vi. 3.

frequently in the Kadish and in other parts of the Jewish Morning Service.[1]

For a list of Hebrew words surviving in use in the Christian Liturgy, see § 29, p. 230.

Dr. J. F. Young, Bishop of Florida, has printed in parallel columns portions of the Jewish Sabbath Morning Service and of the Greek Liturgy of St. Basil; and also the Jewish supplications used during the Ten Days of Penitence (the Sabbath excepted) at the morning service and the Greek Ektene. In each case there is a general resemblance, but that resemblance seems to be too vague to justify the conclusion that the Christian formula of devotion has been borrowed from the Jewish, or that there is any direct connection between them.[2]

The Rev. J. E. Field has written many pages to prove the Jewish origin of the Christian Liturgy, but his proof of such origin is made up mainly of slender coincidences of diction or similarities of subject-matter, in the case of single sentences or even of single words, and does not carry conviction.[3]

§ 39. GOSPEL FOR THE TENTH SUNDAY AFTER TRINITY.—The selection of the passage from St. Luke xix. 41–48, in which our Lord's prophecy of the destruction of Jerusalem occurs, as the Gospel for the Tenth Sunday after Trinity is said to have been

[1] The author is indebted to the Rev. Duncan MacGregor for this suggestion. See *Antiphonary of Bangor*, Part ii. (London, 1895), pp. 75-77, and p. 257 of this book.
[2] *Papers on Liturgical Enrichment* (New York, 1883), p. 17.
[3] *The Apostolic Liturgy and the Epistle to the Hebrews* (London, 1882), Appendix v. p. 622.

determined by its near coincidence with one of the days of prayer and fasting (the ninth of Ab), on which the Jews bewail the fall of their capital and the destruction of the temple.[1]

A review of the facts accumulated in this chapter will, we think, bring most readers to the conclusion that on some points there has been deliberate imitation of Jewish usage on the part of the Christian Church; while on other points an unintentional resemblance exists, a resemblance based on an instinct of reverence, which, whether in the Jewish or the Christian, or indeed in any non-Jewish and non-Christian religion, would naturally show itself in the same or in a similar way.

§ 40. HEATHEN WORSHIP SUGGESTED AS THE SOURCE OF CHRISTIAN RITUAL.—In connection with the subject-matter of this chapter, it is desirable to mention the fact that a totally different theory of the origin and development of Christian ritual, and of the growth of Christian terminology in connection with the sacramental ordinances of the Church, has been recently put forward both in this country and abroad. Take up the *Hibbert Lectures* for 1888. Their author, Dr. Hatch, selects for his title, *The Influence of Greek Ideas and Usages upon the Christian Church.* In chapter x. he maintains that

---

[1] Kingsbury (T. L.), *The Holy Tears of Jesus* (London, 1892), p. 12. This passage forms the Gospel for the Eleventh Sunday after Pentecost in the Leofric Missal, and for the Ninth Sunday after Pentecost in the present Roman use.

the sacramental ritual and terms of the Christian Church, as developed from the second to the fifth centuries of the Christian era, were borrowed from the Eleusinian mysteries. He dwells especially upon—

(*a*) Eleusinian baptism, with its various titles, with the preparation of its recipients, and the ritual of its administration.

(*b*) The processions with lights.

(*c*) The offerings of worshippers laid upon a holy table.

(*d*) The common or communion feast which followed.

(*e*) The secrecy, resembling that of Freemasons, with which the Eleusinian rites were conducted.

(*f*) The exclusion of the unworthy from initiation into and participation in the mysteries.

(*g*) The formula or password only told to the initiated.

(*h*) The mystic crown worn by them.

These and other Eleusinian observances are compared to the ritual, nomenclature, and practices of the Christian Church as commencing to be developed directly after the Apostolic age, and as fully developed in the fifth and sixth centuries; and the latter are concluded to be derived from the former.

We cannot do justice to Dr. Hatch's argument in a short summary. It is thoughtfully worked out, and finished with the following eloquent passage :—

'In the splendid ceremonial of Eastern and Western worship, in the blaze of lights, in the separation of the central point of the rite from common view, in the procession of torch-bearers, chanting their sacred hymns, there is the survival, and in some cases the galvanized survival, of what I cannot find it in my heart to call a pagan ceremonial; because though it was the expression of a less enlightened faith, yet it was offered to God from a heart that was not less earnest in its search after God, and in its effort after holiness, than our own.'[1]

Although a *primâ facie* case is made out by Dr. Hatch in a·chapter which deserves to be read through carefully by every person interested in the subject, yet we are convinced that on further consideration the whole theory will break down on the following grounds:—

1. It seems to be a moral impossibility that a religion like Christianity, the *raison d'être* of which was a protest against heathen theology and heathen morality, which threw unmeasured ridicule and contempt upon the heathen gods, especially in the pages of its earlier apologists, Aristides, Minucius Felix, etc., should have borrowed its ritual practices and terminology from a heathen source. This remark applies to the Church in the ante-Nicene period. No doubt in later days, when Christianity came more widely in contact with heathenism, and when heathenism had lost the power, if not the will, to persecute, there may have been some adaptation of heathen ritual observances.[2]

---

[1] Hatch (E.), *Hibbert Lectures* for 1888. The theory of an Eleusinian origin of the Eucharist is persuasively and ingeniously supported by Dr. P. Gardner, *The Origin of the Lord's Supper* (London, 1893).

[2] As has been shown by Mr. Bass Mullinger, in his article on

2. The cause why the earliest Christian rites were performed with secrecy, both as to manner and time and place, was the danger of persecution and martyrdom which always attended or was liable to attend the profession and practice of Christianity until it became a *religio licita*. This characteristic of secrecy lingered on as against the heathen and catechumens long after the dangers in which it originated had passed away.

3. Such words as φωτίζειν, φωτισμός, σφραγίζειν, σφραγίς, μυεῖσθαι, μυστήριον, are derived directly from the New Testament, and not from the Eleusinian mysteries. It is not necessary here to discuss the further question, Whence did the writers of the New Testament, especially St. Paul, derive the use of the words?

The similarity between certain parts of the ritual and liturgical language of heathenism and both Judaism and Christianity, was noticed long ago by a famous Christian thinker and writer, who offered a far more probable explanation of it than the Hibbert Lecturer, viz. that the false religion is an imitation of the true, and not *vice versâ*.

Tertullian said—

'The question will arise, By whom is the sense of the passages which make for heresies interpreted? By the devil, of course, to whom pertain those wiles which pervert the truth, and who, by the mystic rites of his idols, vies even with the essential portions of the Divine sacraments. He

---

'Paganism' in Smith and Cheetham's *Dictionary of Christian Antiquities*.

too baptizes some, that is, his own believers and faithful followers; he promises the putting away of sin by a laver; and, if my memory still serves me, their Mithra sets his mark on the foreheads of his soldiers; he celebrates also an oblation of bread, and introduces an image of a resurrection, and beneath a sword wreathes a crown. What must we also say of the fact that he limits his high priest to a single marriage, and that he has his virgins and his votaries professing continence. But if we consider the superstitions of Numa Pompilius, his priestly offices, badges, and privileges, his sacrificial services, and the instruments and vessels of the sacrifices themselves, and the curious rites of his expiations and vows, shall we not clearly see that the devil imitated the well-known moroseness of the Jewish law? Satan, therefore, who showed such great eagerness to express in the rites of idolatry those very things of which the administration of Christ's sacraments consists, possessing still the same genius, set his heart upon and succeeded in adapting to his profane and rival creed the very instruments of Divine things and of the Christian saints, his interpretation from their interpretations, his words from their words, his parables from their parables,' etc.[1]

A theory of the heathen origin of Christian vestments has been sometimes put forward, e.g. by a recent writer, who says—

'The mitre is the head-dress of the Persian priests, and of the Mithra worshippers of Commagene, on statues of the early Roman period. This is by no means the only instance in which Pagan vestments came to be used by Christian priests. The scarlet robes of the flamens were adopted by cardinals; the alb was an Egyptian sacred dress; the dalmatic, a short-sleeved skirt, was worn by

---

[1] *Liber de Præscriptionibus Adversus Hæreticos*, cap. xl.; *P. L.*, tom. ii. col. 54.

Commodus and by Elagabalus, the emperor who was priest of the Sun-God, symbolized by the black stone brought from Emesa in Syria to Rome. The practice of kissing the foot of an emperor was introduced by Caligula from Persia.'[1]

There is no proof offered for these statements except in the case of a supposed etymological connection between 'Mithras' and 'Mitre.' They are extremely improbable. It would not be more fanciful to connect the scarlet robes of the flamens with the academic full dress of Doctors of Divinity.

The Puritans at the time of the Reformation denounced the surplice as heathenish, as well as popish. It was described not only as 'the white linen garment that the Mass-priest wears in the popish religion,' but also as 'the mark of the *linigeri calvi* of Isis,' as 'a kind of garment used by the priests of Isis' and as 'the costume of the priests of Baal.'[2]

The threefold constitution of the Christian ministry has been referred to a heathen origin in recent times by many distinguished writers, including Hatch in England,[3] and Harnack in Germany;[4] but the *à priori*

---

[1] *Edinburgh Review*, Jan. 1895, p. 225.
[2] For authorities, see note in Mullinger (J. B.), *History of the University of Cambridge*, ii. 195.
[3] *The Organization of the Early Christian Churches*, Bampton Lectures (London, 1888), 3rd ed.
[4] *Ibid.*, translated, with introduction and appendices, by Adolf Harnack, Giessen, 1883. Renan holds a similar view of the evolution and development of the Christian ministry, but he does not trace the borrowing process from the civil organization and surroundings of heathen society (*L'Église Chrétienne* (Paris, 1879), chap. vi.).

improbability of early Christianity condescending to borrow from the heathenism which it denounced, and by which it was persecuted, applies to this as well as to all other cases of alleged or supposed borrowing, apart from difficulties which may arise peculiar to the particular loan or debt under consideration.

APPENDIX.

FROM THE APOSTOLIC CONSTITUTIONS.

§ 1. Gloria in Excelsis—§ 2. Triumphal Hymn—§ 3. A Widow's Thanksgiving—§ 4. A Eucharistic Thanksgiving—§ 5. A Post-Communion Thanksgiving—§ 6. A Thanksgiving for the Holy Oil—§ 7. A General Prayer—§ 8. Baptismal Formula of Renunciation—§ 9. Baptismal Creed—§ 10. Consecration of the Water at Baptism—§ 11. Consecration of the Oil at Baptism—§ 12. A post-Baptismal Prayer—§ 13. A Prayer at the Consecration of a Bishop—§ 14. The Clementine Liturgy—§ 15. Another Description of the Liturgy—§ 16. A Prayer at the Ordination of a Presbyter—§ 17. A Prayer at the Ordination of a Deacon—§ 18. A Prayer at the Ordination of a Deaconess—§ 19. A Prayer at the Ordination of a Sub-Deacon—§ 20. A Prayer at the Ordination of a Reader—§ 21. A Consecration of Water and Oil—§ 22. An Evening Prayer—§ 23. A Morning Prayer—§ 24. A Thanksgiving at the Presentation of the Firstfruits—§ 25. A Prayer for the Faithful Departed.

IN this appendix we place before the reader the devotional formulæ—anthems, prayers, etc., including the so-called Clementine Liturgy—which are contained in the compilation known as the Apostolic Constitutions. As that compilation dates from the second half of the fourth century, we have not ventured to include any of its contents in Chapter iii., unless known to us through earlier writings, although much of the following devotional material may be, and much of it no doubt is, ante-Nicene.

§ 1. GLORIA IN EXCELSIS.

The following is a very ancient hymn of unknown authorship. The two earliest forms in which it is known to us occur in the seventh book of the Apostolic Constitutions, and in the Codex Alexandrinus of the Bible, now in the British Museum. In the latter it is labelled 'A Morning Hymn.' In the former the context would imply its use at eventide; but the one MS. which gives it any title describes it as 'A Morning Hymn.' In the *Antiphonary of Bangor*, a seventh-century Irish service-book, it is headed, 'For the Evening and for the Morning,' or as we might say, 'At Vespers and Matins'; for its connection was with the Divine office. The Eucharistic use of it, now prevalent in Western Christendom, is of later origin.

We give in parallel columns translations of the three earliest texts of 'Gloria in Excelsis,' to which reference has been made, together with the anthems or other devotional formulæ appended to them.

Further information about the origin, growth, and use of this hymn will be found in Julian's *Dictionary of Hymnology* (London, 1892), pp. 425, 459; Smith and Cheetham's *Dictionary of Christian Antiquities* (London, 1875), vol. i. p. 736.

GLORIA IN EXCELSIS.

I. Apostolic Constitutions (lib. vii. caps. 47-49. pp. 187, 188. 4th century).	II. Codex Alexandrinus (fol. 569, 2nd col. 5th century).	III. Antiphonary of Bangor (fol. 33r. 7th century).
Glory to God in the highest, and on earth peace, goodwill among men. We praise Thee, we hymn Thee, we bless Thee, we glorify Thee,	Glory to God in the highest, and on earth peace, goodwill among men. We praise Thee, we bless Thee, we worship Thee, we glorify Thee,	Glory to God in the highest, and on earth peace to men of good will. We praise Thee, we bless Thee, we worship Thee, we glorify Thee, we magnify Thee, we give thanks to Thee,
we worship Thee, through the great High Priest, Thee the one unbegotten God, alone, unapproachable through Thy great glory. O Lord, heavenly King, God the Father Almighty.	we give thanks to Thee for Thy great glory. O Lord, heavenly King, God the Father Almighty. O Lord, the only-begotten Son, Jesus Christ, and Holy Spirit,	for Thy great pity. O Lord, heavenly King, God the Father Almighty. O Lord, the only-begotten Son, Jesus Christ, Holy Spirit of God, and we all say, Amen. O Lord, Son of God the Father, Lamb of God,
O Lord God, the Father of Christ, the spotless Lamb,	O Lord God, Lamb of God, Son of the Father,	

GLORIA IN EXCELSIS—continued.

I.—Apostolic Constitutions.	II.—Codex Alexandrinus.	III.—Antiphonary of Bangor.
which taketh away the sin of the world,	that takest away the sins of the world, have mercy upon us. Thou that takest away the sins of the world, have mercy upon us.[4]	that takest away the sin of the world, have mercy upon us.
receive our prayer. Thou that sittest upon the Cherubim,	Receive our prayer. Thou that sittest at the right hand of the Father,	Receive our prayer. Thou that sittest at the right hand of God the Father,
[have mercy upon us.] For Thou only art holy, Thou only art the Lord, Jesus Christ;	have mercy upon us. For Thou only art holy, Thou only art the Lord, Jesus Christ,	have mercy upon us. For Thou only art holy, Thou only art the Lord. Thou only art glorious, with the Holy Ghost,
of the God of all created nature, our King, through whom be glory, honour, and worship to Thee. Praise the Lord, ye servants, O praise the name of the Lord.[1] We praise Thee, we hymn Thee, we bless Thee, for Thy great glory, O Lord, King, Father of Christ, the spotless Lamb, which taketh away the sin of the world. It becometh us to praise Thee, it becometh us to hymn Thee, it becometh us to glorify Thee,	to the glory of God the Father. Every day will I bless Thee, and praise thy name for ever, and for ever and ever.[5] Vouchsafe, O Lord, this day also, that we be kept without sin.[6] Blessed art Thou, O Lord God of our fathers, and praised and glorified be Thy name for ever.[7] Amen. Blessed art Thou, O Lord; teach me Thy statutes.[8] Blessed art Thou, O Lord; teach me Thy statutes.[8]	in the glory of God the Father. Amen. Every day we bless Thee, and praise Thy name for ever, and for ever and ever.[5] Amen. Vouchsafe, O Lord, to keep us this day without sin.[6] Blessed art Thou, O Lord God of our fathers, and praised and glorified be Thy name for ever.[7] Amen. Have mercy upon us, O Lord, have mercy upon us.[14] Hearken unto my words, O Lord; hear my cry; incline unto the voice

God and Father, through Thy Son, in the all-holy Spirit, for ever and ever. Amen.

Lord, now lettest Thou Thy servant depart in peace, according to Thy word. For mine eyes have seen Thy salvation, which Thou hast prepared before the face of all people,

A light to lighten the Gentiles, and the glory of Thy people Israel.[2]

Blessed art Thou, O Lord, that nourishest me from my youth up, and givest food to all flesh.[3]

Fill our hearts with joy and gladness, that having always all sufficiency, we may abound unto every good work in Christ Jesus our Lord; through whom glory, honour, and power be unto Thee for ever. Amen.

Blessed art Thou, O Lord; teach me Thy statutes.[8]

Lord, Thou hast been our refuge from generation to generation.[9]

I said, Lord, have mercy upon me; heal my soul, for I have sinned against Thee.[10]

Lord, I have fled unto Thee for refuge; teach me to do Thy will, for Thou art my God.[11]

For with Thee is the well of life; and in Thy light shall we see light.[12]

Continue forth Thy loving-kindness unto them that know Thee.[13]

of my prayer, my King and my God.[15]

In the morning also shalt Thou hear my prayer.[16]

In the morning shall my prayer come before Thee, O Lord.[17]

Day and night, hourly and momently, have mercy upon us, O Lord.[18]

By the prayers and merits of Thy saints have mercy on us, O Lord.[18]

[By the prayers and merits] of angels, archangels, patriarchs, prophets, have mercy on us, O Lord.[18]

[By the prayers and merits] of apostles, martyrs, and confessors, and of the whole hierarchy of the saints, have mercy [on us, O Lord].[18]

Glory and honour to the Father, and to the Son, and to the Holy Ghost, both now, and ever, and for endless ages. Amen.[19]

---

[1] Ps. cxiii. 1.   [2] St. Luke ii. 29-32.   [3] Is. cxxxvi. 25.
[4] The repetition of this clause also occurs in the present Anglican version of this hymn, but not in the usual Latin versions. It has never been ascertained on what authority, or for what reason, the compilers of the Book of Common Prayer made the change in the text. It is interesting to see that they have the authority of the Codex Alexandrinus for it, though that MS. can hardly have been known to them.
[5] Ps. cxlv. 2.   [6] *Te Deum*, ver. 26.   [7] Tobit viii. 5, or Song of the Three Children, 29, 30.   [8] Ps. cxix. 12.
[9] Ps. xc. 1.   [10] Ps. xli. 4.   [11] Ps. cxliii. 9, 10.   [12] Ps. xxxvi. 9.   [13] Ps. xxxvi. 10.
[14] Ps. cxxiii. 3.   [15] Ps. v. 1, 2.   [16] Ps. v. 3.   [17] Ps. lxxxviii. 13.   [18] Origin unknown.
[19] The Mozarabic form of *Gloria Patri*. For further notes, see *Antiphonary of Bangor*, pt. ii., in vol. x. of the Henry Bradshaw Society Publications, p. 75.

§ 2. Triumphal Hymn.

The 'Triumphal Hymn,' or 'Tersanctus,' or 'Sanctus,' is a constituent portion of all Liturgies. From its being found in the Apostolic Constitutions, where it forms part of the Clementine Liturgy, we know that it is as old as the fourth century. It is probably older still, perhaps almost as ancient as Christianity. It will be found printed on p. 297 in a shape nearly resembling that in our present English Liturgy. It must be distinguished from the 'Trisagion,' which occurs in most Eastern Liturgies, but in a different position, and which is also found among the Reproaches on Good Friday in the Roman Missal. Its words are—

'Holy God, holy and mighty, holy and immortal, have mercy upon us.'

This Trisagion is not found in the Clementine Liturgy, and the date of its composition is unknown.

The following formulæ of devotion are also contained in the Apostolic Constitutions:—

§ 3. A Widow's Thanksgiving.

'Blessed art Thou, O God, who hast refreshed my fellow widow. Bless, O Lord, and glorify him that ministered unto her, and let his good work ascend in truth before Thee, and remember him for good in the day of his visitation. Add glory to my bishop who hath well fulfilled his ministry before Thee, and hath directed a seasonable alms to be given to my fellow widow in her destitution; grant unto him a crown of rejoicing in the day of the revelation of Thy visitation.'[1]

[1] Lib. iii. cap. 13, p. 102.

§ 4. A Eucharistic Thanksgiving.

'We thank Thee, O our Father, for that life which Thou hast made known to us, through Thy Son Jesus, through whom also Thou makest all things, and takest thought for the whole world; whom too Thou didst send to become man for our salvation, and didst permit Him to suffer and to die, whom Thou didst also raise up and wast pleased to glorify, and hast seated Him on Thy right hand, through whom also Thou hast promised unto us the resurrection of the dead. Do Thou, O Lord Almighty, eternal God, as this grain was once scattered, and afterwards gathered together so as to form one loaf, so gather Thy Church together from the ends of the earth into Thy kingdom. Furthermore, we thank Thee, O our Father, for the precious blood of Jesus Christ which was shed for us, and for His precious body whereof we celebrate the antitype, He Himself having commanded us to show forth His death; for through Him glory is to be given to Thee for ever. Amen.'[1]

§ 5. A Post-Communion Thanksgiving.

'We give thanks to Thee, O God and Father of Jesus our Saviour, for that holy thing which Thou hast made, to tabernacle within us, and for the knowledge, and faith, and love, and immortality, which Thou hast given to us through Thy Son Jesus. Thou, O Almighty God, the God of the universe, didst create the world, and the things which are therein, through Him, and didst implant a law in our souls, and didst prepare things beforehand for their reception by men. O God of our holy and blameless fathers, Abraham, Isaac, and Jacob, Thy faithful servants, Thou art powerful, and faithful, and true, and without deceit

---

[1] Lib. vii. cap. 25. A shorter form of this prayer is given in the *Didaché* (see p. 173). Its use, as here expanded, is necessarily Eucharistic.

in Thy promises. Thou didst send upon earth Jesus, Thy Christ, to converse among men as man, and to take away error by the roots, being Himself both God the Word and man. Do Thou, even now, through Him, remember this holy Church, which Thou hast purchased with the precious blood of Thy Christ, and deliver it from all evil, and perfect it in Thy love and Thy truth, and gather us all together into Thy kingdom which Thou hast prepared. Maranatha. Hosanna to the Son of David; blessed is He that cometh in the Name of the Lord. God is the Lord who was manifested to us in the flesh. "If any one be holy, let him approach; if any one be not holy, let him become so by repentance." Permit also to your presbyters to offer thanksgiving.'[1]

§ 6. A Thanksgiving for the Holy Oil.[2]

'We give thanks to Thee, O Lord, the Creator of all things, both for the fragrancy of the oil, and for the immortality which Thou hast made known unto us through Thy Son Jesus.'[3]

§ 7. A General Prayer.

It is plain from chap. xxx. that it was intended for Sunday use, and it is probable, from expressions in the prayer itself, that it was intended to be used on the sabbath, or seventh day of the week.

Chap. xxx. is short, and is worthy of being given in full—

'On the day of the resurrection of the Lord, which we call the Lord's day, assemble yourselves together, unintermittingly giving thanks to God, and confessing the benefits

---

[1] Lib. vii. cap. 26, p. 170. This is an enlargement and an alteration of the form of prayer, and of the directions contained in the *Didaché*, cap. x. (see p. 173). Some of the alterations are of much interest, and betoken a later date.

[2] Μύρον.   [3] Lib. vii. cap. 27, p. 171.

which God hath conferred upon us through Christ, having delivered us from ignorance, from error, and from bondage, so that your sacrifice may be unblamable and acceptable to God, who has said concerning His ecumenical Church, " In every place shall incense be offered unto Me and a pure offering ; for I am a great King, saith the Lord Almighty, and My Name is dreadful among the heathen."' [1]

Then after two chapters devoted to the characteristics of true bishops, presbyters, and deacons, and of those false prophets who will arise in the latter days, the following lengthy form of prayer is provided for general use in chapters xxxiii.-xxxviii. :—

[CAP. XXXIII.] ' O our eternal Saviour, King of gods, who alone art Almighty and Lord, the God of all things that exist, the God of our holy and blameless fathers, and of those that were before us, the God of Abraham, Isaac, and Jacob, who art merciful and compassionate, long-suffering and of great pity, to whom all hearts are open and all secret desires are known, the souls of the righteous call upon Thee, and the hopes of holy men are fixed on Thee, Thou Father of the blameless, who hearest those that call on Thee in righteousness, who knowest the supplications which are not uttered, for Thy forethought reacheth to the innermost recesses of human hearts, and by Thy knowledge Thou searchest the hearts of each man, and in every region of the world the incense of prayer and supplication is sent up to Thee. O Thou who has appointed this present world as the place where men should run the race of righteousness, and hast opened the gate of mercy unto all, and hast demonstrated unto every man, by implanted knowledge and natural judgment, and from the exhortation of the law, that the possession of wealth is not everlasting, that the ornament of beauty is not perpetual, that the force of power is easily

---

[1] Mal. i. 11.

dissolved, that everything is smoke and vanity, and that only the good conscience of faith passes without guile through the midst of heaven, and returning with truth seizes the right hand of future nourishment,[1] and before the promise of the regeneration is fulfilled, the soul itself exults in hope and rejoices. For from the beginning of the truth which was in our forefather Abraham, when he changed his laborious journey, Thou didst guide him with a vision, and didst teach him what kind of a world this world is, and knowledge preceded his faith, and faith succeeded his knowledge, and the covenant was the consequence of his faith. For Thou saidst, "I will multiply thy seed as the stars of the heaven, and as the sand which is upon the seashore."[2] Moreover, when Thou hadst given him Isaac, and knewest him to be like Abraham in his way of life, then wast Thou also called his God, saying, "I will be a God unto thee, and to thy seed after thee."[3] And when our father Jacob was sent into Mesopotamia, Thou shewedst him Christ, and spakedst by him, saying, "Behold, I am with thee, and I will increase and multiply thee exceedingly."[4] And thus Thou spakedst unto Moses, Thy faithful and holy servant in the vision of the bush, saying, "I AM THAT I AM : this is My Name for ever, and this is My memorial unto all generations."[5] Champion of the seed of Abraham, blessed art Thou for ever.

[CAP. XXXIV.] Blessed art Thou, O Lord, the King of æons,[6] who by Christ has made the whole world, and by Him at the beginning didst reduce into order the disordered parts ; who dividedst the waters from the waters by the firmament, and didst infuse into them the spirit of life ; who didst fix the earth, and extend the heavens, and dispose each creature by an accurate constitution. For at Thy desire, O Lord, the world was beautified, and the heavens,

---

[1] It is impossible to make any sense of this sentence, and it has been suggested to read τρυφῆς (enjoyment), for τροφῆς (nourishment).
[2] Gen. xxii. 17.   [3] Gen. xvii. 7.   [4] Gen. xlviii. 4.
[5] Exod. iii. 14, 15.   [6] For 'æons,' see p. 292, note 1.

fixed as an arch, were decorated with stars for our comfort in darkness; and the light and the sun were created for the demarcation of days, and for the production of fruits; and the waxing and waning moon for the revolving seasons; and the one was called "night," and the other was entitled "day." And the firmament was exhibited in the midst of the abyss, and Thou commandedst the waters to be gathered together and the dry land to appear. As for the sea itself, how can any one describe it? which comes in furiously from the ocean, and retreats from the sand, where it is stayed at Thy command, for Thou hast said that on it shall its waves be broken.[1] And Thou didst make it a highway for little and for great living creatures, and for ships. Then the earth became green, picked out with all kinds of flowers, and with a variety of different trees; and the glittering luminaries, the nourishers of these plants, preserve their unchangeable path, in nothing departing from Thy command. Where Thou biddest them, there do they rise and set, for signs of seasons and years, regulating by alternation the labours of men. Afterwards the different kinds of animals were created, inhabiting the dry land, or the water, or the air, or amphibious; and the cunning wisdom of Thy providence imparts a corresponding providence to each of them. For as He was not unable to produce different kinds of animals, so neither did He disdain to exercise a different providence towards each one. And as the conclusion of creation, Thou gavest direction unto Thy Wisdom, and createdst a rational living creature, the citizen of the world, saying, "Let us make man in our image, after our likeness,"[2] exhibiting him as the ornament of the world,[3] fashioning a body for him out of the four elements, the primary substances, and furnishing it with a soul created out of nothing, and endowing it with the five senses, and setting the mind over the senses as the charioteer

[1] Job xxxviii. 11.   [2] Gen. i. 26.
[3] It is impossible to preserve the play in the original words, κόσμου κόσμον. They occur again in the Clementine Liturgy, p. 285, note 1, and p. 293, note 2.

of the soul. And in addition to all these things, O Lord God, who shall worthily describe the course of clouds big with rain, the shining of lightning, the noise of thunder, providing an appropriate supply of food, and an all-harmonizing temperature of the air? And when man was disobedient Thou didst deprive him of the reward of life; yet didst Thou not totally destroy him, but laidest him to sleep for a little time, and then didst summon him with an oath to a resurrection, having loosed the bond of death, O Thou quickener of the dead, through Jesus Christ, our hope.

[CAP. XXXV.] Great art Thou, O Lord Almighty, and great is Thy power, and of Thy understanding there is no count. Creator, Saviour, rich in graces, long-suffering and full of pity, who dost not take away salvation from Thy creatures; for Thou art good by nature, and sparest sinners, and invitest them to repentance, and Thy admonition is pitiful. For how should we abide if we were required to come to judgment immediately, when after so much long-suffering we hardly get clear of our own weakness? The heavens declare Thy power, and the quivering earth, suspended upon nothing, Thy security. The wave-tossed sea, feeding the myriad host of living creatures, is bound with sand, standing in awe of Thy command, and compels all men to cry, "O Lord, how manifold are Thy works! in wisdom hast Thou made them all: the earth is full of Thy riches."[1] And the flaming host of angels, and the intellectual spirits say to Palmoni,[2] "One is holy," and the holy seraphin, together with the six-winged cherubin, sing to Thee the triumphal hymn, and cry with voice unceasing, "Holy, holy, holy is the Lord of Hosts; heaven and earth are full of Thy glory."[3] And the other multitudes of the orders, angels, archangels, thrones, dominions, principalities, authorities, powers, cry aloud and say, "Blessed be the

---

[1] Ps. civ. 24.
[2] Dan. viii. 13. 'Unto that certain saint which spake' (A. V.) in LXX., Τῷ φελμουνί. The meaning is not known.
[3] Isa. vi. 3.

glory of the Lord from His place." [1] But Israel, Thy Church on earth, taken out of the Gentiles, emulating the heavenly powers night and day, with a full heart and a willing soul, sings, "The chariots of God are twenty thousand, even thousands of angels: and the Lord is among them, as in the holy place of Sinai." [2] The heaven knows Him who fixed it in the form of an arch as a cube of stone upon nothing, who united land and water to one another, and poured the vitalizing air abroad, and conjoined fire therewith, for warmth and for comfort under darkness. The choir of the stars strikes us with admiration, declaring Him that numbered them, and showing forth Him that named them, as living creatures declare Him that breathed life into them, and trees Him that made them grow; all of which having come into existence by Thy word, show forth the might of Thy power. Wherefore every man ought to send up to Thee through Christ, the hymn of thanksgiving for all these benefits, as he has power over them all by Thine appointment. For Thou art kind in Thy benefits, and beneficent in Thy compassions, who alone art Almighty; for Thy eternal power both quenches flame, and stops the mouths of lions, and tames the monsters of the deep, and raises the sick, and overturns powers, and overthrows the army of the enemy, and the people numbered in pride.[3]

Thou art He that is in heaven, upon the earth, in the sea, in all finite things, Thyself confined by nothing, for there is no limit to Thy greatness. This is not our saying, O Lord; it is the oracle of Thy servant, which saith, "And thou shalt know in thy heart and consider, that the Lord thy God is God in heaven above, and upon the earth beneath: there is none else beside Him." [4] For there is no God beside Thee alone; there is none holy beside Thee, O Lord God of knowledge, God of saints, holy above all holy beings, for they are sanctified under Thy hands.[5]

---

[1] Ezek. iii. 12. [2] Ps. lxviii. 17. [3] See 2 Sam. xxiv. 1-17.
[4] Deut. iv. 39. [5] See Deut. xxxiii. 3.

Thou art glorious and highly exalted, invisible by nature, unsearchable in Thy judgments. Thy life is without want, Thy duration neither alters nor fails, Thy operation is without toil, Thy greatness is unbounded, Thy excellency is perpetual, Thy habitation is unapproachable, Thy dwelling-place is unchangeable, Thy knowledge is without beginning, Thy truth is immutable, Thy work is unassisted, Thy might is unassailable, Thy monarchy is without succession, Thy kingdom is without end, Thy strength is irresistible, Thy host is very numerous. Thou art the Father of wisdom, the Creator of the world by a Mediator as the original Cause, the Bestower of providence, the Giver of laws, the Fulfiller of want, the Punisher of the ungodly, the Rewarder of the just, the God and Father of Christ, and the Lord of them that reverence Him; whose promise is infallible, whose judgment is not open to bribes, whose decision is incapable of change, whose piety is incessant, and His thanksgiving is everlasting; through whom adoration is worthily due to Thee from every rational and holy nature.

[CAP. XXXVI.] O Lord Almighty, Thou didst create the Christ, and didst ordain the sabbath day in memory of this fact that, on it Thou didst rest from Thy works, in order to meditate upon Thy laws. Thou hast also appointed festivals for the rejoicing of our souls, that we might come to remember that Wisdom which was created by Thee; how for our sakes He condescended to be born of woman, and appeared in life, and manifested Himself at His baptism, as one who appeared as both God and man; He suffered by Thy permission on our behalf, and died, and rose again by Thy power. Wherefore we solemnly celebrate the feast of the resurrection on the Lord's day, and rejoice over Him that conquered death, and brought life and immortality to light. For through Him Thou hast brought the Gentiles to Thyself for a peculiar people, the true Israel, beloved of God and seeing Him.[1] For Thou, O Lord, didst bring

[1] See p. 306, note 2.

our fathers out of the land of Egypt, and didst deliver them out of the iron furnace, and from the clay and brickmaking. Thou didst ransom them from the hand of Pharaoh and his subordinates, and didst lead them through the sea as through dry land, and didst bear with their manners in the wilderness, supplying them with all good things. Thou didst give them the law or the decalogue which was spoken by Thy voice and written down with Thy hand. Thou didst enjoin the observation of the sabbath, not as affording to them an occasion for idleness, but an opportunity of piety, for increasing the knowledge of Thy power and the hindrance of evils, having limited them, as it were, within a holy circuit, for the sake of instruction, and for a rejoicing every seven days. On this account there was appointed one week, and seven weeks, and the seventh month, and the seventh year, and the revolution of this year in the jubilee, which is the fiftieth year for remission; so that they might have no excuse for pretending ignorance. On this account He permitted men to rest on every sabbath, so that no man might be willing to send forth an angry word out of his mouth on the sabbath day. For the sabbath is the ceasing from creation, the completion of the world, the seeking after laws, and praise and thanksgiving unto God for the gifts which He hath bestowed upon men. The Lord's day surpasses all these, as it exhibits the Mediator Himself, the Provider, the Law-giver, the Cause of the resurrection, the First-born of every creature,[1] God the word, and man, born of the Virgin Mary alone without a man, who lived a holy life, and was crucified under Pontius Pilate, and died, and rose again from the dead. Thus, the Lord's day, O Lord, commands us to offer unto Thee thanksgiving for all things. For this is the grace afforded by Thee, which by its greatness has obscured all other blessings.

[1] Col. i. 15. Yet much of the preceding language in this long prayer seems to set forth inadequately the co-equal divinity of God the Son.

[CAP. XXXVII.] Thou who hast fulfilled the promises made by the prophets, and hast had mercy upon Sion and compassion upon Jerusalem, by exalting the throne of David Thy servant in the midst of her, by the birth of Christ who was born of his seed, according to the flesh, of a virgin alone, do Thou now, O Lord God, accept the prayers which proceed from the lips of Thy people, which are of the Gentiles, which call upon Thee in truth; as Thou didst accept the gifts of righteous men in their generations. In the first place, Thou didst favourably regard and accept the sacrifice of Abel; of Noah on his coming out of the ark; of Abraham after his leaving the land of the Chaldees; of Isaac at the well of the oath; of Jacob in Bethel; of Moses in the desert; of Aaron betwixt the quick and dead; of Jesus the son of Nave in Gilgal; of Gideon at the rock and the fleeces before his sin; of Manoah and his wife in the field; of Samson in his thirst before his transgression; of Jephthah in the war before his rash vow; of Barak and Deborah in the time of Sisera; of Samuel at Mizpeh; of David at the threshing-floor of Ornan the Jebusite; of Solomon at Gibeon and at Jerusalem; of Elias at Mount Carmel; of Elisæus at the barren spring; of Jehoshaphat in war; of Ezekias in sickness and in the time of Sennacherib; of Manasses in the land of the Chaldeans after his transgression; of Josias in Phassa;[1] of Esdras at the return from the captivity; of Daniel in the lions' den; of Jonas in the whale's belly; of the three children in the fiery furnace; of Anna in the tabernacle before the ark; of Neemias at the rebuilding of the walls, and of Zerubbabel; of Mattathias and his sons in their zeal for Thee; of Jael in blessings; now, therefore, also receive the prayers of Thy people which are offered unto Thee with knowledge through Christ in the spirit.

[CAP. XXXVIII.] We give thanks to Thee for all things, O Lord Almighty, because Thou hast not taken away Thy

---

[1] The reference is not known. It has been conjectured that Φασσᾶ may be a misreading for φασέκ, used for Pascha in 2 Chron. xxxv. 6.

mercies and compassions from us, but in each generation after generation Thou dost save, deliver, assist, and protect us. For Thou didst assist in the days of Enos and Enoch; in the days of Moses and Jesus; in the days of the Judges; in the days of Samuel and Elias, and the prophets; in the days of David and the Kings; in the days of Esther and Mordecai; in the days of Judith; in the days of Judas Maccabæus and his brethren; and in our days Thou hast assisted us by Thy great High Priest Jesus Christ Thy Son. For He hast delivered us from the sword, and hath freed us from famine, and nourished us, and hath healed our sickness, and sheltered us from the evil tongue. For all things we give thanks to Thee through Christ, who hast given to us an articulate voice for confession, and hast supplied a well-adapted tongue to an instrument, like the bow which strikes the lyre, with a proper taste, and a correspondent touch; and sight for seeing, and the hearing of sound, and the smelling of vapours, and hands for work, and feet for walking. Thou mouldest all these members from a little drop in the matrix, and after such formation Thou dost bestow on it an immortal soul, and producest it into the light as a rational living creature, even man. Thou didst instruct him by Thy laws, and brighten him with Thy judgments, and though Thou hast brought upon him dissolution for a little while, Thou didst promise his resurrection. Wherefore, what life is in itself sufficient, or what length of ages will suffice for men to express their thanks? To thank Thee worthily is impossible; to thank Thee according to our ability is meet and right. For Thou hast redeemed us from the impiety of polytheism, and hast brought us out from the heresy of those that slew Christ, delivering us from error and ignorance. Thou didst send Christ as a man among men, being the only-begotten God.[1] Thou hast

---

[1] This phrase seems to establish the divinity of Jesus Christ, though much of the language used in these Clementine devotions seems to fall short of the full Catholic doctrine of the co-equality of the Persons in the Trinity.

caused the Paraclete to dwell in us. Thou hast given Thine angels charge over us; Thou hast put the devil to shame. Whereas we were not, Thou didst make us; Thou takest care of us when we are made; Thou measurest out life unto us; Thou providest us with food; Thou hast promised repentance. For all these things glory and worship be unto Thee through Jesus Christ, now, and for ever, and throughout all ages. Amen.'[1]

§ 8. Baptismal Formula of Renunciation.

'I renounce Satan, and his works, and his pomps, and his service, and his angels, and his inventions, and all things that are under him.'[2]

§ 9. Baptismal Creed.

'I believe and am baptized into one unbegotten only true God, Almighty, Father of Christ, Creator and Maker of all things, from whom all things do come.

And in the Lord Jesus Christ, His only-begotten Son, the First-born of every creature, begotten before the ages through the good pleasure of the Father, by whom all things were made, things in heaven and things on earth, both visible and invisible; who in those last days came down from heaven, and took flesh, and was born of the holy Virgin Mary, whose conversation was holy according to the laws of His God and Father. He was crucified under Pontius Pilate, and died for us, and rose again from the dead after His passion on the third day; He ascended into heaven, and sat on the right hand of the Father, and is coming again with glory at the end of the world to judge the quick and the dead; whose kingdom shall have no end.

And I am baptised into the Holy Ghost, that is to say, the Paraclete, who wrought in all the saints from the

---

[1] Lib. vii. capp. 33-38, pp. 174-181.
[2] Lib. vii. cap. 41, p. 183.

beginning of the world, and was afterwards also sent from the Father to the Apostles, according to the promise of our Saviour and Lord Jesus Christ; and, after the Apostles, to all believers in the holy and Apostolic Church; into the resurrection of the flesh, and into the remission of sins, and into the kingdom of heaven, and into the life of the world to come.'[1]

§ 10. CONSECRATION OF THE WATER AT BAPTISM.

'Look down from heaven, and sanctify this water, and give to it grace and power, so that he that is baptized therein according to the commandment of Thy Christ, may be crucified with Him, and may die with Him, and be buried with Him, and may rise again with Him unto the adoption of sonship which is in Him, by becoming dead unto sin and living unto righteousness.'[2]

§ 11. CONSECRATION OF THE OIL AT BAPTISM.

'O Lord God, who art without generation, and without a superior, the Lord of the whole world, who hast caused the sweet odour of the knowledge of the gospel to extend to all nations, do Thou grant now that this oil may be efficacious upon him that is being baptized, so that the fragrance of Thy Christ may remain firm and fixed upon him, and that having died with Christ, he may rise and live with Him.'[3]

§ 12. A POST-BAPTISMAL PRAYER.

'O God Almighty, the Father of Thy Christ, Thy only-begotten Son, give me a body undefiled, a pure heart, a watchful mind, unerring knowledge, the descent upon me of the Holy Spirit, for the acquirement and full possession of the truth through Thy Christ, through whom be glory to Thee in the Holy Ghost for ever. Amen.'[4]

---

[1] Lib. vii. cap. 41, p. 183.
[2] *Ibid.*, cap. 43, p. 185.
[3] *Ibid.*, cap. 44, p. 185.
[4] *Ibid.*, cap. 45, p. 186.

§ 13. A Prayer at the Consecration of a Bishop, *To be used while Deacons are holding the Book of the Gospels over the newly elected Bishop's Head.*

'Thou self-existent One, our Master and Lord, God Almighty, who alone art unbegotten, and ownest allegiance to no other king, who always art, and wast before the ages, who standest in need of nothing, and art above all causation and generation; who alone art true; who alone art wise; who alone art most highest; who art by nature invisible; whose knowledge is without beginning; who alone art good and incomparable; who knowest all things before they come into being; who art acquainted with hidden things; who art unapproachable, owning no lord above Thee; the God and Father of Thy only-begotten Son, our God and Saviour; the Creator of all things by Him, the Forethinker, the Care-taker, the Father of mercies, and the God of all comfort,[1] who hast Thy dwelling on high, and yet humblest Thyself to behold the things that are on the earth;[2] Thou that dost set bounds to Thy Church, by the presence of Thy incarnate Christ, of which the Holy Ghost is witness, through Thy Apostles, and through us the Bishops who by Thy grace are here present; Thou who from the beginning didst fore-ordain priests for the government of Thy people, Abel in the first place, Seth, and Enos, and Enoch, and Noe, and Melchisedech, and Job; who didst appoint Abraham, and the rest of the patriarchs, together with Thy faithful servants Moses and Aaron, and Eleazar, and Phinees; who didst appoint from among them rulers and priests in the tabernacle of the testimony; who didst choose out Samuel to be a priest and a prophet; who didst not leave Thy sanctuary without ministers in sacred things; who wast well-pleased with those in whom Thou chosest to be glorified;—Do Thou Thyself now through us, by the mediation of Thy Christ, pour down the power of Thy guiding Spirit, which waiteth on Thy beloved Son Jesus Christ, which He bestowed

---

[1] 2 Cor. i. 3. [2] Ps. cxiii. 5.

according to Thy will upon the holy Apostles of Thee, the eternal God. Grant in Thy name, O God, that searchest the hearts, that this Thy servant, whom Thou hast chosen to be bishop, may feed Thy holy flock, and fill the office of high priest before Thee, serving Thee without blame night and day; that with the approbation of Thy countenance He may gather together the number of those that shall be saved,[1] and may offer to Thee the gifts of Thy holy Church. Grant unto him, O Lord Almighty, through Thy Christ, the Communion of the Holy Ghost, so that he may have power to remit sins according to Thy command, to give forth lots according to Thy direction, and to loose every band according to the power which Thou gavest unto the Apostles; and that he may please Thee by meekness and purity of heart, steadfastly, unblameably, irreprovably offering unto Thee the pure and unbloody sacrifice, which Thou didst ordain through Christ, the mystery of the New Testament, for a sweet-smelling savour, through Thy holy Child, Jesus Christ, our God and Saviour, through whom glory, honour, and worship be to Thee in the Holy Ghost, now, and for ever, and for endless ages. ℞. Amen.'[2]

§ 14. 'The Clementine Liturgy.'[3]

We now come to the famous Liturgy embedded in the Apostolic Constitutions, and known as 'The Clementine Liturgy.' The following features in its structure or wording imply a very early date for its composition, and for the most part point to an ante-Nicene origin:—

1. The length of many of the prayers, and especially of the Preface, with its exhaustive commemoration of God's providential dealings in creation and

---

[1] Τῶν σωζομένων.

[2] Lib. viii. cap. 5, pp. 195-197. A shorter form of this prayer is given in the Canons of Hippolytus, c. iii. § 11, p. 42. See p. 193.

[3] Lib. viii. capp. 5-15, pp. 197-217.

redemption, and in the Old Testament and New Testament history generally.[1]

2. The elaborate forms of the dismissal of the Catechumens, Energumens, Competentes, and Penitents. The presence of these forms implies a date when the disciplinary system of the primitive Church was in full force.

3. The repeated references to the sufferings of persecuted Christians in exile, or in prison, or at work, or in the mines, together with prayer for the emperors that persecute them.[2]

4. The inexactness of the theological language used, indicating an ante-Arian and a pre-Nicene age.

5. The absence of a Creed.

6. The non-mention of incense.

7. The omission of the Lord's Prayer.

The Lord's Prayer, having been delivered by the Founder of Christianity to His Apostles and others, would naturally form an integral portion of Christian worship from the earliest times. In the *Didaché*, where it is given with the doxology in a curtailed form, it is ordered to be repeated three times a day.[3] Its omission from the Clementine Liturgy, as its text has reached us, is liturgically unique, and has never been satisfactorily explained. There are several passages in that Liturgy which are adaptations from or which refer to various petitions in the Lord's Prayer.[4]

[1] See p. 291, etc.
[2] See pp. 287, 300, 301. The first section of Bk. v. of the Apostolic Constitutions is 'Concerning the Martyrs,' and was evidently written before heathen persecutions had ceased.
[3] Cap. viii. *ad finem*. So Apostolic Constitutions, lib. vii. cap. 24.
[4] There are nine passages quoted by F. H. Chase, which incorporate or echo phrases in the Lord's Prayer. In some of them the echo is certainly faint (*The Lord's Prayer in the Early Church*, Cambridge, 1891, pp. 142, 143).

It is contained in the Apostolic Constitutions[1] in a form similar to, but not verbally identical with, the form given in the *Didaché*.[1] It is there also ordered to be used by the newly baptized person directly after the post-baptismal anointing.[2] It is to be said by him standing, and with face turned towards the East.

Guided then, so far as guidance is given, by the Clementine Liturgy, we see the following to have been the main features and order of the Christian Liturgy in the earliest complete form in which it has come down to us:—

Mass of the Catechumens.

[Preparation and approach to the altar.]
Lections (p. 278).
Sermon (p. 279).
Dismissal of Catechumens, Energumens, Competentes, Penitents (pp. 279-285).

Mass of the Faithful.

Deacon's Bidding Prayer, or Eucharistic Litany for all sorts and conditions of men (p. 285).
Prayer of the Faithful (p. 288).
Kiss of Peace (p. 289).
Lavabo (p. 290).
Offertory (p. 290).
Secret Prayer (p. 290).
Sursum Corda (p. 290).
Preface (p. 291).
Triumphal Hymn, or Tersanctus (p. 297).
Consecration Prayer—
    (*a*) Commemoration of the work of Redemption (p. 297).
    (*b*) Commemoration of the Institution (p. 299).

---

[1] Lib. vii. cap. 24, p. 169.   [2] *Ibid.*, cap. 44, p. 185.

(c) The Great Oblation (p. 299).
(d) The Epiklesis, or Invocation of the Holy Ghost (p. 299).

The Great Intercession, for the whole State of Christ's Church Militant on earth and at rest in Paradise, followed by another Deacon's Bidding Prayer (p. 300).

Prayer of humble access (p. 303).
Sancta Sanctis (p. 303).
Communion of Celebrant and People (p. 304).
Thanksgiving after reception, with bidding thereto (p. 304).
Benediction (p. 306).
Dismissal (p. 306).

Another description of the primitive Liturgy, differing in some of its details, is given in another part of the Apostolic Constitutions. It is of great interest, and will be found translated on page 307.

We translate from the text as given in the Eighth Book of the Apostolic Constitutions.[1] More recent reprints of the Greek text may be seen in Hammond's (C. E.) *Liturgies, Eastern and Western* (Oxford, 1878), pp. 3-23 ; and in Maskell's (W.) *Ancient Liturgy of the Church of England*, 3rd Edition (Oxford, 1882), pp. 281-293.

[MASS OF THE CATECHUMENS.]

[LECTIONS.]

'*And after the reading of the Law, and the Prophets, and our*[2] *Epistles, and the Acts, and the Gospels,*[3]

[1] Capp. 5-15, Ueltzen's ed. Suerini et Rostochii, 1853, pp. 197-217.

[2] The various directions in the Apostolic Constitutions are, by a sort of pious fraud, very common in early ecclesiastical literature, and not considered dishonest by the public opinion of the day, referred to the Apostles themselves, who are introduced as speaking in the first person. In this translation we have omitted the passages which introduce them.

[3] Three lections appear to be intended here : an Old Testament Lection, the Epistle, the Gospel—perhaps more.

let the [newly] ordained [Bishop][1] salute the Church, saying:

[SALUTATION.]

The grace of our Lord Jesus Christ, and the love of God the Father, and the communion of the Holy Ghost, be with you all.[2]

And let all answer:

And with thy spirit.

[THE SERMON.]

And after this let him address to the people words of exhortation, and when he hath finished the word of instruction, let all stand up, and let the Deacon, ascending up to some high place, proclaim:[3]

[DISMISSAL OF THE CATECHUMENS.]

Let none of the hearers,[4] let none of the unbelievers [be present].

And let all the faithful pray for them in their hearts, saying:

Lord, have mercy.

---

[1] The Clementine Liturgy is embedded in an office for the Consecration of a Bishop. This may account for the absence of any reference to any preliminary prayers, or to an Introit, or to the Little Entrance; *i.e.* the procession of the Gospel in the Eastern Church at Mass.

[2] 2 Cor. xiii. 14.

[3] This rubric and what follows is attributed in the original Greek to St. Andrew. We have omitted this and other passages which claim an Apostolic origin for the whole or any part of this Liturgy.

[4] There are believed to have been four grades of Catechumens, but the existence of the first class, as a class, is uncertain.

  I. Ἐξωθούμενοι ... *Externi* ... Outsiders.
  II. Ἀκροώμενοι ... *Audientes* ... Hearers.
  III. Γονυκλίνοντες ... *Genuflectentes* ... Kneelers.
  IV. Φωτιζόμενοι ... *Competentes* ... Candidates for baptism.

Hefele, however, will not allow that there ever were more than two grades of Catechumens, viz. Class II. and Class IV., with which Class III. is identical (*History of the Christian Councils*, Edinburgh, 1872, 2nd edit., p. 421).

And let him minister on their behalf, saying:

Let us all beseech God for the Catechumens, that He, who is good and the lover of men, may mercifully hear their prayers and supplications, and, receiving their requests, may assist them, and grant them their hearts' desires, in such way as may be expedient for them; that he may reveal to them the gospel of His Christ, may enlighten [1] them and cause them to understand, may instruct them in the knowledge of God, may teach them His commandments and judgments, may implant in them His holy and salutary fear, and may open the ears of their hearts to occupy themselves in His law day and night; [2] that He may stablish them in piety, may unite and number them together in His holy fold, may count them worthy of the laver of regeneration, of the vestment of immortality, and of the true life; and that He may preserve them from all impiety, and may give no place to the enemy against them; and that He may purify them from all pollution of flesh and spirit,[3] and may dwell in them and walk in them,[4] through His Christ; that He may bless their coming in and their going out,[5] and may direct that which lies in front of them, as may be expedient for them. Furthermore, let us earnestly supplicate on their behalf, that having obtained remission of their sins through the initiation of baptism,[6] they may be found worthy of participation in the holy mysteries, and of perseverance with the saints.

[Silent prayer.]

Catechumens, stand up.

Ask for the peace of God through His Christ, and that this day and all the time of your life may be peaceful and sinless, that your ends may be Christian, that God may be merciful and gracious; and for the remission of your sins. Commend yourselves to the only unbegotten God, through His Christ.

Bow down, and receive the blessing.

[1] Φωτίσῃ, φωτισμός was a recognized title of baptism.
[2] Cf. Ps. i. 2; cxix. 97.   [3] 2 Cor. vii. 1.
[4] 2 Cor. vi. 16.   [5] Cf. Ps. cxxi. 8.   [6] Διὰ τῆς μυήσεως.

And, as we have prescribed before, let the people say for each of those whom the Deacon addresses:
Lord, have mercy.
And before all let the children[1] say it. And while the Catechumens bow down their heads, let him that ha'h been elected Bishop bless them with the following blessing:
Almighty God, the Unbegotten and Unapproachable, the only true God, the God and Father of Thy Christ, Thy only begotten Son, the God of the Paraclete, and Lord of all, who didst by Christ constitute Thy disciples as teachers for instruction in piety, do Thou Thyself also now look down upon these Thy servants, the Catechumens of the gospel of Thy Christ. Give to them a new heart, and renew a right spirit within them,[2] to know and to do Thy will with a full heart and willing soul. Make them worthy of[3] the initiation of holy baptism,[3] and unite them to Thy holy Church, and make them partakers of the Divine mysteries, through Christ, our hope, who died for them, through whom be glory and worship to Thee, in the Holy Ghost for ever. Amen.

After this let the Deacon say:
Depart, ye Catechumens, in peace.

[DISMISSAL OF THE ENERGUMENS.]
And after they have departed let him say:
Pray, ye Energumens, who are vexed with unclean spirits:
Let us all earnestly pray for them, that the merciful God through Christ would rebuke the unclean and evil spirits, and deliver his supplicants from the oppression of the adversary; that He who rebuked the legion of devils,[4]

---

[1] Τὰ παιδία. It is not known what children are referred to; they were possibly the children of the choir; but more probably the children mentioned later on (pp. 290, 308) as present with their mothers.
[2] Ps. li. 10.   [3] Τῆς ἁγίας μυήσεως.
[4] Cf. St. Mark v. 2–20.

and the devil, the fount of evil, would now rebuke these apostates from piety, and deliver the works of His own hands from the active hostility of Satan, and cleanse them whom He hath created with great wisdom.

Let us, further, earnestly pray for them.

Save them, and raise them up, O God, in Thy might.

Bow down, ye Energumens, and receive the blessing.

And let the Bishop pray over them, saying:

Thou who didst bind the strong man and spoil all his goods;[1] Thou who didst give us power to tread upon serpents and scorpions, and upon all the power of the enemy;[2] Thou who didst deliver up unto us the murdering serpent a prisoner, as a sparrow unto children;[3] before whom all things shake and tremble at the presence of Thy power; Thou that didst cast him down as lightning to earth from heaven,[4] not with a local fracture, but from honour to dishonour, through his deliberate evil-mindedness; whose look drieth up the depths, and whose indignation maketh the mountains to melt away, and whose truth remaineth for ever;[5] whom infants praise, and sucklings bless; whom angels worship and adore; who lookest upon the earth and makest it to tremble; who touchest the hills and they smoke;[6] who rebukest the sea and makest it dry, and driest up all its rivers, and the clouds are the dust of Thy feet;[7] who walkest upon the sea as upon a pavement, the only-begotten God, Son of the mighty Father;—rebuke the evil spirits and deliver the works of Thy hands upon the activity of an adverse spirit; for to Thee belongeth glory, honour, and adoration, and through Thee to Thy Father in the Holy Ghost, for ever. Amen.

Then let the Deacon say:

Depart, ye Energumens.

[1] St. Mark iii. 27.
[2] St. Luke x. 19.
[3] Job. xli. 5.
[4] St. Luke x. 18.
[5] 2 Esdras viii. 23.
[6] Ps. civ. 32.
[7] Nahum i. 4, 3.

[DISMISSAL OF THE COMPETENTES, OR CANDIDATES FOR BAPTISM.]

And after they have gone let him proclaim:

Pray, ye candidates, for baptism.[1]

Let us, the faithful, all pray earnestly for them, that the Lord would make them worthy to be baptized [2] into the death of Christ, and to rise again with Him, and to be made members of His kingdom, and partakers of His mysteries; that He would unite them and enrol them along with such as shall be saved [3] in His holy Church.

Save them and raise them up by Thy grace.

Then having been sealed [4] to God through His Christ, let them bow down, and be blessed by the Bishop with his blessing:

O God, who didst say beforehand through Thy holy prophets to them that are to be baptized,[5] "Wash you, make you clean," [6] and didst through Christ appoint a spiritual regeneration, look down now Thyself upon these persons who are to be baptized. Bless them and sanctify them, and prepare them that they may be worthy of Thy spiritual gift, and of their true adoption as sons, and of Thy spiritual mysteries, and of being gathered into the number of those that shall be saved, through Christ our Saviour, through whom to Thee in the Holy Ghost be glory, honour, and adoration for ever. Amen.

Then let the Deacon say:

Depart, ye candidates for baptism.

[DISMISSAL OF THE PENITENTS.]

Afterwards let him make this proclamation:

Pray, ye that are in penitence.

Let all of us earnestly pray on behalf of our brethren who are in penitence, that the God of mercy would show unto them the way of repentance; that He would receive

---

[1] Φωτιζόμενοι. [2] Μυηθέντας. [3] Σωζομένων.
[4] Κατασφραγισάμενοι. [5] Μυουμένοις. [6] Isa. i. 16.

their recantation and confession; that He will bruise Satan under their feet shortly,[1] and ransom them from the snare of the devil,[2] and from the despitefulness of demons, and deliver them from every unlawful word, and from every unseemly deed and wicked thought; that He would forgive them all their offences, both voluntary and involuntary, and blot out the handwriting that is against them,[3] and write their names in the book of life,[4] and cleanse them from all filthiness of the flesh and spirit,[5] and restore and unite them to His holy flock; for He knoweth whereof we are made: for who will boast, "I have made my heart clean?" Who will claim, "I am pure from my sin?"[6] For we are all worthy of punishment.[7]

Let us pray for them yet more earnestly, because there is joy in heaven over one sinner that repenteth,[8] that turning away from every unlawful work, they may become associated with every good action, in order that God, the Lover of men, may speedily and favourably accept their supplications, may restore them to their former position, and may give them back the joy of His salvation, and stablish them with His free[9] spirit,[10] so that their footsteps no more slip,[11] but that they be deemed worthy to be partakers of His most holy things, and sharers of the Divine mysteries; in order that being proved worthy of the adoption of sons, they may attain life eternal.

Let us all still earnestly say on their behalf:

Lord, have mercy.

Save them, and raise them up by Thy grace.

Rise up, and bow down before God through His Christ and receive the blessing.

[1] Rom. xvi. 20.   [2] 2 Tim. ii. 26.   [3] Col. ii. 14.
[4] Phil. iv. 3.   [5] 2 Cor. vii. 1.   [6] Prov. xx. 9.
[7] Ecclus. viii. 5.   [8] St. Luke xv. 10.
[9] 'Ηγεμονικῷ. Here, as elsewhere in quotations, we have substituted the A.V. rendering for a literal translation of the Greek word or words.
[10] Ps. li. 12, 14.   [11] Ps. xvii. 5.

Then let the Bishop pray over them as followeth:

Almighty and everlasting God, Lord of the whole world, Creator and Governor of all things, who through Christ didst consecrate man to be the ornament of the world,[1] and didst give him a law implanted and written, that he might live, as a reasonable being, according to Thy statutes; and when he had sinned didst give him Thine own goodness as a pledge to repentance, look down upon those who have bowed to Thee the necks of their souls and bodies; because Thou wouldest not the death of a sinner, but rather that he should repent, so that he should return from his evil way and live,[2] Thou who didst receive the repentance of the Ninevites; who willest that all men should be saved, and come to the knowledge of the truth;[3] who didst through Thy fatherly pity receive the son who devoured his substance in riotous living because of his repentance;[4] do Thou Thyself now accept the repentance of Thy supplicants, for there is none that sinneth not against Thee,[5] and if Thou, Lord, will be extreme to mark what is done amiss, O Lord, who may abide it? for there is mercy with Thee:[6] and restore them to Thy holy Church in their former reputation and honour, through Christ our God and Saviour, by whom in the Holy Ghost be glory and honour to Thee for ever. Amen.

Then let the Deacon say:

Depart, ye penitents.

[MASS OF THE FAITHFUL.]
Let the Deacon add:

Let none of those who are not able to pray with us draw near.

Let those of us who are among the faithful kneel:

---

[1] It has not been found possible to preserve the play upon words contained in the Greek expression κόσμου κόσμον. See p. 265, note 3; p. 293, note 2.

[2] Cf. Ezek. xviii. 23.   [3] 1 Tim. ii. 4.   [4] Cf. St. Luke xv. 11–32.
[5] 2 Chron. vi. 36.   [6] Ps. cxxx. 3, 4.

[EUCHARISTIC LITANY, OR DEACON'S BIDDING PRAYER.]
Let us entreat God through His Christ.
Let us all earnestly beseech God through His Christ.

Let us pray for the peace and good condition of the world and holy churches, that He who is God of all may bestow His own peace upon us, eternal and that cannot be taken away, to the end that He may preserve us, persevering in the fulness of that virtue which is according to godliness.

Let us pray for the holy, Catholic, and Apostolic Church, which extends from one end of the world to another, that the Lord would preserve it and guard it continually, unshaken and unstormed, till the end of the world, founded upon the Rock.[1]

Let us pray for the holy parish [2] here, that the Lord of all would vouchsafe to us to pursue unfailingly His heavenly hope, and to pay to Him unceasingly the debt of our prayer.

Let us pray for the whole episcopate which is under heaven of those who rightly divide the word of Thy truth.[3]

Let us pray for our bishop James [4] and his parishes.

Let us pray for our bishop Clement [5] and his parishes.

Let us pray for our bishop Evodius [6] and his parishes.

That the merciful God would vouchsafe to preserve them to their holy Churches, in safety, honour, and length of days, and would grant to them an honourable old age in piety and righteousness.

Let us pray for our presbyters, that the Lord would deliver them from all unseemly and wicked deeds, and would grant to them a presbyterate both safe and honourable.

Let us pray for the whole diaconate and ministry in Christ, that the Lord would vouchsafe to them an unblamable diaconate.

[1] St. Matt. vii. 25 ; xvi. 18.   [2] Παροικία.   [3] 2 Tim. ii. 15.
[4] First Bishop of Jerusalem.
[5] First, second, or third Bishop of Rome, after SS. Peter and Paul.
[6] First Bishop of Antioch.

Let us pray for the readers, singers, virgins, widows, and orphans, for married women, for women with child, that the Lord would have mercy upon them all.

Let us pray for eunuchs walking in holiness of life.

Let us pray for those in a state of continence and piety.

Let us pray for those who bring forth fruit in the holy Church, and who give alms to the poor.

Let us pray for those who bring offerings and firstfruits to the Lord our God:

That God, Who is the Fountain of all goodness, would recompense them with His heavenly gifts, and would give unto them a hundredfold more in the present world, and in the world to come life everlasting,[1] and would grant unto them eternal things instead of temporal, and things of heaven instead of things of earth.

Let us pray for our newly baptized[2] brethren, that the Lord would strengthen and confirm them.

Let us pray for our brethren tried with weakness, that the Lord would deliver them from all sickness and all infirmity, and restore them sound to His holy Church.

Let us pray for those who travel by land or water.

Let us pray for those who are in mines, in exile, in prison, or in bonds for the name of the Lord.[3]

Let us pray for those who travail in the bitterness of servitude.

Let us pray for our enemies and for them that hate us.

Let us pray for those who persecute us for the name of the Lord, that the Lord would soften their anger and scatter their wrath against us.

Let us pray for those that are without and wandering, that the Lord would bring them back.

Let us pray for the children of the Church, that the Lord would perfect them in His fear, and would bring them to the full measure of their age.

---

[1] Cf. St. Matt. xix. 29.   [2] Νεοφωτίστων.

[3] This petition implies an early date, in the times of heathen persecution.

Let us pray for each other, that the Lord would guard us and preserve us by His grace unto the end, and deliver us from evil,[1] and from all the scandals of those that work iniquity, and that He would preserve us unto His heavenly kingdom.

Let us pray for every Christian soul.

Save us and raise us up, O God, by Thy pity.

Let us rise up.

With earnest prayer let us commit ourselves and each other to the living God through His Christ.

[PRAYER OF THE FAITHFUL.]

Then let the Bishop add this prayer, and say:

O Lord, Almighty, Most Highest, who dwellest on high, Holy One resting in holy ones, without beginning, the only Potentate, who hast given to us by Christ the preaching of knowledge, to the acknowledgment of Thy glory and of Thy name, which He hath made known to us for our comprehension; do Thou also now look down through Him upon this Thy flock, and deliver it from all ignorance and evil-doing, and grant that they may fear Thee with fear, and lovingly love Thee, and be reflected on from the face of Thy glory. Be gracious unto them, and merciful, and hearken unto their prayers, and keep them immovable, unblamable, irreprovable, that they may be holy both in body and spirit, not having spot, or wrinkle, or any such thing,[2] but that they may be complete, and that not one of them may be defective or imperfect. Thou that art mighty to help, and no respecter of persons, be Thou the Assister of this Thy people, whom Thou hast purchased with the precious blood of Thy Christ; be Thou their Protector, Aider, Provider, Guardian, their most Strong Wall of defence, their Bulwark of security, because none is able to pluck them out of Thy hand;[3] for there is no other

---

[1] St. Matt. vi. 13. But τοῦ πονηροῦ in the Clementine text is almost certainly masculine. It is to be noted that we have here part of the Lord's Prayer embedded in the Liturgy.

[2] Eph. v. 27. [3] Cf. St. John x. 29.

God than Thou, and in Thee is our hope. Sanctify them through Thy truth; Thy word is truth.[1] Thou who dost nothing for favour, Thou who canst not be deceived, deliver them from every sickness, and from every weakness, from every offence, from all injury and deceit, from fear of the enemy, from the arrow that flieth by day, from the pestilence [2] that walketh in darkness;[3] and deem them worthy of eternal life, which is in Christ, Thy only-begotten Son, our God and Saviour, by whom in the Holy Ghost be glory and honour to Thee, now, and for ever, and for endless ages. Amen.

After this, let the Deacon say:
Let us attend.

Then let the Bishop salute the Church, and say:
The peace of God be with you all.

And let the people answer:
And with Thy spirit.

[THE KISS OF PEACE.]
Then let the Deacon say to all:
Greet one another with an holy kiss.

Then let the clergy kiss the Bishop, and the laymen kiss the laymen, and the women kiss the women; and let the children[4] stand at the reading desk;[5] and let another Deacon stand by them, that they may not be disorderly, and let other Deacons watch the men, and the women, that there be no disturbance; that no one nod, or whisper, or sleep. And let Deacons be stationed at the doors of the men, and Sub-Deacons at the doors of the women, to see that no one go out, and that no door be opened, even by one of the faithful, during the time of the Anaphora.[6]

---

[1] St. John xvii. 17.   [2] Πράγματος.   [3] Ps. xci. 5, 6.

[4] It is doubtful whether the children mentioned here are the children of the congregation or the children of the choir. See p. 281, note 1.

[5] Βήματι. The bema, ambo, or reading-desk, from which the liturgical lessons were read.

[6] The Anaphora of the Eastern Liturgy is the equivalent of the Canon in the Latin Mass.

[THE LAVABO.]

Then let a Sub-Deacon bring water to wash the hands of the Priests, which is a symbol of the purity of souls devoted to God.

Then let the Deacon say: [1]

Let none of the catechumens, let none of the hearers, let none of the unbelievers, let none of the heterodox remain. Ye who have joined in the former prayer depart. Mothers, take up your children. Let no one have aught against any man. Let no hypocrite remain. Let us stand upright before the Lord to present unto Him our offerings with fear and trembling.

[THE OFFERTORY.]

When this is done, let the deacons bring the gifts to the bishop at the altar, and let the presbyters stand on his right hand and on his left, as disciples stand by their Master. And let two deacons, on each side of the altar, hold a fan of thin membranes, or of peacocks' feathers, or of fine linen, and let them gently drive away the small winged insects, so that they may not touch the cups.

Then let the Bishop,[2] *having prayed in secret, accompanied by the Priests,*[3] *put on a splendid vestment, and stand at the altar. There, having made the sign of the cross with his hand upon his forehead, let him say:*

The grace of Almighty God, and the love of our Lord Jesus Christ, and the fellowship of the Holy Ghost be with you all.[4]

Then let all with one voice say:

And with thy spirit.

[SURSUM CORDA.]

Bishop. Lift up your mind.[5]

---

[1] Mr. Maskell begins to print at this point: *Ancient Liturgy of the Church of England*, 3rd ed. p. 282.

[2] Ἀρχιερεὺς.   [3] Ἱερεῦσιν.   [4] 2 Cor. xiii. 14.

[5] For the Versicle, 'Lift up your hearts' (Sursum Corda), and the Response, 'We lift them up unto the Lord,' etc., see pp. 107, 1c8.

People. We lift it up unto the Lord.
Bishop. Let us give thanks unto the Lord.
People. It is meet and right so to do.

[PREFACE.]

Then let the Bishop say:

It is very meet and right before all things to sing praises unto Thee, who art the true God, existing before all things that are, of whom the whole family in heaven and earth is named,[1] who alone art unbegotten, without beginning, without a ruler, without a master, standing in need of nothing, the Author and Giver of all good things, who art beyond all cause and all generation, the same yesterday, to-day, and for ever, from whom all things, as from a starting point, came into existence. For Thou art knowledge without beginning, eternal sight, unbegotten hearing, untaught wisdom; the first in nature, alone in existence, and beyond all number; who through Thy only-begotten Son didst bring all things into existence out of nothing, having begotten Him before all ages by Thy will, and power, and goodness, without any medium, the only-begotten Son, God the Word, the living Wisdom, the First-born of every creature,[2] the Angel of Thy great counsel,[3] Thy High priest, the King and Lord of all intellectual and sensible nature, who was before all things,[4] by whom all things were made.

For Thou, O eternal God, didst make all things by Him, and by Him dost vouchsafe a suitable providence over the whole world; for by the same Person that Thou didst graciously bring all things into being, by Him Thou hast granted that all things should continue in well-being. O God and Father of Thy only-begotten Son, who by Him before all things didst create Cherubim and Seraphim, æons and hosts, principalities and powers, dominions and thrones,

---

[1] Eph. iii. 15.
[2] Col. i. 15.
[3] Isa. ix. 6.
[4] Col. i. 17.

archangels and angels,[1] and after all these things didst create by Him this visible world, and all things that are therein. For Thou art He that did fix the heavens as an arch, and did spread them out as a curtain,[2] and did found the earth upon nothing by Thy will alone. Thou hast established the firmament, and hast prepared the night and the day, bringing forth light out of Thy treasures, and superinducing darkness to overshadow it, to provide rest for the living creatures which roam to and fro in the world. Thou hast appointed the sun in the heaven to rule the day, and the moon to rule the night;[3] Thou hast inscribed in the heaven the choir of stars to praise Thy great glory. Thou createdst water for drink and cleansing, the vital air for respiration, and for the manufacture of the voice by the tongue striking the air, and the hearing which co-operates with it, so as to receive and perceive the words which fall upon it. Thou hast made the fire for our consolation in darkness, for the relief of our necessities, for warmth and light. Thou hast divided the great sea from the land, and hast made the one navigable, and the other a basis for our feet in walking;[4] the former Thou hast replenished with

[1] (i.) Hierarchy of Dionysius (*De Cœlesti Hierarchia*, caps. vii.-ix.).

1. Σεραφίμ ... Seraphim.
2. Χερουβίμ ... Cherubim.
3. Θρόνοι ... Thrones.
4. Κυριότητες ... Dominions.
5. 'Εξούσιαι ... Authorities.
6. Δυνάμεις ... Powers.
7. 'Αρχαί ... Principalities.
8. 'Αρχάγγελοι ... Archangels.
9. ῎Αγγελοι ... Angels.

(ii.) Hierarchy of Clementine Liturgy.

1. Χερουβίμ ... Cherubim.
2. Σεραφίμ ... Seraphim.
3. Αἰῶνες ... Æons.
4. Στράτιαι ... Hosts.
5. Δυνάμεις ... Powers.
6. Εξούσιαι ... Authorities.
7. 'Αρχαί ... Principalities.
8. Θρόνοι ... Thrones.
9. 'Αρχάγγελοι ... Archangels.
10. ῎Αγγελοι ... Angels.

The addition of æons in list (ii.) is curious, and suggestive of Gnostic influence on the Clementine Liturgy.

[2] Ps. civ. 2. [3] Gen. i. 16.

[4] Compare the accounts of the creation in the long Prefaces in the early Gallican *Missale Richenovense*, Missa vi.; Neale and Forbes, *The Ancient Liturgies of the Gallican Church* (Burntisland, 1855), pt. i. pp. 17, 18.

small and great beasts, and the latter Thou hast filled with the same both tame and wild; and Thou hast wreathed it with various plants, and crowned it with herbs, and beautified it with flowers, and enriched it with seeds. Thou didst collect together the great deep, and surround it with a mighty cavity, seas of salt water heaped together, hedged round with barriers of finest sand. Sometimes Thou dost crest it with Thy winds to the height of mountains, sometimes levelling it as a plain, sometimes making it rage with a storm, sometimes stilling it with a calm, making it easy for sea-faring voyagers to traverse. Thou hast girdled round with rivers the world which was made by Thee through Christ, and hast watered it with mountain-streams, and hast moistened it with everflowing springs, and hast bound it round with mountains, to make the earth most secure and unmoved. Thou hast replenished Thy world and adorned it with fragrant and medicinal herbs, with many and different kinds of living creatures, strong and weakly, edible and workable, tame and wild; with the hissing of serpents, and the cries of many-coloured birds; with the revolutions of years and the numbers of months and days, the succession of seasons, and the courses of clouds big with rain, for the production of fruits, and the support of living creatures. Thou hast appointed the station of the winds,[1] which blow at Thy command, and the multitude of plants and herbs.

And not only hast Thou created the world, but Thou didst also make man the citizen therein, exhibiting him as the ornament thereof.[2] For Thou didst say to Thy Wisdom, "Let us make man in our image, after our likeness; and let them have dominion over the fish of the sea, and over the fowl of the air."[3] Wherefore, too, Thou madest him of an immortal soul and a perishable body, the soul out of

[1] Job xxviii. 25.
[2] Κόσμον κόσμου. It has not been found possible to preserve the play upon the words in a translation. See pp. 265, note 3; 285, note 1.
[3] Gen. i. 26.

nothing, the body out of the four elements; and as to the soul, Thou didst endow him with rational knowledge, with the power of discerning between piety and impiety, and of observing right and wrong; and, as to the body, Thou didst grant him five senses, and the power of progressive motion. For Thou, O Almighty God, didst by Christ plant a garden eastwards in Eden,[1] adorned with every kind of edible food, and into it as into a sumptuous dwelling-place Thou didst introduce man. And when Thou madest him, Thou didst give him an implanted law, that at home and within himself he might have the seeds of divine knowledge. And when Thou hadst brought him into this paradise of luxury,[2] Thou didst allow unto him the power of partaking of all things, forbidding him only the taste of a single tree, in hope of greater blessings, in order that if he kept the commandment, he might receive the reward of his obedience in immortality. But when he neglected the commandment and tasted the forbidden fruit by the guile of the serpent and the counsel of his wife,[3] Thou didst justly cast him out of paradise; yet in Thy goodness Thou didst not suffer him to fall into utter destruction, for he was the work of Thy hands, but Thou didst subject creation to him, and didst grant unto him that he should procure sustenance for himself by the sweat of his brow and the labour of his hands, while Thou didst cause all the fruits of the earth to spring up, and grow, and ripen. At length, having laid him to sleep for a little while, Thou didst promise with an oath to recall him to a regeneration, having loosed the bond of death, and promised him life after resurrection. Nor was this all, but Thou didst also multiply his posterity without number, glorifying those who remained true to

[1] Gen. ii. 8.
[2] Παράδεισος τρυφῆς. This phrase is found in Gen. ii. 15; iii. 24.
[3] This long account of the fall is paralleled by a similar but still more detailed account of the same event in the fragment of a Copto-Thebaic Liturgy published by F. A. A. Georgius (Rome, 1789), and assigned by him to the end of the fourth century (*Fragmentum Evangelii S. Iohannis*, pp. 301-315).

Thee, and punishing those who rebelled against Thee. And while Thou didst accept the sacrifice of Abel as of an holy man, Thou didst reject the offering of Cain who slew his brother as of an accursed person. Besides these Thou didst accept of Seth and Enos, and didst translate Enoch. For Thou art the Creator of men, and the Supplier of life, and the Fulfiller of want, and the Giver of laws, and the Rewarder of those who keep them, and the Avenger of those who break them. Thou didst bring the great flood upon the world because of the number of the ungodly, saving righteous Noe from it in the ark with eight souls,[1] the last of the foregoing and the first of succeeding generations. Thou didst kindle a fearful fire upon the five cities of Sodom,[2] and didst turn a fruitful land into a salt lake for the wickedness of them that dwell therein,[3] but didst snatch holy Lot out of the burning. Thou art He who didst deliver Abraham from the impiety of his forefathers, and madest him heir of the world, and revealedst unto him Thy Christ.[4] Thou didst beforehand ordain Melchisedech to be the high priest in Thy service. Thou didst render Thy much-suffering servant Job conqueror over the serpent, the originator of evil. Thou madest Isaac the son of the promise, and Jacob the father of twelve sons, whose descendants Thou didst multiply exceedingly, bringing him into Egypt with seventy-five souls. Thou, O Lord, didst not overlook Joseph, but gavest him, as a reward for his chastity for Thy sake, the government of the Egyptians. Thou, O Lord, didst not overlook the Hebrews when they were evil-entreated by the Egyptians, on account of the promises made unto their fathers, but Thou didst deliver them, and punish the Egyptians. And when men corrupted the law of nature, sometimes deeming creation to be an automaton, sometimes honouring it more than was meet, and marshalling it against Thee who art

---

[1] Cf. 1 Pet. iii. 20; 2 Pet. ii. 5.
[2] Wisdom x. 6.
[3] Ps. cvii. 34.
[4] Cf. St. John viii. 56.

the God of all things,[1] Thou didst not suffer them to err; but Thou didst raise up Thy holy servant Moses, and by him didst give the written law to assist the law of nature, showing the creation to be Thy handiwork, and abolishing the error of polytheism. Thou didst adorn Aaron and his sons with the honour of the priesthood. Thou didst punish the Hebrews when they sinned, and didst receive them again when they returned to Thee. Thou didst take vengeance on the Egyptians with ten plagues. Thou didst divide the sea, causing the Israelites to pass through, destroying the Egyptians who pursued them beneath its waves. With wood Thou didst make the bitter water sweet. Thou didst bring water out of the precipice of stone. Thou didst rain down manna from heaven, and broughtest food from the air in the form of quails.[2] Thou gavest them a pillar of fire by night to give them light, and a pillar of cloud by day as a shadow from the heat. Thou appointedst Jesus to be the leader of their hosts, and through Him didst destroy the seven nations of the Canaanites. Thou didst divide Jordan, and dry up the rivers of Etham,[2] and overthrow walls without machinery, and without the aid of human hands.[3]

For all these things glory be to Thee, O Lord Almighty. Countless hosts of angels, archangels, thrones, dominions, principalities, authorities, powers, hosts, æons[4] worship Thee; the Cherubim and six-winged Seraphim, with twain covering their feet, and with twain covering their heads, and with twain flying,[5] together with thousand

---

[1] Cf. Rom. i. 21-25.   [2] Ps. lxxiv. 15.

[3] For the historical portion of this Preface compare the confession of the Levites in Neh. ix. and ch. xi. of the Epistle to the Hebrews.

[4] Both in Dr. Neale's translation of this Liturgy (*The Liturgies of St. Mark*, etc., London, 1859, p. 82), and in the translation contained in *A. C. L.* (Edinburgh, 1870, vol. xvii. p. 230), the mention of æons is omitted, αἰώνων being read as αἰωνίων, and made to agree with στρατιῶν.

[5] Isa. vi. 2.

thousands of archangels, and ten thousand times ten thousand of angels, saying incessantly with unsilenced shouts of praise :

[TRIUMPHAL HYMN, OR TERSANCTUS.[1]]

And let all the people say together:

"Holy, holy, holy, is the Lord of hosts. Heaven and earth are full of His glory." [2] Blessed is He for ever. Amen.[3]

[COMMEMORATION OF THE WORK OF REDEMPTION.]

After this let the Bishop [4] *say:*

For truly Thou art holy, and most holy, the most highest and highly exalted for ever. Holy also is Thy only-begotten Son, our Lord and God, Jesus Christ, who in all things doing service to Thee His God and Father, both in the creation of different things, and in taking care of them as they required, did not overlook the perishing human race ; for after the law of nature, and the warnings of the positive law, and the reproofs of prophets, and the superintendence of angels, when men were corrupting both natural law and the positive law, and were banishing from their memory the burning [of Sodom], and the plagues of Egypt, and the slaughter of the nations of Palestine, being just ready to perish universally, the Creator of man was pleased Himself with Thy consent to become man, the Law-giver to become a subject, the High Priest to become a victim, the Shepherd to become a sheep. And He appeased Thee His God and Father, and reconciled Thee to the world,[5] and freed all

---

[1] This is the more correct title ; the title of 'Trisagion' belongs to another hymn, for some account of which see p. 260.

[2] Isa. vi. 3.

[3] This short form of the Hymn without the full Benedictus closely resembles the form in the Anglican Liturgy.

[4] Ὁ ἀρχιερεύς.

[5] This is a curious phrase, inverting St. Paul's order of words in 2. Cor. vi. 19. It points to an early date when liturgical language had not acquired theological exactness. See p. 276.

men from the impending wrath. He was born of a Virgin, incarnate, God the Word, the beloved Son, the First-born of every creature,[1] and, according to the prophecies spoken before concerning Him by Himself, of the seed of David and Abraham, and of the tribe of Judah. He who fashioneth all who are born into this world was formed in the Virgin's womb; He took flesh who was without flesh; He who was begotten in eternity was born in time. He was holy in His conversation, and taught according to the law. He drove away all manner of sickness and all manner of disease from among the people.[2] He wrought signs and wonders in their midst.[3] He who nourisheth all that stand in need of nourishment, and filleth all things living with plenteousness,[4] partook of food, and drink, and sleep. He made manifest Thy Name to them that knew it not; He put ignorance to flight; He kindled the light of piety; He fulfilled Thy will, finishing the work which Thou gavest Him to do.[5] And having accomplished all these things, He was seized by the hands of wicked men, priests and high priests, falsely so called, and a lawless mob, through the treachery of one who was possessed by wickedness as by a disease. And He suffered many things at their hands, and endured all manner of indignity by Thy permission, and was delivered over to Pilate the governor. And the Judge was judged, the Saviour was condemned, the impassible One was nailed to the cross; He who was by nature immortal died; the Giver of life was buried,[6] that He might loose from suffering and deliver from death those for whose sake He came, and that He might break the chains of the devil, and deliver mankind from his deceit. And on the third day He rose again from the dead, and after continuing forty days with His disciples, He was received up

---

[1] Col. i. 15. [2] St. Matt. iv. 23. [3] Acts v. 2.
[4] Ps. cxlv. 16. [5] St. John xvii. 4.
[6] The language of the original Greek is here very beautiful. There is a terse antithesis in repeated clauses which it is impossible to preserve fully in a translation.

into heaven, and sat on the right hand of Thee His God and Father.[1]

[COMMEMORATION OF THE INSTITUTION.]

Mindful therefore of what things He suffered on our behalf, we give thanks to Thee, Almighty God, not as we ought, but as we are able, and we fulfill His institution. For in the same night in which He was betrayed, He took bread in His holy and spotless hands, and looking up to Thee His God and Father, He brake it, and gave it to His disciples, saying, " This is the mystery of the New Testament. Take of it, eat; this is My body, which is broken for many for the remission of sins." Likewise also having mingled the cup with wine and water, and having blessed it, He gave it to them, saying, " Drink ye all of it; this is My blood, which is shed for many for the remission of sins. Do this in remembrance of me ; for as often as ye eat this bread, and drink this cup, ye do show My death until I come." [2]

[THE GREAT OBLATION.]

Remembering therefore His passion, and death, and resurrection from the dead, and ascension into heaven, and His future second coming, in which He cometh with glory and power to judge the quick and the dead, and to render to every man according to his deeds,[3] we offer to Thee, our King and our God, according to His institution, this bread and this cup, giving thanks to Thee through Him that Thou hast thought us worthy to stand in Thy presence, and to offer as priests before Thee.

[THE INVOCATION.]

And we beseech Thee that Thou wouldest look graciously on these gifts now lying before Thee, O God, who needest naught : and that Thou wouldest be well-pleased to accept them to the honour of Thy Christ, and that Thou wouldest send down Thy Holy Spirit, the witness of the sufferings of

[1] St. Mark xvi. 19.
[2] Chiefly based on St. Matt. xxvi. 26-28, and 1 Cor. xi. 23-26.
[3] Rom. ii. 6.

the Lord Jesus,[1] upon this sacrifice, that He may make[2] this bread the body of Thy Christ, and this cup the blood of Thy Christ; so that they who partake thereof may be confirmed in piety, may obtain remission of their sins, and be delivered from the devil and his wiles, may be filled with the Holy Ghost, may be made worthy of Thy Christ, and may obtain eternal life, Thou, O Lord Almighty, being reconciled to them.[3]

[GREAT INTERCESSION.]

We further beseech Thee, O Lord, for Thy holy Church universal,[4] which Thou hast purchased with the precious blood of Thy Christ, that Thou wouldest keep it, unshaken and unstormed, until the end of the world, and for every episcopate rightly dividing the Word of truth.[5]

We further beseech Thee on behalf of myself, who am nothing, who now offer unto Thee, and on behalf of the whole presbyterate, on behalf of the deacons, and of all the clergy, that Thou wouldest endue them all with wisdom, and fill them with the Holy Ghost.

Furthermore, we beseech Thee, O Lord, for the king and those that are in authority,[6] and for the whole army, that they may be peaceably disposed towards us,[7] in order that leading all the rest of our life in peace and quietness we may glorify Thee through Jesus Christ our hope.

Furthermore, we offer unto Thee on behalf of all Thy saints who have pleased Thee from the beginning of the world, patriarchs, prophets, just men, apostles, martyrs, confessors, bishops, presbyters, deacons, sub-deacons,

---

[1] 1 Pet. v. 1.

[2] Ἀποφήνῃ, which may also be rendered 'may show this bread to be.'

[3] This curious expression reminds us of the previously used phrase on p. 297, where see note 5.

[4] Ἀπὸ περάτων ἕως περάτων.

[5] 2 Tim. ii. 15. [6] 1 Tim. ii. 2.

[7] This petition implies an early date, when the king and the army were still heathen and hostile to the Christian religion.

readers, singers, virgins, widows, laity, and all those whose names Thou Thyself knowest.

Furthermore, we offer unto Thee, on behalf of this people, that Thou wouldst make them,[1] to the praise of Thy Christ, a royal priesthood, a holy nation;[2] on behalf of those who are living in virginity and purity; on behalf of the widows of the Church; on behalf of those who are living in holy matrimony, and who are labouring with child; and on behalf of the infants among Thy people, that Thou wilt not suffer any of us to be cast away.

Furthermore, we entreat Thee also on behalf of this city,[3] and them that dwell therein; for the sick; for those who are in the bitterness of slavery;[4] for those in banishment;[4] for those in prison;[4] for those who are travelling by land or water, that Thou wouldest be the Helper, Assister, and Supporter of them all.

Furthermore, we beseech Thee also on behalf of those who hate us and persecute us for Thy Name's sake; on behalf of those that are without, and wandering out of the way; that Thou wouldest convert them to that which is good, and appease their wrath against us.

Furthermore, we beseech Thee also on behalf of the catechumens of the Church, and for those who are vexed by the adversary,[5] and on behalf of our brethren who are penitents, that Thou wouldest perfect the former in the faith, and cleanse the second from the possession of the evil one, and accept the repentance of the last, and forgive unto them and unto us our trespasses.

Furthermore, we also offer unto Thee that we may experience a seasonable temperature and receive the fruits of the earth in due season, in order that perpetually

---

[1] Ἀναδείξῃς.   [2] 1 Pet. ii. 9.

[3] Jerusalem, Rome, or Antioch, the Bishops of which cities have been previously named on page 286.

[4] These expressions imply an early date, in the times of heathen persecution.

[5] *i.e.* possessed by the devil, energumens.

partaking of good things from Thee, we may praise Thee unceasingly, Who givest food to all flesh.[1]

Furthermore, we beseech Thee also' on behalf of those who are absent for a just reason, that Thou wouldest keep us all in piety, and gather us immovable, unblamable, irreproachable, within the kingdom of Thy Christ, the God of all sensible and intelligent nature; for to Thee be all glory, worship and thanksgiving, honour and adoration, to Father, and Son, and Holy Ghost, both now and ever, and for unceasing and unending generation after generation.

And let all the people say :

Amen.

Then let the Bishop say:

The peace of God be with you all.

And let all the people say:

And with Thy Spirit.

Then let the Deacon proclaim again:

Let us again and again beseech God through His Christ.

Let us pray to the Lord our God on behalf of the gift which has been offered, that the good God would receive it through the mediation of His Christ upon His heavenly altar for a sweet-smelling savour.[2]

Let us beseech Him on behalf of this church and people.

Let us beseech Him for the whole episcopate, the whole presbyterate, the whole diaconate and ministry in Christ, and for the whole body which fills up the church, that the Lord would preserve and keep them all.

Let us beseech Him for kings and those in authority, that they may be peaceably disposed towards us, that we may lead a quiet and peaceable life in all godliness and honesty.[3]

Let us remember the holy martyrs, that we may be found worthy to become partakers of their trial.

[1] Ps. cxxxvi. 25.   [2] Eph. v. 2.   [3] 1 Tim. ii. 2.

Let us pray for those who have passed to their rest in faith.

Let us pray for a seasonable temperature, and for the full maturing of the fruits of the earth.

Let us pray on behalf of the newly baptized,[1] that they may be confirmed in the faith.

Let us entreat God on behalf of one another. Raise us up, O God, by Thy grace.[2]

Let us stand up, and dedicate ourselves to God through His Christ.[3]

[PRAYER OF HUMBLE ACCESS.]

Then let the Bishop say:

O God, who art great, and whose Name is great, who art great in counsel and powerful in works, the God and Father of Thy holy Child Jesus,[4] our Saviour, look upon us, and upon Thy flock, which Thou hast chosen through Him to the glory of Thy Name; sanctify us both in body and soul, and grant that being cleansed from all filthiness of flesh and spirit,[5] we may partake of the good things spread before us; and judge none of us unworthy of them, but be Thou our Supporter, and Helper, and Protector, through Thy Christ, with whom to Thee and to the Holy Ghost, be glory, honour, praise, adoration, and thanksgiving for ever. Amen.

And after all have said ' Amen,' *let the Deacon say:*

Let us attend.

[SANCTA SANCTIS.]

Then let the Bishop make this proclamation to the people:

Holy things to holy persons.

And let the people reply:

There is one holy One, one Lord, one Jesus Christ, to the glory of God the Father, blessed for ever. Amen. Glory

---
[1] Νεοφωτίστων.
[2] This is the people's response to the deacon's invitation.
[3] This is another invitation on the part of the deacon.
[4] Acts iv. 30.　　[5] 2 Cor. vii. 1.

to God in the highest, and on earth peace, good will towards men.[1] Hosanna to the Son of David, blessed is He that cometh in the name of the Lord.[2] God is the Lord who hath also appeared unto us.[3] Hosanna in the highest.

[THE COMMUNION.]

After this, let the Bishop receive; then the Presbyters, and Deacons, and Sub-Deacons, and Readers, and Singers, and Ascetics, and among the women the Deaconesses, and the Virgins, and the Widows; then the children, and afterwards all the people in order with fear and reverence, without tumult:

Then let the Bishop administer the oblation, saying:

The Body of Christ.

And let the person receiving say:

Amen.

Then let the Deacon take the cup, and as he administers it let him say:

The Blood of Christ, the cup of life.

And let him that drinketh say:

Amen.

And let the thirty-third Psalm[4] be said while all the rest are receiving, and when all, both men and women have received, let the Deacons take up what remains [of the consecrated elements] and bear it to the sacristy:

[THE POST-COMMUNION THANKSGIVING.]

And when the Singer has finished let the Deacon say:

Having received the precious body and the precious blood of Christ, let us give thanks unto Him who hath deemed us worthy to partake of His holy mysteries, and let us beseech Him that it may not be to us for condemnation, but for salvation, to the benefit of soul and body, for

---

[1] St. Luke ii. 14.   [2] St. Matt. xxi. 9.
[3] Ps. cxviii. [lxx. cxvii.] 27.
[4] *I.e.* Ps. xxxiv. in A.V.; especially suitable on account of verse 8.

the preservation of godliness, for the forgiveness of sins, and for the life of the world to come.

Let us arise. In the grace of Christ let us commend ourselves to God, the only unbegotten God, and to His Christ.

[THANKSGIVING.]

And let the Bishop give thanks:

O Lord God Almighty, Father of Thy Christ Thy blessed Son, who art ready to hear them that with uprightness call upon Thee, and who knowest the petitions of them that are silent, we yield Thee thanks for that Thou hast vouchsafed unto us to partake of Thy holy mysteries, which Thou hast given unto us, for the fulfilment of good resolutions, for the preservation of piety, and for the remission of transgressions; because the name of Thy Christ hath been called over us, and we have been enrolled in Thy family. Thou who hast separated us from fellowship with the ungodly, unite us with those who have been sanctified to Thee, establish us in the truth by the descent of the Holy Ghost; that which we do not know do Thou reveal; that which is wanting do Thou fill up; in that which is known to us do Thou strengthen us; preserve Thy priests[1] blameless in Thy service; maintain kings in peace, and rulers in righteousness; preserve the atmosphere in a good temperature, the fruits of the earth in fertility, the world in Thy all-powerful providence. Soften the nations that delight in war, turn back that which has gone astray; hallow Thy people; guard the virgins; keep married people faithful; strengthen the continent; bring infants to riper years; confirm the newly baptized;[2] instruct the catechumens; cause them to become worthy of initiation,[3] and lead us all into the kingdom of heaven, through Christ Jesus our Lord, with whom to Thee and to the Holy Ghost be glory, honour, and worship for ever. Amen.

---

[1] Ἱερεῖς. See chap. ii. § 16, p. 140. [2] Τοὺς νεοτελεῖς.
[3] Τῆς μυήσεως, *i.e.* baptism.

[BENEDICTION.]
Then let the Deacon say:

Bow down to God through His Christ, and receive the blessing.

And let the Bishop pray over them, saying:

O God Almighty, true and incomparable, who art everywhere, and art present in all things, though existing in nothing as part hereof, Thou who art not circumscribed by place or aged by time, who art not limited by ages, or led aside by words, who art not subject to generation and needest no guard, who art superior to corruption, and unsusceptible of change, who art immutable by nature, dwelling in the light which no man can approach unto,[1] naturally invisible, yet comprehensible to all reasonable natures that with good will seek for Thee, the God of Israel, Thy people which truly seeth Thee,[2] and which hath believed in Christ, be favourable and hear me for Thy name's sake, and bless those that have bowed their necks unto Thee, and grant unto them their hearts' desires so far as may be expedient for them, and suffer none of them to be cast away out of Thy kingdom, but sanctify them, guard them, shelter them, assist them, rescue them from the adversary and from every enemy, protect their houses; keep them in their coming in and in their going out; for to Thee belongeth glory, praise, majesty, worship, and adoration, and to Thy Son Jesus Christ, our Lord, and God, and King, and to the Holy Ghost, now and ever, and for endless ages. Amen.

[DISMISSAL.]
And the Deacon shall say:

Depart in peace.'

§ 15. ANOTHER DESCRIPTION OF THE LITURGY.

This will perhaps be the most convenient point at which to append the description of the early

---

[1] 1 Tim. vi. 16.

[2] According to a popular but erroneous derivation, 'Israel' was believed to mean 'one who sees God.'

Christian Liturgy, as found in Book ii. chap. 57 of the Apostolic Constitutions. The person addressed is the bishop.

'When thou callest together the Church of God, as the commander[1] of a great ship, order the assemblies to be made with all knowledge, charging the Deacons as mariners to assign places to the brethren as passengers, with all carefulness and solemnity.

And, in the first place, let the building be long, turned towards the East, with vestries on both sides at the east end; and it will be like a ship. Let the Bishop's throne[2] be placed in the middle, and the Presbyters be seated on each side of him, while the Deacons stand by in for the most part closely girt vestments, because they correspond to the sailors and to the overseers of the rowers on each side of the ship. Let these so arrange that the laymen be seated in a different part of the church, in a silent and orderly way; and let the women be seated apart by themselves, they also keeping silence.

[LECTIONS.—(a) *Old Testament.*]

In the middle let the Reader, standing in some elevated position, read the Books of Moses and of Jesus the son of Nave, Judges, Kings, Chronicles, and Books connected with the return from the Captivity; and in addition to these the Books of Job, of Solomon, and of the sixteen prophets.

[(b) *Acts and Epistles.*]

And when two lessons have been read, let some one else sing the hymns of David,[3] and let the people join at the conclusion of the verses.[4] Afterwards let our Acts be read,

---

[1] Κυβερνήτης.

[2] Θρόνος. This word does not necessarily mean 'a throne,' or 'chair of state;' any seat is a θρόνος.

[3] Evidently the Book of Psalms.

[4] This is probably not the 'Gloria Patri,' but the verse, or portion of a verse, sung over again by the people after a certain number of verses in the old responsorial mode of chanting.

and the Epistles of Paul, our fellow-labourer, which he sent to the Churches under the conduct of the Holy Ghost.

[(c) *Gospel.*]

After this, let a Deacon or Presbyter read the Gospels, both those which we Matthew and John have delivered to you, and those which the fellow-labourers of Paul received and left to you, Luke and Mark.

And when the Gospel is read, let all the Presbyters, and Deacons, and all the people stand in perfect silence, for it is written, "Take heed, and hearken, O Israel,"[1] and again, "Do thou stand here and hearken."[2]

[SERMON.]

Next let the Presbyters exhort the people, one by one, not all together, and last of all the Bishop who resembles the commander.[3]

Let the door-keepers stand at the men's entrances and guard them, and the deaconesses at the women's entrances, like persons taking seamen on board. For the same [description and] pattern was also in the tabernacle of the testimony, [and in the temple of God.][4] And if any person be found sitting in a wrong place, let him be rebuked by the Deacon, as by the man standing at the ship's head, and let him be transferred to his proper place. For the church is not only like a ship, but it is also like a sheepfold. For as shepherds place these brute beasts, goats and sheep, separately according to their kind and age, and each of them has a tendency to run together, the like to his like ; so let it be in the church ; let the younger people sit by themselves, if there be a place for them, if not let them stand upright ; and let those who are already advanced in years be seated in order. As to the children who are standing, let their fathers and mothers take charge of them. The younger women again let them sit by themselves, if there be room, but, if not, let them stand behind the women. And

---

[1] Deut. xxvii. 9.   [2] Deut. vi. 31.   [3] Κυβερνήτης.
[4] The words within brackets are omitted in some MSS.

let the women who have been already married, and have borne children, be placed by themselves. The virgins, and widows, and the older women should stand or be seated first of all. The Deacon should be the disposer of places beforehand, in order that every one who enters may go into his proper place, and may not sit at the entrance. In the same way let the Deacon superintend the people, in order that no one may whisper, or slumber, or laugh, or nod; for people ought to stand in church wisely, and soberly, and watchfully, having their attention fixed on the word of the Lord.

[EXPULSION OF CATECHUMENS AND PENITENTS.—
PRAYER OF THE FAITHFUL, ETC.]

After this, let all rise up with one consent, and looking eastward, after the departure of the catechumens and penitents, pray in the eastward position to God who ascended up to the heaven of heavens, remembering also the original situation of paradise in the East, whence the first man was expelled, after he had broken the commandment, persuaded by the serpent's guile.

After the prayer, let some of the Deacons attend upon the oblation of the Eucharist, waiting upon the body of the Lord with fear, and let others of the Deacons keep watch on the congregation,[1] and ensure silence among them.

Then let the Deacon who is in attendance on the Bishop[2] say to the people:

Let no one have a quarrel against any, let no one come in hypocrisy.

[KISS OF PEACE.]

Then let the men salute each other, and the women salute each other with the kiss of peace, but let no one act deceitfully, as Judas betrayed the Lord with a kiss.

[DEACON'S BIDDING PRAYER.]

After this, let the Deacon pray for the whole Church, and for the whole world, with the parts thereof and the fruits

[1] Τοὺς ὄχλους. [2] Ἀρχιερεύς.

thereof, for priests and rulers, for the Bishop,[1] and the king, and for universal peace.

[BENEDICTION OF THE PEOPLE.]

After this, let the Bishop[1] pray for peace upon the people, and bless them, as Moses commanded the priests to bless the people with these words, " The Lord bless thee, and keep thee. The Lord make His face to shine upon thee, and give thee peace."[2]

Then let the Bishop pray over the people, and say, "Save Thy people, O Lord, and bless Thine inheritance, which Thou hast purchased and acquired with the precious blood of Thy Christ, and hast called a royal priesthood and a holy nation."[3]

[GREAT OBLATION.—COMMUNION.]

After this, let the sacrifice follow, all the people standing, and praying silently ; and when the oblation has been made, let each rank by itself partake of the body of the Lord and His precious blood, in order, with reverence, and godly fear.

Let the women approach with their heads covered, as becometh the rank of women. The doors should be guarded, lest any unbeliever, or any unbaptized[4] person should come in.'

[1] 'Αρχιερεύς.
[2] Abbreviated from Numb. vi. 24-26. This Levitical Benediction appears in the old Gallican Liturgy; Germanus, *Expositio brevis Antiquæ Liturgiæ Gallicanæ*, given in Martene, *De Antiquis Ecclesiæ Ritibus*, lib. i. cap. iv. art. xii. ordo. i. ; in the old Irish Liturgy as represented by the Book of Dimma, Book of Mulling, and the Stowe Missal ; Warren (F. E.), *Liturgy and Ritual of the Celtic Church*, pp. 171, 172, 225 ; in the Anglo-Saxon Liturgy, where it occurs among the Episcopal Benedictions at Mass for special days in the Leofric Missal (p. 248), and for the first Sunday after Pentecost in the Benedictional of St. Ethelwold. It occurs in its present abbreviated form at the end of the Commination Service in the Book of Common Prayer.
[3] 1 Pet. i. 19 ; ii. 9.   [4] 'Αμύητος.

§ 16. A Prayer at the Ordination of a Presbyter.

This prayer is to be said by the bishop while he is laying his hands on the candidate in the presence of the presbyters and deacons—

'O Lord Almighty, our God, who hast created all things by Christ, and who, with mutual love, takest care of the whole world by Him; for He who had power to make different creatures, has also power to take care of them in different ways. Wherefore, O God, Thou providest for immortal beings by bare protection, but for mortal beings by succession—in the case of the soul by attention to laws, in the case of the body by the supply of its wants. Do Thou now, therefore, also look down Thyself upon Thy holy Church, and increase it, and multiply those that preside over it, and grant them power to labour, both in word and deed, for the edification of Thy people. Look down also now upon this Thy servant, who is advanced to the presbyterate by the vote and decision of the whole clergy, and fill him with the spirit of grace and counsel, that he may help and guide Thy people with a pure heart, as Thou didst look down upon Thy chosen people, and didst command Moses to choose elders,[1] whom Thou didst fill with Thy spirit. Do Thou also now, O Lord, grant this, and preserve in us the unfailing spirit of Thy grace, in order that Thy servant, being filled with the gifts of healing and the word of teaching, may in meekness instruct Thy people, and may serve Thee sincerely with a pure mind and a willing heart, and may blamelessly discharge the priestly ministrations on behalf of Thy people;[2] through Thy Christ, with whom to Thee and the Holy Ghost, be glory, honour, and worship for ever. Amen.'[3]

---

[1] Πρεσβυτέρους. We have translated it by the word 'elders,' as found in Ex. xxiv. 9 (A.V.).

[2] Καὶ τὰς ὑπὲρ τοῦ λαοῦ ἱερουργίας ἀμώμους ἐκτελῇ.

[3] Lib. viii. cap. 16, pp. 217, 218.

§ 17. A Prayer at the Ordination of a Deacon.

This prayer is to be said by the bishop, laying his hands on the candidate in the presence of the presbyters and deacons—

'O God Almighty, true and without guile, who art rich unto all them that call upon Thee in truth,[1] fearful in counsels, wise in understanding, powerful and great, hear our prayer, O Lord, and hearken unto our supplication, and cause the light of Thy countenance to shine upon this Thy servant, who is being ordained to the office of deacon in Thy service; and replenish him with the Holy Spirit and with power, as Thou didst replenish Stephen the martyr and follower of the sufferings of Thy Christ. Do Thou make him worthy to discharge acceptably the office of a deacon now committed unto him, steadily, unblamably, without reproach, that so he may become worthy of a higher degree; through the mediation of Thy only-begotten Son, with whom glory, honour, and worship be unto Thee and the Holy Spirit for ever. Amen.'[2]

§ 18. A Prayer at the Ordination of a Deaconess.

This prayer is to be said by the bishop, laying his hand upon the candidate in the presence of the presbyters, deacons, and deaconesses—

'O eternal God, the Father of our Lord Jesus Christ, Creator of man and woman, who didst fill with Thy spirit Miriam, and Deborah, and Anna, and Huldah; who didst not disdain that Thy only-begotten Son should be born of a woman; who in the tabernacle of witness and in the temple, didst ordain women to be the keepers of Thy holy gates,[3] do Thou now also look down upon this handmaiden, who is being ordained to the office of deaconess;

---

[1] Rom. x. 12.   [2] Lib. viii. cap. 18, pp. 218, 219.
[3] There is no mention of these female doorkeepers in the Bible.

give unto her the Holy Spirit, and cleanse her from all filthiness of the flesh and spirit,[1] so that she may worthily accomplish the work committed to her hands, to Thy glory, and to the praise of Thy Christ, with whom to Thee, and to the Holy Spirit, be glory and worship for ever. Amen.'[2]

§ 19. A PRAYER AT THE ORDINATION OF A SUB-DEACON. This prayer is to be said by the bishop as he lays his hands upon the head of the candidate—

'O Lord God, the Creator of heaven and earth, and of all things that are therein; who also in the tabernacle of witness didst appoint the vergers to be the guardians of Thy holy vessels;[3] do Thou also now look down upon this Thy servant elected to the office of sub-deacon; and give unto him the Holy Spirit, that he may worthily handle Thy sacred[4] vessels, and do Thy will always; through Thy Christ, with whom to Thee, and to the Holy Ghost, be glory, honour, and worship for ever. Amen.'[5]

§ 20. A PRAYER AT THE ORDINATION OF A READER. This prayer is to be said by the bishop as he lays his hands upon the head of the candidate—

'O eternal God, who art plenteous in mercy and compassions, who hast made manifest the constitution of the world by Thy operations therein, and who keepest the number of Thine elect; do Thou also now look down upon Thy servant who is ordained to the office of reading Thy Holy Scriptures to Thy people, and grant to him Thy Holy Spirit and the spirit of prophecy. Thou who didst give Thy servant Esdras skill to read Thy law to Thy people,[6] now also hear our prayers, and give Thy servant skill, and grant unto him, that he may fulfil, without blame, the work

---

[1] 2 Cor. vii. 1.   [2] Lib. viii. cap. 20, p. 219.
[3] Viz. the Kohathites. Numb. iii. 31.
[4] Τῶν λειτουργικῶν σου σκευῶν.   [5] Lib. viii. cap. 21, p. 220.
[6] Neh. viii. 1-8.

which hath been entrusted to him, and be found worthy of higher advancement, through Christ, with whom to Thee, and to the Holy Ghost, be glory and worship for ever. Amen.'[1]

§ 21. A Consecration of Water and Oil.

'O Lord of hosts, the God of powers, Creator of the waters, and Supplier of oil, who art merciful and a Lover of man, who gavest water for drink and for purification, and oil to make him a cheerful countenance,[2] do Thou now also sanctify this water and this oil through Thy Christ, in the name of him [or her] that hath offered it; and give to them a power to restore health, to banish diseases, to put devils to flight, and to bring to nought every hostile design, through Christ our hope, with whom to Thee, and to the Holy Ghost, be glory, honour, and worship for ever. Amen.'[3]

§ 22. An Evening Prayer.

It will be easier to understand its character, if we reproduce here the preliminary directions and arrangements. When it is evening the bishop is directed to assemble the Church; during the lighting of the lamps a psalm is to be sung; then the deacon is to bid prayers for the catechumens, the energumens, competentes, and penitents. After the dismissal of these, the deacon invites the faithful to pray, and uses these words—

'Save us, O God, and raise us up by Thy Christ. Let us stand up, and pray for the mercies and compassions of the Lord, for the angel of peace, for what things are good and profitable, for a Christian end, for an evening and night peaceful and without sin, and let us pray that the whole course of our life may be without condemnation. Let us commend ourselves and each other to the living God, through His Christ.'[4]

---

[1] Lib. viii. cap. 22, p. 220.
[2] Ps. civ. 15.
[3] Lib. viii. cap. 29, p. 223.
[4] Lib. viii. cap. 36, p. 229.

Then let the Bishop add this prayer, and say:

O God, who art without beginning and without end, who madest the whole world through Christ, and who carest for it, but who art before all things His God and Father, the Lord of the Spirit, the King of all things known to our intelligence or our sense; who hast made the day for the works of light and the night for rest, for our weakness; for the day is Thine, and the night is Thine: Thou hast prepared the light and the sun;[1] O Lord, Thou Lover of men, and full of all goodness, accept favourably this our evening thanksgiving.[2] Thou who hast led us through the length of the day, and hast brought us to the beginning of the night, guard us through Thy Christ, give us a peaceful evening, and a night free from sin; and make us worthy of eternal life, through Thy Christ; through whom to Thee, and to the Holy Ghost, be glory, honour, and worship for ever. Amen.[3]

And let the Deacon say:

Bow down for the laying on of hands.

And let the Bishop say:

O God of our fathers, and Lord of mercy, who by Thy wisdom didst form man as a reasonable creature, beloved of God above all other creatures on the earth, and gavest him power to rule over all things that are in the world; who hast willed to appoint rulers and priests, the former for the security of life, the latter for the regularity of worship, do Thou now also stoop down, O Lord Almighty, and make the light of Thy countenance to shine upon Thy people, who bow the neck of their hearts before Thee. Bless them through Christ, through whom Thou hast enlightened us with the light of knowledge, and hast revealed unto us Thyself, with whom worthy adoration is due to Thee, and

---

[1] Ps. lxxiv. 16.

[2] Εὐχαριστία. The strictly liturgical use of this term seems to be Western only.

[3] Lib. viii. cap. 37, p. 229.

to the Spirit, which is the Paraclete, from every reasonable and holy nature for ever. Amen.¹

And let the Deacon say:

Depart in peace.'

§ 23. A Morning Prayer.

After the repetition of the morning Psalm,² and the dismissal of the catechumens, energumens, competentes, and penitents, and after the usual bidding, the deacon is directed to say—

'Save them, O Lord, and raise them up by Thy grace.

Let us beg the mercies and compassions of the Lord, that this morning, and this day, and the whole time of our sojourning here, may be peaceful and without sin; that He will send to us the angel of peace, and grant to us a Christian end, and the mercy and lovingkindness of God. Let us commend ourselves and each other to the living God, through His only-begotten [Son].³

And let the Bishop add this prayer, and say:

O God, the God of the spirits and of all flesh, incomparable, and in want of nought, who gavest the sun to rule the day, and the moon and the stars to govern the night,⁴ do Thou now also look down upon us with the eyes of pity, and receive our morning thanksgivings, and have mercy upon us. For we have not holden up our hands to any strange God,⁵ neither is there among us any new god, save Thou only the Eternal and Everlasting. Thou who hast given to us our being through Christ, and hast granted to us our well-being through the same, deign also to make us worthy of eternal life through Him, with whom to Thee, and to the Holy Ghost, be glory, honour, and worship for ever. Amen.⁶

---

[1] Lib. viii. cap. 37, p. 229.
[2] Ps. lxiii.
[3] Lib. viii. cap. 37, p. 230.
[4] Ps. cxxxvi. 7, 8.
[5] Ps. xliv. 21.
[6] Lib. viii. cap. 38, p. 230.

And let the Deacon say:
Bow down for the laying on of hands.

And let the Bishop add this prayer, and say:
O God, faithful and true, who hast mercy on thousands, and ten thousands in them that love Thee,[1] Lover of the humble and Protector of them that want, of whom all things stand in need, because all things are subject unto Thee: look down upon this Thy people, who have bowed down their heads to Thee, and bless them with spiritual blessings; keep them as the apple of an eye;[2] preserve them in piety and righteousness; and deem them worthy of eternal life in Christ Jesus Thy well-beloved Son; with whom to Thee and the Holy Ghost, be glory, honour, and worship, now, and for ever, and for endless ages. Amen.[3]

And let the Deacon say:
Depart in peace.'

§ 24. A Thanksgiving at the Presentation of the Firstfruits.

'We give thanks to Thee, O Lord Almighty, Creator and Provider of the universe, through Thy only-begotten Son Jesus Christ our Lord, for the firstfruits now offered unto Thee, not in such manner as we ought, but to such extent as we are able. For who among men can worthily give thanks unto Thee for those things which Thou has given unto them to partake of? O God of Abraham, Isaac, and Jacob, and of all the saints, who madest all things bear to perfection by Thy word, and didst command the earth to bring forth every kind of fruit for our refreshment and our food, giving juices for more sluggish and sheepish natures, grass for animals that eat grass, flesh for some, and seed for others; but corn to us, as advantageous and suitable for our food; and many different things, some for use, some for health, and some for our delight. On all these accounts

---

[1] Exod. xx. 6.   [2] Ps. xvii. 8.   [3] Lib. viii. cap. 39, p. 231.

Thou art worthy to be exalted in hymns of praise, for Thy beneficence unto all, through Christ, through whom to Thee in the Holy Ghost be glory, honour, and worship for ever. Amen.'[1]

§ 25. A Prayer for the Faithful Departed.[2]

First of all, the deacon is directed to bid as follows :—

'Let us pray for our brethren who have passed to their rest in Christ, that God, the Lover of men, who hath received his soul, may forgive him every sin, both voluntary and involuntary, and may be merciful and gracious unto him, and may assign him a place in the country where the pious range at large, in the bosom of Abraham, Isaac, and Jacob, with all those that have pleased Him, and done His will from the beginning of the world, whence grief, and sorrow, and sighing have fled away. Let us arise and commend ourselves and each other to the eternal God through the Word which was in the beginning.

And let the Bishop say:

O Thou, who art by nature immortal and unending, from whom every creature, both immortal and mortal, hath its being; who hast made man, the reasonable living creature, the denizen of this world, in his constitution mortal, therewithal adding the promise of a resurrection; who didst suffer Enoch and Elias not to taste of death; the God of Abraham, the God of Isaac, and the God of Jacob, Thou art their God, not as of the dead, but as of the living;[3] for the souls of all live unto Thee, and the spirits of the righteous are in Thy hand, and there shall no torment touch them;[4] for they are all sanctified under Thy hands;[5] do Thou now also regard this Thy servant, whom Thou hast selected and received into another state, and pardon him whatever sin

---

[1] Lib. viii. cap. 40, p. 231. [2] Lib. viii. cap. 41, p. 231.
[3] St. Matt. xxii. 32. [4] Wisdom iii. 1.
[5] Deut. xxxiii. 3. See LXX.

he hath committed voluntarily or involuntarily; and send angels of mercy to him, and place him in the bosom of the patriarchs and prophets, and apostles, and all who have pleased Thee from the foundation of the world, where there is no grief, nor pain, nor sighing, but the place where pious souls range at large, and a land where the righteous are at rest, and the inhabitants whereof see the glory of Thy Christ, through whom to Thee, in the Holy Spirit, be glory, honour, and worship, thanksgiving, and adoration for ever. Amen.

And let the Deacon say:
Bow down and receive the blessing.

And let the Bishop offer thanksgiving over them in the words which follow:

O Lord, save Thy people, and give Thy blessing unto Thine inheritance,[1] which Thou hast purchased with the precious blood of Thy Christ. Shepherd them under Thy right hand, and cover them under Thy wings, and grant unto them to fight the good fight, and to finish their course, and to keep the faith,[2] immutably, unblamably, and irreprovably, through our Lord Jesus Christ, Thy beloved Son, with whom to Thee, and to the Holy Ghost, be glory, honour, and worship for ever. Amen.'[3]

[1] Ps. xxviii. 10.   [2] 2 Tim. iv. 7.
[3] Lib. viii. cap. 41, pp. 231-233.

INDEX OF BIBLICAL QUOTATIONS AND REFERENCES.

NOTE.—In cases where an asterisk (*) has been prefixed the Septuagint numeration of the Psalms has been followed.

I.—OLD TESTAMENT.

	PAGE		PAGE
GENESIS i. 16	292	Gen. xlviii. 9–20	2
26	265, 293	14	232
ii. 3	2	Exodus iii. 5	224
8	294	14–15	264
15	294	vi. 1	169
iii. 24	294	xii. 15, 18–20	32
iv. 3–5	2	29	229
vii. 2	2	xv. 1–19	203
viii. 20	2	xix. 6	42
xv. 8–18	2	xx. 6	317
xvii. 7	264	xxii. 22	229
10–14	2	xxvii. 2	229
xxii. 17	264	20	208
xxiii. 17–20	3	xxviii. 33–35	221
xxiv. 26	3	xxix. 4	220
65	235	xxx. 22–25	3
xxvi. 25	3	xxx. 34–38	3
xxvii. 27–29	2	xl. 1–11	228
xxviii. 1–4	2	15	70
18	3	Levit. iv. 17	229
20–22	3	25	229
xxxv. 2–3	3	xii. 6–8	65
14	3	xvi. 4, etc.	220
xli. 42	235	Numb. iii. 31	313
xlviii. 4	264	vi. 22–26	4

Y

Numb. viii. 7	69
xv. 37–41	210
xix. 18	69
Deut. iv. 39	267
vi. 4–9	210
31	308
x. 8	237
xi. 13–21	210
xiii. 18	169
xxvi. 3	4
5–10	4
13–15	5
xxvii. 9	308
xxxii. 1–43	203
39	168
xxxiii. 3	267, 318
xxxiv. 9	232
Josh. v. 15	224
2 Sam. xxiv. 1–17	267
1 Kings ii. 7	168
viii. —	228
60	169
ix. 3	6
1 Chron. xiii. 8	6
xv. 14, 16, 28	6
xxiii. 5	6
xxv. 5–6	6
xxviii. 11–19	5
2 Chron. iii. 3	6
vi. 36	285
viii. 14	7
Ezra vi. 16, 17	228
Neh. viii. 1–8	313
ix. 2–4	237
3	236
Job xxviii. 25	293
xxxviii. 11	265
xli. 5	282
Psalm i. 2	280
v. 1, 2, 3	259
vi. 3	245
xvii. 5	284
8	317
xix. —	204
Psalm xxiv. —	203
xxviii. 10	319
xxxii. 6	86, 87
*xxxii. 10	168
xxxiv. —	204, 304
8	304
xxxvi. 9	259
10	259
*xxxix. 2	169
xl. 8, 9	7
xli. 4	259
xliv. 21	316
xlviii. —	203
li. 5	65
10	281
12, 14	284
lv. 18	236
lxiii. —	316
lxviii. 17	267
lxxiv. 8	206
15	296
16	315
lxxxi. —	203
lxxxii. —	203
lxxxviii. 13	259
xc. —	204
1	259
xci. —	204
5, 6	289
xcii. —	203, 204
xciii. —	203, 204
xciv. —	203
*xcix. 3	169
civ. 2	292
15	314
24	266
32	282
cvii. 34	295
cxiii. —	216
5	274
cxiv. —	216
cxviii. 27	304
*cxviii. 114	168
*cxviii. 133	169

BIBLICAL QUOTATIONS AND REFERENCES. 323

	PAGE		PAGE
Ps. cxix. 12	259	Prov. xx. 9	284
62	236	Cant. iii. 11	235
97	280	v. 3	176
164	236	Isaiah i. 16	60
cxxi. 8	280	vi. 2	296
cxxiii. 3	259	3	171, 266, 297
cxxx. 3, 4	285	ix. 6	291
cxxxii. 3	245	xiii. 11	168
cxxxv. —	204	xxxiii. 2	245
cxxxvi. —	204	lvii. 15	168
7, 8	316	lxiv. 4	171
25	259, 302	Jer. xxi. 10	169
cxli. 2	115	Lam. ii. 19	236
cxliii. 9, 10	259	Ezek. iii. 12	267
*cxliv. 18	170	xviii. 23	285
cxlv. —	204	xxi. 26	168
2	259	xxxvi. 25	69
16	298	Dan. vi. 10	236
cxlvi. —	204	vii. 10	171
cxlvii. —	204	Dan. viii. 13	266
cxlviii. —	204	Nahum i. 3, 4	282
cxlix. —	204	Zech. viii. 19	229
cl. —	204	Mal. i. 11	7, 130, 263
Prov. ix. 5	124		

II.—APOCRYPHA.

2 Esd. viii. 23	282	Ecclus. xvi. 18, 19	168
Tobit viii. 5	259	xlvii. 9, 10	7
Judith ix. 11	168	Song of the 3 Ch. 29, 30	259
Wisdom iii. 1	318	1 Macc. i. 54	79
vii. 17	169	iv. —	228
x. 6	295	2 Macc. x. —	228
Ecclus. viii. 5	284	xii. 44, 45	238

III.—NEW TESTAMENT.

St. Matt. iv. 23	298	St. Matt. vii. 25	286
v. 23, 24	37	x. 1, 7, 8, 40	39
vi. 5	237	9, 10	47
12	86	17	207
13	288	xvi. 18	286
14, 15	86	xvi. 19	24
vii. 6	173	xviii. 18	24

INDEX.

	PAGE
St. Matt. xix. 13, 15	17
. 29	287
. xxi. 3	25
9	304
12, 13	42
xxii. 32	318
xxiii. 3, 4	207
xxiv. 31	173
xxvi. 26-28..26, 33, 87, 299	
30	33
xxvii. 66	22
xxviii. 19-20	10
St. Mark i. 4	10
iii. 27	282
v. 2-20	281
vi. 13	46
x. 9	38
xi. 15	42
xiv. 22-24	26
26	33
49	42
xvi. 15, 16	10
19	299
St. Luke i. 49, 51, 52, 54, 55	243
68, 69, 71-73	243
77-79	244
ii. 14	244, 304
29, 30	244
29-32	259
42	222
iv. 16, 33	42
17	205
18	21
vii. 47	86
x. 1	40
18	282
19	282
26, 27	210
xi. 41	86
xii. 11	207
xv. 10	284
11-32	285
22	235
xviii. 8	25

	PAGE
St. Luke xix. 45	42
xxi. 12	206
xxii. 19-20	26
41	143
xxiv. 50	17
52, 53	43
St. John ii. 13-16	42
iii. 3	60
5	9, 13, 64
22	10
33	22
iv. 1, 2	10
24	8
vi. 27	22
viii. 56	295
x. 22	229
29	288
xiii. 13, 14	25, 48, 176
xvii. 4	298
17	289
xx. 21-23	24, 40, 87
Acts i. 3	45
5, 8	10
ii. 15	236
41	11, 14
42	30, 44
46	30, 31, 43
iii. 1	43, 236
iv. 27	21, 71, 90
30	303
v. 2	298
vi. 6	41
viii. 12, 13	11
12, 14, 15, 17	19
16	11
27	15
38	11, 13
ix. 18	11
x. 3	236
9	236
38	21
47, 48	11
xii. 8	47
xiii. 3	41

BIBLICAL QUOTATIONS AND REFERENCES.

	PAGE		PAGE
Acts xiii. 24	10	1 Cor. xi. 25–28	18
xiv. 23	42	26	25
xv. 21	45, 205	27–29	32
23	42	34	9
xvi. 15, 33	11	xii. 26	31
25	33	29	42
xviii. 8	11	xiv. 1–28	164
25	10	16	31
xix. 5, 6	11, 20	19	44
xx. 7	31, 44, 46, 115, 133	29	42
		34, 35	44
28	42	40	9, 45
xxii. 16	14	xv. 3–5	15
17	43	29	12, 96
19	207	xvi. 1, 2	39, 44, 46
xxvi. 11	207	20	36
Rom. i. 21, 25	296	2 Cor. i. 3	274
ii. 6	299	21	20
iv. 11	22	22	21
vi. 3	12	ii. 6–11	24
4	14	vi. 16	280
17	23	vii. 1	280, 284, 303, 313
x. 4	7	xi. 24	207
12	312	xiii. 12	36
xiii. 11, 12	35	14	17, 279, 290
xv. 16	42	Gal. iii. 24	7
28	22	Eph. i. 13	21
xvi. 16	36	iii. 15	291
20	284	iv. 11	42
1 Cor. i. 14, 16	11	30	21
ii. 9	171, 172	v. 2	302
iv. 1, 2	42	14	35
v. 3–5	24	19	34
vi. 11	14	22–32	39
vii. 39	38	25, 26	13
ix. 2	22	27	288
x. 16	18, 30	Phil. iv. 3	284
21	18, 19, 32	7	17
xi. 2, 4, 5	44	Col. i. 15	269, 291, 298
17–34	37, 133	17	291
20	30, 38, 133	ii. 11, 12	14, 220
23	16	14	284
23–26	26, 299	iii. 16	34
25	33	1 Thess. v. 12	42

	PAGE		PAGE
1 Thess. v. 26	37	Heb. x. 23	23
1 Tim. i. 20	24	25	45
ii. 1	31	xiii. 10	19
2	300, 302	17	42
4	285	St. Jas. ii. 2	45
7	42	v. 14–15	46, 86, 87
iii. 16	35	16	87
iv. 10	36	1 St. Pet. i. 19	310
14	41	ii. 5	42
22	25, 41	9	42, 301, 310
vi. 12	16	iii. 20	295
16	306	21	16
2 Tim. i. 6	41	v. 1	300
13	23	14	37, 38
18	237	2 St. Pet. ii. 5	295
ii. 11–13	35	13	38
15	286, 300	1 St. John ii. 20	20
19	22	27	20
26	284	2 St. John 9	23
iv. 5	42	St. Jude 3	23
7	319	12	38
13	47, 48	Rev. i. 6	42
Titus iii. 5	15	10	46
8	36	ii. 1	42
Heb. i. 9	21	9	45
vi. 1, 2	20	iii. 9	45
x. 1	8	xix. 8	235
22	13		

INDEX OF GREEK WORDS.

ἀγάπη, 38, 110, 135
ἄγγελοι, 292
ἄγγελος, 42
ἁγία μύησις, 281
ἁγία τράπεζα, 81
Αἰῶνες, 292, 296
ἀκροώμενοι, 279
ἀμύητος, 310
ἀναγνώστης, 108
ἀναδεικνύναι, 301
ἀνάμνησις, 108
ἀπόστολος, 42
ἀποφαίνειν, 300
ἀῤῥαβών, 108
ἄρτος τῆς εὐχαριστίας, 109
ἀρχάγγελοι, 292
ἀρχαί, 292
ἀρχιερεύς, 42, 140, 170, 233, 290, 297, 309, 310
ἄρχων ἐκκλησίας, 140

βῆμα, 289
βωμὸς, 79

γένοιτο, 52
γονυκλίνοντες, 279
γραμματικός, 108

διάκονος, 42, 141
διδάσκαλος, 42
δυνάμεις, 292

ἐκλεκτή, 123
ἐξομολόγεισθαι, 82
ἐξομολόγησις, 57, 82, 108
ἐξορκισμός, 108
ἐξούσιαι, 292
ἐξωθούμενοι, 279
ἐπίκλησις, 120
ἐπίσκοπος, 42, 70, 140, 141
ἐπισυναγωγή, 45
ἐσθὴς λαμπρά, 163
εὐαγγελιστής, 42
εὐχαριστεῖν, 106, 119
εὐχαριστία, 30, 106, 108, 111, 315
εὐχαριστία ἐπιλύχνιος, 191
εὐχή, 119
εὐχὴ διὰ σιωπῆς, 224
ἐφόδιον, 113

ἡγούμενος, 42

θεατρικός, 108
θρόνοι, 292
θρόνος, 307 ; δόξης, 168
θυσία, 112
θυσιαστήριον, 78, 79, 81

ἱερεύς, 42, 140, 141, 233, 290, 305
ἱερουργεῖν, 42

κατασφραγισάμενοι, 283
κέρασμα, 123
κήρυξ, 42
κλήρος, 108
κλίσις γονάτων, 145
κοιμητήριον, 108
κόσμος, 265, 285, 293
κυβερνήτης, 307, 308
κυνηγός, 108
κυριακή, 108, 157
κυριακὴ ἡμέρα, 46
κύριε ἐλέησον, 245
κύριος, 25
κυριότητες, 292

λαϊκός, 233
λειτουργεῖν, 30, 171
λειτουργία, 30, 197
λειτουργός, 42
λευῖται, 233
λόγος, 119, 120
λουτρόν, 62
λυχνικός, 108

μαθητεύειν, 63
μυεῖσθαι, 250, 283
μύησις, 305
μύρον, 161
μυστήριον, 250

νεοτελής, 305
νεοφώτιστοι, 287, 303

οἰκονόμος, 42
οἰωνιστής, 108
ὄχλος, 309

παιδία, 281
παιδία νεόγονα, 63
πάλλιον, 108
παράδεισος, 294
παράκλητος, 108
παροικία, 286
πάσχα, 108

πέταλον, 163
ποιμήν, 42
πονηρός, 288
πρεσβύτερος, 42, 140, 311
προεστώς, 140
προηγούμενος, 140
προϊστάμενος, 42
προκαθεζόμενος, 140
προσευχή, 205
προστάτης, 170
προφήτης, 42

σεραφίμ, 292
σκεύη λειτουργικά, 313
στράτιαι, 292
συναγωγή, 45, 223, 224
σφραγίζειν, 22, 70, 250
σφραγίς, 22, 61, 101, 250
σωζόμενοι, 275, 283

τέλειον, 62
τράπεζα, vide ἁγία

ὕδωρ ζωῆς, 61
ὑμνίζειν, 33
ὕμνος, 33
ὑποδιάκονος, 108

φαιλόνης, 47
φασέκ, 270
φασσᾶ, 270
φελμουνί, 266
φωτίζειν, 250, 280
φωτιζόμενοι, 279, 283
φώτισμα, 62
φωτισμὸς, 60, 61, 250, 280

χάρισμα, 62
χειρεπιθεσία, 139
χειροθεσία, 96, 161
χερουβίμ, 292
χρηστός, 160
χρίσμα, 21, 96
χρίσμα εὐχαριστίας, 161
χριστός, 160

GENERAL INDEX.

GENERAL INDEX.

Aaron, 3, 70, 90, 221, 233, 270, 274, 296
Abel, 2, 186, 270, 274
Abercius, xi, 122, 123, 146
Ablution (Agapé), 136
Ablutions (Eucharistic, baptismal), 226
Abraham, 2, 193, 238, 264, 270, 274, 295
Absolution, 24, 56, 85
Acolytes, 139
Acts of Apollonius, xi, 112
—— *Callistratus*, 125
—— *Eugenia*, xi, 115
—— *Fructuosus*, etc., xi, 103, 144
—— *Paul and Thecla*, xi, 61, 69, 100, 109, 125, 145, 149
—— *the Scillitan Martyrs*, xi, 174, 175
—— *Thomas*, xi, 88, 107, 109, 112, 129
—— *Xanthippe, Polyxena, and Rebecca*, xi, 58, 69, 100
Adæus and Maris, Liturgy of, 29, 172, 195
Advent, 230
Æons, 264, 291, 292, 296
Affusion, 14, 70
African Church, 57, 66, 80, 116
Africanus, Julius, xii
Agapé, 31 : see *Love-feast*
Agonothetes, 161

Alba (Alb), 241, 251
Alexander, 24
Alexandria, 81, 127, 206
Alexandrian Liturgies, 17, 29
Almsgiving, 46, 54, 85
Alpha and Omega, 150
Altar, 19, 78–82, 229
Altare, 79
Ambo, 82, 289
Ambrose, St., 74
Ambrosian Divine Office, 203 ; *Liturgy*, 27, 165
Amen (Eucharistic), 121, 231
Anatolius, 153
Andrewes, Bishop, 58
Angel (a ministerial title), 42
Angel (a title of Christ), 291
Angels, 266, 292, 296, 297
Anglican Liturgy, 17, 27, 259, 297, 310, 360
Anglo-Saxon Liturgy, 310
Anicetus, Bishop of Rome, 104, 111, 127
Anna, 270, 312
Anointing: see *Unction*
Antioch, 196, 286, 301
Anthems, 195
Antiphonal chanting, 75
Antiphonary of Bangor, 246, 256–259
Antistes, 140
Antoninus Pius, xii, 51, 177

GENERAL INDEX.

Apollinaris, xii
Apollonius : see *Acts of Apollonius*
Apostle, 42
Apostles, 300
Apostolic Canons, xii, 59, 104, 131, 233
—— *Constitutions*, xii, 12, 58, 62, 64, 72, 96, 101, 102, 129, 133, 139, 141, 146, 156, 159, 161, 163, 169, 181, 193, 195, 227, 233, 255-319
Aquarii, 122
Aquilinus, 175
Ara, 79, 80
Arbith, 204
Arca, 126
Archangels, 266, 292, 296
Aristides, xii, 103, 177, 249
Arles, Synod of, 95
Armenian Divine Office, 245
—— *Liturgy*, 17, 29, 225
Arnobius, xii, 77, 130, 148
Ascetics, 304
Ashes, 83
Aspersion, 14
Athanasius, St., 96
Athenagoras, xii, 178
Audientes, 279 : see *Hearers*
Augurius, xi
Augustine, St., 122
Aurelius, 178
Authorities, 266, 292
Avircius, 122 : see *Abercius*

Baal, 252
Baptism, in Holy Scripture, 9-16 ; in Early Church, 58-74 ; Jewish use of, 219, 220 ; of St. John Baptist, 10 ; fasting at, 72 ; formula of, 11 ; kiss at, 132 ; of infants, 62-65, 220 ; by immersion or affusion, 14, 69 ; milk and honey at, 67 ; minister of, 73 ; profession of faith at, 15, 65 ; sign of the cross at,
68 ; sponsors at, 66 ; times for, 72 ; titles of, 61 ; unction at, 68, 70, 71, 87-90, 98, 160, 161
Barak, 270
Barnabas : see *Epistle of Barnabas*
Basil, St., of Cæsarea, 107, 125, 191, 198, 199 ; Coptic Liturgy of, 29 ; Greek Liturgy of, 27, 30, 168, 197, 246 ; Syriac Liturgy of, 29
Basilides, (i) 73, (ii) 81
Bede, 80
Beleth, 162
Bells, 220
Bema, 208, 289
Benediction, 16, 17, 129 ; formulæ of, 192, 306, 310
Benedictional of St. Ethelwold, 310
Benedictions before and after Lessons, 221
Benedictus, 243
Bible : see *Scripture*
Bickell's theory, 218
Bishops, 300, 302 ; titles of, 42, 140 ; prayer at the consecration of, 193
Book of Common Prayer, iii-v : see *Anglican Liturgy*
—— *Dimma*, 310
—— *Lismore*, 225
—— *Mulling*, 310
Bowing, at name of Jesus, 224 ; to the altar, 225
Breaking of Bread, 30, 109
Brightman, F. E., xii, xiii, 199
Byzantine Ritual, 232

Cain, 2
Callistratus : see *Acts of Callistratus*
Candidates for baptism, 279, 283
Canons of Hippolytus, xiii, 62, 65, 67, 72, 81, 88, 100, 104, 105, 108, 116, 127, 131, 132, 133, 136, 139, 140, 141, 148, 154,

GENERAL INDEX.

155, 161, 163, 165, 181, 192-194, 227, 240, 275
Capa, 241
Cardinals' scarlet robes, 251
Carpos (Carpis), 92
Carthage, second Council of, 117, 118
—— *third Council of*, 94
Cassian, 225
Casula, 242
Catacombs, 137, 141, 149, 152-153, 232
Catechumens, 276, 277, 279, 280, 281, 290, 305, 309, 314, 316
Celerina, 147
Celerinus, 147
Celestinus, 175
Celsus, 164
Celtic Liturgy, 151, 225, 310
Chalice (*Cup*), 18, 125, 137, 290, 304
Chasuble, 240, 242
Cherubim, 266, 291, 292, 296
Children, 284, 289, 290, 304, 308
Choir, seq.
Choral service, in the Jewish temple, 6; in Christian worship, 74, 75
Chrism, 90, 98, 160, 161: see *Unction*
Christian religion, a description of, 77
Christiani perfecti, 89
Christmas Day, 156, 229
Chrysostom, St., 27, 47, 199
——, *Greek Liturgy of*, 27, 172
——, *John, I. Syriac Liturgy of*, 28
——, *John, II. Syriac Liturgy of*, 28
Church furniture, 17, 75-82
Cingulum, 242
Circumcision, 65, 220
Cittinus, 175
Clement, St., of Alexandria, xiii,

62, 64, 68, 75, 79, 80, 90, 96, 102, 111, 113, 136, 138, 145, 154, 158, 181, 182
Clement, St., Bishop of Rome, 196, 286; First Epistle of, xiii, 83, 140, 141, 143, 167-172, 233
——, Second Epistle of, xiii, 151,
——, *Syriac Liturgy of*, 28
Clementine Homilies, xiii, 72, 111, 140
—— *Liturgy*, xiii, 17, 27, 61, 109, 121, 131, 141, 168-171, 195-197, 199, 219, 260, 265, 275-306
—— *Recognitions*, xiii, 72
Clodia, 115
Cock-crow, 154
Codex Alexandrinus, 195, 256-259
Colours, sequence of, 221
Columba, St., 225
Commodianus, xiii, 83
Commodus, 178, 252
Communion, 30; of newly baptized, 89; in both kinds, 117: see *Eucharist*
Competentes, 276, 279, 283, 314, 316
Compline, 236
Confession, 3-7, 82-87
Confessors, 156, 300
Confirmation, 19, 20, 21, 87-98, 161, 222
Consecration, of baptismal water, 73, 273; of baptismal oil, 273; of a bishop, 274; of churches, 228-229; of water and oil, 314
Consignare, 70
Constantine the Great, 76, 78, 240
Conybeare, F. C., xi, 125
Cope, 241
Coptic ritual, 225; Liturgy, 294
Cornelius (1), 11
—— (2), *Bishop of Rome*, 69, 118, 121, 139
Cosmos, 265, 285, 293

Councils, ante-Nicene, xiii
Creed, baptismal, 16, 23, 272;
  forms of, 177–181
Crispus, 11
Cross : see *Sign of the Cross*
Crowns, 138 ; Jewish, 235
Cup : see *Chalice*
Cyprian, St., of Carthage, xiv, 57,
  63, 64, 66, 69–71, 73, 77, 80,
  82, 83, 91–93, 95, 99, 100, 107,
  112–114, 117, 118, 120, 123–5,
  126, 128, 132, 140–142, 144,
  147, 150, 151, 156, 179
Cyril, St., Coptic Liturgy of, 29,
  172
———, *Syriac Liturgy of*, 28

Dalmatic, 251
Daniel, 270
David, 5, 7, 270, 271
Day of Atonement, 238
Deacon, prayer at the ordination
  of a, 194, 312
Deacon's Bidding Prayer, 286
Deacons, 141, 279, 281–283, 285,
  289, 290, 300, 302–304, 306–
  309
Deaconesses, 234, 304, 312
Deborah, 270, 312
Dedication, Feast of the, 229
——— *of churches*, 228
Deprecatio, 150
Diaconus, 141
Didaché, The, xiv, 12, 70, 102,
  106, 109, 115, 135, 141, 157,
  172-4, 261, 262, 276, 277
Dinocrates, 148
Diognetus: see *Epistle to Diognetus*
Dionysius of Alexandria, xiv, 81,
  127
——— *St. Barsalibi, Syriac Liturgy
  of*, 29
——— *of Corinth*, xiv, 158
——— *Pseudo-Areopagita*, xiv, 131,
  133, 292

*Dionysius, Pseudo - Areopagita,
  Syriac Liturgy of*, 28
*Dioscorus, St., of Alexandria,
  Syriac Liturgy of*, 28
——— *of Cardou, Syriac Liturgy of*,
  29
Diptychs, 172, 175
Discipline, system of, 82–85
Divine Office, 154–155 : see *Ambrosian, Anglican, Armenian,
  Irish, Mozarabic, Roman*
Divorce, 137
Dominicum, 77
Dominions, 266, 291, 292, 296
Domus Dei, 77
Donata, 175
Doorkeepers, 139, 234, 308, 312 :
  see *Ostiarii*
Dormitio, 150
Durandus, 230, 240

Easter Day, 156
Easter Even, 104, 105, 156, 157,
  159
Eastern Church, 230: see *Divine
  Office, Liturgy*
Eastward position, 145–146, 226,
  307
Ebionites, xiii, 122
Eden, 294
Egnatius, 147
Egypt, 295, 297
Egyptian Church Order, xiv, 109,
  128, 139, 193
Egyptian monks, 225
Eighteen Benedictions, The, 210–
  214, 243
Elagabalus, 252
Eleazar, 274
Eleusinian mysteries, 248–249
Elias, 270, 271, 318
Eliseus, 270
Elvira, Council of, 166
Ember seasons, 229
Encratites, xi, xvi

GENERAL INDEX. 335

Energumens, 276, 281, 301, 314, 316
Enlightenment, 60
Enoch, 271, 274, 295, 318
Enos, 271, 274, 295
Ephodion, 113
Epiklesis: see *Invocation*
Epiphany, 73, 156
Episcopacy, 140
Epistates, 161
Epistle of Barnabas, xiii, 157
Epistle to Diognetus, xiv
Epitaphs, 122, 146, 149-154
Esdras, 270, 313
Esther, 271
Etham, 296
Ethiopic Apostolic Constitutions, 29
Ethiopic Liturgy, 29, 172
Eucharist, The Holy, 25-33, 52, 58, 59, 105-129; consecration of, 118-122; fast before, 127; frequency of celebration of, 31, 115-117; in both kinds, 32, 117, 118; in private houses, 43; mixed chalice at, 122-125; mode of reception, 127; reception by infants, 128, 129; reservation of, 125-127; time of celebration, 113-115; titles of, 109-113
Eucharist of Christ, 112
Eucharistia (εὐχαριστία), 106, 191, 315
Eucharistic thanksgivings, 261
Eugenia: see *Acts of Eugenia*
Eulogius, xi
Eunuchs, 287
Eusebius, 77, 78, 144
Evangelist, 42
Evodius, St., Bishop of Antioch, 286
Excommunication, 23: see *Absolution*
Exomologesis, 57, 82
Exorcism, 101; bread of, 148

Exorcists, 139
Extempore prayer, 106, 107, 142
Externi, 279
Ezekias, 270

Fabian, 139
Falconilla, 149
False hair, 91
Fan, 290
Fasting, 126; before baptism, 72; before the Eucharist, 127; before ordination, 41; before the Paschal Supper, 232; on Wednesday and Friday, 101-105; on Easter Even, 104; at four seasons, 229, 230
Fasts, Jewish, 229
Feast of the Lord, 113
Felix, 175
Firmilian, St., 56, 93, 94, 121, 140, 223
Firstfruits, 287; Jewish formula of offering, 4; Christian prayers at reception of, 193, 317
Fish (emblem), 123
Font, 82, 89
Friday, 102, 103, 104, 116, 157, 230
Fructuosus, St.: see *Acts of Fructuosus, etc.*
Furniture: see *Church*

Gaius, 11
Gallican Liturgy, 27, 49, 151, 165, 169, 172, 292
Gallicinium, 154
Gallienus, 76
Gardner, Dr. P., 31, 249
Gemara, 202
Generosa, 175
Genuflectentes, 279
Germanus, St. Parisiensis, 228, 240, 310
Gideon, 270
Glass cups, 137

Gloria in Excelsis, 195, 244, 245, 256–259; Anglican version of, 259
Gloria Patri, 192, 259, 307
Gnostic, 158
Gnosticism, xi, 96, 292
Good Friday, 104, 128, 132, 156, 260
Good Shepherd, the, 125
Gospel of St. Peter, xvi, 157
Gospel, procession of the, 227
——, standing at the, 226
—— for Tenth Sunday after Trinity, 246
Gratiarum actio, 112
Greek Ektene, 246
—— *language,* liturgical use of, 108, 164, 231
—— *Liturgy and Ritual,* 98, 220, 235: see *Liturgy*
Gregory, St. (Catholicus), Syriac Liturgy of, 29
Gregory, St. (Thaumaturgus), xv, 179, 180
Gregory, St. (Theologus), Coptic Liturgy of, 30
—— ——, *Greek Liturgy of,* 30

Haggadah, 231
Hallel, 33, 216, 217
Hallelujah, 216, 231
Hatch, Dr. E., 247–250
Hearers, 279, 290
Heathen worship, as the source of Christian ritual, 247–253
Hebrew language, use of, 52, 230, 231
Hegesippus, xv, 144
Hel, 231
Hermas, Shepherd of, xv, 61, 102, 138, 140, 143, 223
Hierapolis, xii, 122, 123
Hieropolis, xi, 28, 123
High priest, 42, 233
Hilaris, 149

Hippolytus, xiv, xv, 179: see *Canons of Hippolytus*
Holy Communion: see *Eucharist*
Holy Doctors, Syriac Liturgy of the, 29
Holy Orders: see *Orders, Ordination*
Holy Saturday: see *Easter Even*
Holy Scripture: see *Scripture*
Holy Table: see *Table*
Honey, 67, 68, 89
Horns of the altar, 229
Hosanna, 174, 231, 262, 304
Hosts, 291, 292, 296
Hot water: see *Water, Warm*
Huldah, 312
Hymenæus (1), 24
Hymenæus (2), Bishop of Jerusalem, 180
Hymns, 33–35, 181, 183, 191: see *Tersanctus, Trisagion*
Hyssop, 229

Ignatius, St., of Antioch, xv, 75, 78, 79, 83, 109, 110, 134, 137, 157, 223; Acts of the Martyrdom of, xv, 143; Syriac Liturgies of, 28, 29
Ignatius the Patriarch, Syriac Liturgy of, 29
Ignatius, pseudo-, xii, 199
Illumination, 60–62, 250
Immersion, 13, 69; trine, 70, 88, 181
Imponere manum, 57, 70
Imposition of hands, in absolution, 24, 56–58; baptism, 88; benediction, 16, 129; confirmation, 19, 20, 87–98, 129, 192; exorcism, 101; ordination, 129, 139; Jewish origin of, 220, 231, 232
Incense, 129–131
Infants, Communion of, 128
Institution, words of, 25–27, 121, 299

Instrumental music, 75
Intercession, the Great, 300
Interrogations at baptism, 15, 65, 181
Invocation, baptismal, 73; eucharistic, 119-121, 198, 278, 299
Irenæa, 150
Irenæus, St., of Lyons, xv, 15, 63, 66, 74, 80, 111, 112, 120, 122, 142, 158, 159, 178
Irene, 232
Irish Liturgy or Ritual, 13, 49, 165, 221, 225, 245, 256, 310
Isaac, 238, 270, 295
Isidore, St. (of Seville), 97
Isis, 252
Israel, meaning of the word, 268, 306

Jacob, 238, 270, 295
Juel, 270
James, St., Greek Liturgy of, 27, 169, 197
——, *Syriac Liturgy of*, [i] 27, 172, 219, [ii] 27
James, St., the Less, 144, 163, 286
James, St. (Baradatus), Syriac Liturgy of, 28
James, St. (of Botnan), Syriac Liturgy of, 28
James, St. (of Edessa), Syriac Liturgy of, 28
Januaria, 175
Januarius, 179
Jehoshaphat, 270
Jephthah, 270; his daughter, 187
Jerome, St., 97, 233
Jerusalem, church of, 286, 301
Jessopp, Dr., 15, 36
Jesus (Joshua), 270, 271, 296, 307
Jewish, origin of, or influence on Christian Liturgy and Ritual, 200-247
Job, 274, 295
John, St., the Divine, 163; prac-

tice of, claimed to be followed by Asiatic Churches, 111
John, St., Basorensis, Syriac Liturgy of, 29
John, St., Evangelist, Syriac Liturgy of, 28
John, St., the Patriarch, Syriac Liturgy of, 29
Joining of hands, 138
Jonas, 270
Jordan, 296
Joseph, 187, 295
Josias, 270
Jubaianus, 92
Judas Iscariot, 309
Judas Maccabæus, 228, 237, 271
Judith, 187, 271
Julius, St., Syriac Liturgy of, 28
Justin Martyr, xv, 51, 59, 61, 62, 65, 72, 74, 98, 106, 110, 114, 115, 119, 122, 125, 131, 134, 138, 140, 142, 158, 164

Kadish, the, 214, 244, 246
Kalemeros, 150
Kedusha, the, 215, 245
Keriath Shema: see *Shema*
Kiss of Peace, in Holy Scripture, 36, 37; in early Church, 131-133; at baptism, 61, 89, 132; at Eucharist, 52, 61, 131, 132, 289, 309; at marriage, 133; at ordination, 133
Kneelers, 279
Kneeling, 143
Kohathites, 313
Kyrie eleyson, 245

Lactantius, xv, 105, 131
Laetantius, 175
Laity, 301, 307; priesthood of, 42, 74, 301, 310
Laodicea, Council of, 79, 224
Lauds, 204, 236
Laurentius, 147

Z.

Lavabo, 164, 165, 226, 231, 290
Laying on of hands: see *Imposition of hands*
Leah, 238
Lebar Brecc, 221
Lections, 278, 307
Lent, 104, 156, 230
Leofric Missal, 247, 310
Leonian Sacramentary, 140
Levita, 141
Levites, 233, 234
Levitical: see *Mosaic*
Lightfoot, Bp., xv, 168, 171
Litany, Eucharistic, 286
Liturgy, use of term in Holy Scripture, 30; when first committed to writing, 105-109: see SS. *Adaeus and Maris, Ambrosian, Anglican, Anglo-Saxon, Armenian, Ethiopic, St. Basil, Celtic, St. Chrysostom, St. Clement, Clementine, St. Cyril, Gallican, Irish, St. James, St. Mark, Mozarabic, Roman*
Lord's Day, the, 157-159, 262: see *Sunday*
Lord's Prayer, the, *215, 245, 276
Lord's Supper, the, 30
Love-feast (Agapé), in Holy Scripture, 37, 38; in early Church, 110, 133-137, 174, 232
Low Sunday, 156
Loyalty, of early Christians, 170
Luciferians, 97

Macarius, 240
Maccabees, Third Book of, 206
Magnificat, 243
Magnus, 179
Manum imponere, 57, 70: see *Imposition of hands*
Manasses, 270
Manipulus (Maniple), 242
Manoah, 270

Maranatha, 174, 262
Marcionite inscription, 223
Marcus, 120
Mark, St., Greek Liturgy of, 29, 168, 169, 172, 175, 195
Mark, St., Syriac Liturgy of, 28
Marriage, in Holy Scripture, 38, 39; in early Church, 115, 137-139; of the clergy, 139; Jewish, 235; kiss at, 133; mixed, 99, 126
Martyrs, 155, 156, 276, 300, 302
Marutas, St., Syriac Liturgy of, 28
Mary (the B.V.M.), 123, 156, 205, 269
Matronata Matrona, 153
Mattathias, 270
Matthew, St., The Shepherd, Syriac Liturgy of, 28
Maundy Thursday, 49, 156, 165, 226
Melchisedech, 111, 274
Melitine legion, 144
Melito of Sardis, xv, 158
Mensa, 81
Methodius of Tyre, xv, 182-191
Michael, St. (of Antioch), Syriac Liturgy of, 29
Midnight, celebration, 114; hour of prayer, 33, 154, 236
Milanese: see *Ambrosian*
Milk, 13
Milk and honey, at baptism, 67, 68, 89
Minchah, 204
Minister (title), 42; of baptism, 73
Minucius Felix, xv, 76, 79, 99, 142, 249
Miriam, 228, 312
Mischna (Mishnah), 202, 231
Missale Gothicum, 169
Mithras (Mithra), 53, 251, 252
Mitre, 163, 251, 252

GENERAL INDEX.   339

Mixed chalice, 32, 33, 52, 53, 122-125, 231, 299; symbolism of, 124
Mixed marriages, 99, 126
Moel Caich, 27
Monday, 230
Mordecai, 271
Mosaic benediction, 3, 310
Moses, 3, 70, 90, 99, 221, 270, 271, 274
Moses, St., Bar-Cephas, Syriac Liturgy of, 29
Mozarabic Breviary, 172, 203, 259
Mozarabic Liturgy or Ritual, 27, 49, 165
Mnsaph, 204
Music, Jewish origin of Christian, 228: see Choral Service

Nartzalus, 175
Neemias, 270
Nemesianus, 92
Nestorius, Liturgy of, 29
Nicodemus, 9?
Ninevites, 285
Nisibis, 123
Nocturns: see Midnight
Noe (Noah), 2, 270, 295
None, 154, 236
Novatian, 69, 122, 139, 179
Numa Pompilius, 251
Nunc Dimittis, 244, 259

Oblation, the Great, 299, 310
Offerings, weekly, 39, 44
Oil, 86, 88-90, 273, 314; of exorcism, 88; of unction or thanksgiving, 88; a thanksgiving for the holy, 262
Old Testament, Ritual in the, 1-9
Onesiphorus, 109, 237
Optatus, 77
Orarium, 242
Orders, Holy, 232-235; Jewish origin of, 234: see Ordination

Ordination, 133; in Holy Scripture, 39-42; in the early Church, 139-141; of a deacon, 312; of a deaconess, 312; of a presbyter, 311; of a reader, 313; of a sub-deacon, 313
Origen, xvi, 64, 65, 74, 77, 81-85, 87, 95, 96, 98, 100, 101, 102, 104, 111, 118, 121, 125, 127, 129, 131, 132, 140, 141, 143-145, 147, 148, 152, 154, 157, 160, 162-165, 175-177
Ornan, 270
Orphans, 234, 287
Osculum: see Kiss of Peace
Ostiarii: see Doorkeepers
Outsiders, 279

Paganism, loans from, 247-251
Palmoni, 266
Papias, xvi, 122
Paraclete, 272, 281, 316
Paradise, 294
Paschal Supper, 216, 217, 231, 232, 245
Passion of |St. Perpetua, xvi, 131, 148, 149
Pastor, 42
Paul, St., 11, 33: see Acts of Paul and Thecla
Paul of Samosata, 180
Pax: see Kiss of Peace
Pedilavium: see Washing of feet
Penitential system, 57, 82-85
Penitents, 276, 283, 309, 314, 316
Pentecost (Pentecostes, or Quinquagesima), 73, 116, 156, 230
Perpetua, St.: see Passion of St. Perpetua
Petalon, 163
Peter, St.: see Gospel of St. Peter
Peter, St. (1), Syriac Liturgy of, 27
Peter, St. (2), Syriac Liturgy of, 28

Peter, St., *of Alexandria*, xvi, 103, 142
Pharaoh, 269
Philaster, or *Philastrius*, 230
Philomelium, xvi
Philoxenus, St., of Bagdad, Syriac Liturgy of, 29
Philoxenus, St., of Hieropolis, Syriac Liturgy of, 28
Philoxenus, St., of Mabuge, Syriac Liturgy of, 28
Phinees, 274
Pilate, 269, 298 (and in the Creeds)
Pliny, Governor of Bithynia, xvi, 51, 75, 113, 115, 134
Pluviale, 242
Poderis, 163
Polycarp, St., xvi, 104, 127, 155; martyrdom of, xvi, 62
Polycrates, xvi, 141
Polyxena, xi, 59, 69
Pontifex, 140
Pontifical of Egbert, 229
Pontifical of Robert of Jumiéges, 229, 240
Powers, 266, 291, 292, 296
Præpositus, 140
Præsul, 140
Prayer, 141-155; attitude at, 141; for the dead, 146-151, 156, 237-239, 303, 318; to the dead, 152-154; hours of, 154, 235, 236; a general, 262-272; a post-baptismal, 273; secret or silent prayer, 224, 277, 280, 290; at presentation of first-fruits, 317; for the evening, 314; for the morning, 316; of humble access, 303
Preacher, 42
Preface (Eucharistic), 245, 291
Presbyter, 42, 141, 300, 302, 304, 307; prayer at the ordination of, 194, 311
President, 42

Prex, 82, 119
Priest, 42, 140, 305
Priesthood of the Laity : see *Laity*
Prime, 236
Primitiva, 150
Princeps Sacerdotum, 140
Principalities, 291, 292, 296
Probst, F., 107
Probus, 58
Proclus, 197
Profession of faith, at baptism, 15, 65, 181
Prophet, 42, 174
Proseuche, 205
Psalms, in the Temple services, 203; in the synagogue, 204
Psalms cxlviii.-cl., 204
Pulpit (*pulpitum*), 82
Puritans, 252

Quadragesima : see *Lent*
Quinquagesima (1) *Paschalis*, 116, 142 : see *Pentecostes*
Quinquagesima (2), 230

Rabanus Maurus, 240
Rachel, 238
Rationale, 163, 240
Readers, 139, 234, 287, 301, 304, 313
Rebecca, [i] xi, 59, [ii] 238
Renunciations at baptism, 65, 88, 272
Reservation of the Eucharist, 53, 114, 125, 126
Responsorial chanting, 75, 307
Ring, 138, 235
Rogatianus, 70
Rogation Days, 230
Roman Divine Office, 203
Roman Liturgy or Ritual, 27, 32, 69, 98, 171, 196, 260
Rome, 78, 123, 134, 286, 301
Rucha, 231
Ruler, 42

GENERAL INDEX. 341

Sabbath, a High, 230: see *Saturday*
Sacerdos, 140, 141
Sackcloth, 83
Sacrament, 113
Sacramentarium Gallicanum, 172
Sacramentarium Gelasianum, 229
Sacramentarium Leonianum, 140
Sacramentum, meaning of term, 51
Sacrifice (as a title), 112, 113
Sacristy, 304
Sahidic Ecclesiastical Canons, xvi
Saints' days, 155-157
Samson, 270
Samuel, 270, 271, 274
Sancta Sanctis, 303
Sanctum, 121
Sanctum Domini, 126
Sandals, 224, 225
Sarah, 238
Saturday, 137, 157
Saul, 11: see *Paul*
Scannlan, 225
Scillitan Martyrs: see *Acts of the Scillitan Martyrs*
Scripture, 155
Seal, 21, 22, 68, 123; of Christ, 58, 61, 69; of faith, 62; of baptism, 62; of the bath, 62; of the Lord, 62
Secret: see *Prayer*
Secunda, 175
Secundinus, 92
Sedatus, 82
Senior, 141
Seraphim, 266, 291, 292, 296
Sermon, 279, 308
Seth, 274, 295
Severus of Antioch, Syriac Liturgy of, 28
Sexes, separation of, 227, 289, 307
Sext, 154, 236
Shacharith, 204
Shema, 204, 209, 210

Shemonah Esrah, 210
Shepherd of Hermas: see *Hermas*
Shoes, removal of, 224
Sibylline Oracles, the, xvi
Sign of the cross, 21, 68, 70, 88, 89, 91, 98-101, 290
Silas, 33
Silent prayer: see *Prayer*
Simon, 11
Singers, 234, 287, 301, 304
Singing, mode of, 228
Skene, W. F., 218
Smyrna, xvi
Socrates, 75, 137
Sodom, 295, 297
Solomon, 6, 7, 228, 270
Song of Moses (1), 203
—— (2), 203
Spanish rite: see *Mozarabic*
Speratus, 175
Sponsors, 66, 67
Stephen, St., protomartyr, 312
Stephen I., Bishop of Rome, 57, 93-95
Stephanas, 11
Steward, 42
Stokes Whitley, 66, 220, 222
Stola, 242
Stone altars, 81, 82
Stowe Missal, 310
Sub-deacons, 139, 300, 304, 313
Summus sacerdos: see *Sacerdos*
Sunday in Scripture, 45, 46; in early Church, 157-159; 53, 115, 116, 137, 142, 145, 262
Surplice, 252
Sursum corda, 107, 108, 290
Susannah, 188
Synagogue, use of the term in Scripture, 45; in early Christian literature, 223, 224; date of, 206; use of, 206, 207; furniture in, 208; hours of service in, 208

GENERAL INDEX.

Table, or Holy Table, 19, 81, 82
Talmud, 202, 204
Tatian, xvi
Tau, 100
-Taylor, Bishop Jeremy, 58
Teacher, 42
Temple Services, 202-204; frequented by Apostles, 43
Terce, 154, 236
Teaching of the Twelve Apostles: see Didaché
Tersanctus: see Triumphal Hymn
Tertullian, xvi, 48, 54, 55, 61, 65, 66, 67, 68, 70, 71, 72, 73, 74, 77, 80, 82, 83, 85, 90, 98, 99, 102, 104, 105, 112-116, 121, 125, 126, 128, 130, 131, 133, 135, 137, 138, 140-142, 144-147, 154, 159, 161, 164, 179, 227, 250, 251
Thanksgiving, Eucharistic, 304, 305
Thebaid, The, 137
Thecla: see Acts of Paul and Thecla
Theodore the Interpreter, Liturgy of, 29
Theodotus, 96, 223
Theophilus, of Antioch, xvi, 160, 223
Thibaris, 101
Thomas, St.: see Acts of Thomas
Thomas, St. (of Heraclea), Syriac Liturgy of, 28
Thorah, 204
Three Children, The, 270
Thrones, 266, 291, 292, 296
Thubunæ, 92
Thuburbum, 82
Thursday, 230
Tiara Sacerdotalis, 163
Timothea, 150
Tithe, offering of (Jewish), 4
Tosiphtha, 202
Traditio symboli, 16

Trajan, 51, 75, 113, 115, 134
Trent, Council of, 151
Trifina, 149
Trisagion, 260
Triumphal Hymn, or Tersanctus, 171, 195, 215, 245, 260, 266, 297
Twelve Apostles, Syriac Liturgy of the, 28

Uncovering heads in prayer, 44
Unction, in Scripture, 20, 46, 86, 90; in early Church, 159-162; at baptism, 68, 70, 71, 87-90, 98, 160, 161; at confirmation, 87, 98, 160, 161; of the sick, 161, 162; Jewish origin of, 90, 220
Unleavened bread, 32

Valentinians, 96, 223
Veiling of women, 44, 227; at marriage, 138
Vespers, 154, 236
Vessels, of glass, 137; of wood, 162
Vestia, 175
Vestments, 239-242, 290, 307; in Scripture, 47; in early Church, 162-164; heathen origin of, 251, 252; Jewish origin of, 240; lay origin of, 241
Veturius, 175
Viaticum, 113
Victor, Bishop of Rome, 111, 126, 158, 163
Vigiliæ nocturuæ: see Midnight
Vincentius, 101
Virgins, 234, 287, 301, 304, 305, 309; Song, 182-191
Vitellianus (Marius), 150
Vitringa's theory, 217, 218
Vulgar tongue, use of, 164
Vulgate, 32, 79, 236

GENERAL INDEX. 343

Walafrid Strabo, 162
Washing, of hands, 164, 165, 226, 231, 290; of feet, 48, 49, 165, 166, 176, 177, 226
Water, baptismal, 13; consecration of, 82, 314; eucharistic, 122–125; warm, 231, 232; for sprinkling, 229
Wednesday, 101–104, 116, 157, 230
White dress, at marriage, 138, 235
Whit Sunday: see *Pentecost*
Widows, 139, 234, 260, 287, 301, 304, 309
Winchester Troper, 231
Wine, red, 231
Women, allowed to enter the sanctuary, 81; to be veiled,

227, 310; not to baptize, 74; not to preach, 227; not to speak in church, 44
Wooden altars, 81, 82; *vessels*, 162

Xanthippe: see *Acts of Xanthippe*
Xystarches, 161
Xystus, St., Syriac Liturgy of, 27
Xystus II., Bishop of Rome, 81, 127, 140

Young, Bishop, 241, 246

Zerubbabel, 228, 270
Zosimus, Narrative of, xvi, 105

PRINTED BY WILLIAM CLOWES AND SONS, LIMITED, LONDON AND BECCLES.

www.ingramcontent.com/pod-product-compliance
Lightning Source LLC
Chambersburg PA
CBHW020325240426
43673CB00039B/917